tial Ro
01962

WITHDRAWN FROM
THE LIBRARY

UNIVERSITY OF
WINCHESTER

KA 0400747 6

THE LIBRARY

UNIVERSITY OF
WINCHESTER

Contemporary Irish Theatre: Transnational Practices

UNIVERSITY OF WINCHESTER
LIBRARY

P.I.E. Peter Lang

Bruxelles · Bern · Berlin · Frankfurt am Main · New York · Oxford · Wien

DRAMATURGIES

Texts, Cultures and Performances

Series Editor

Marc Maufort, *Université Libre de Bruxelles*

Editorial Board

Christopher Balme, *University of Munich*
Franca Bellarsi, *Université Libre de Bruxelles*
Judith E. Barlow, *State University of New York-Albany*
Johan Callens, *Vrije Universiteit Brussel*
Jean Chothia, *Cambridge University*
Birgit Däwes, *Europa-Universität-Flensburg*
Harry J. Elam, *Stanford University*
Albert-Reiner Glaap, *University of Düsseldorf*
André Helbo, *Université Libre de Bruxelles*
Ric Knowles, *University of Guelph*
David O'Donnell, *Victoria University of Wellington*
Alain Piette, *Université de Mons*
John Stokes, *King's College, University of London*
Joanne Tompkins, *University of Queensland-Brisbane*

Editorial Assistants

Audrey Louckx, *Université Libre de Bruxelles*
Gregory Watson, *Université Libre de Bruxelles*

Wei H. KAO

Contemporary Irish Theatre: Transnational Practices

Dramaturgies
Vol. 35

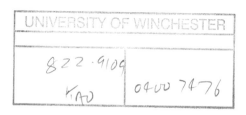

UNIVERSITY OF WINCHESTER

822·9109

KAU   0400 7476

The book was subject to a double blind refereeing process.

No part of this book may be reproduced in any form, by print, photocopy, microfilm or any other means, without prior written permission from the publisher. All rights reserved.

© P.I.E. PETER LANG s.a.
    Éditions scientifiques internationales
    Brussels, 2015
    1 avenue Maurice, B-1050 Brussels, Belgium
    info@peterlang.com; www.peterlang.com

ISSN 1376-3199
ISBN 978-2-87574-300-8
eISBN 978-3-0352-6574-3
D/2015/5678/65

Printed in Germany

CIP available from the British Library and from the Library of Congress, USA.

Bibliographic information published by "Die Deutsche Nationalbibliothek".

"Die Deutsche Nationalbibliothek" lists this publication in the "Deutsche National-bibliografie"; detailed bibliographic data is available on the Internet at <http://dnb.de>.

Contents

Acknowledgments

It is a pleasure to acknowledge the many debts I have incurred during the course of researching and writing this monograph on Irish drama.

First and foremost I would like to extend my gratitude to Professor C.L. Innes, whose abundant knowledge of postcolonial literature has led me to view Irish drama in a global context, following on from my doctoral studies at the University of Kent. Although my thesis was mainly on the Irish novel in the mid-twentieth century, many ideas and observations accumulated that led to the inspiration for this book. Her constant encouragement and friendship are the foundation stones of the current work.

I am also in debt to many colleagues and friends who have long supported me in ways that took one form or another. The discussions I had with them during different phases of the writing, as well as the laughs and parties that occasionally came my way, have added profoundly to enriching this book in many thought-provoking ways. My inspirers (as well as cheerleaders) to whom I owe many thanks are Li-ling Tseng, Kun-liang Chuang, and Yu-chen Lin, Cecilia Hsueh-chen Liu, Belen Sy, Joseph C. Murphy, Raphael Schulte, and Luisa Shu-ying Chang. My graduate students at National Taiwan University and Fu-Jen Catholic University contributed to developing ideas during class discussion and individual consultations. Eamonn Hughes's encouragement of my research in Irish studies has been uplifting.

I am particularly indebted to John Welford, who read most of the early drafts of my articles and patiently helped me with more than just the language editing. I always benefited from the critical comments that he generously made on the drafts.

Participants in the annual conferences of the International Association for the Study of Irish Literatures (IASIL) and at the JM Synge Summer School for Irish Drama are to be credited for their inspiring remarks on my research.

I wish to record my gratitude to the Ministry of Science and Technology of Taiwan and National Taiwan University for their financial support over the years. Without that support, my research could not have been properly carried out.

Alongside many library staff at Trinity College Dublin and my own university, my student assistants, Che-wei Wu, Tak-kei Lai, Chun-wei

Tsai, Chen-wei Han, and Pei-hsuan Chen, significantly facilitated my research. Further, I wish to thank Prof. Marc Maufort, general editor of the series, as well as Emilie Menz, commissioning editor, and Alice de Patoul, Audrey Louckx, Gregory Watson for their editorial advice.

In this book, some of the chapters of this book have previously been published in journals. The comments received from the anonymous reviewers have significantly helped in sharpening my arguments and ideas. I therefore gratefully acknowledge the editors' and publishers' permission to reprint these works: "Transnational Ireland on Stage: America to Middle East in Three Texts" from *Transnational Literature* 6.2 (2014); "A Russian Mirror to Ireland: Migration in Tom Murphy's *The House* and Anton Chekhov's *The Cherry Orchard*" from *Fu-Jen Studies* 46 (2013); "South Africa, Racism and Irish Sectarianism in Dolores Walshe's *In the Talking Dark* and Damian Smyth's *Soldiers of the Queen*" from *English Studies in Africa* 54.2 (2011); "Peace and Beyond in the Middle East: Colin Teevan's War Trilogy" from *War and Cultural Studies* 7.2 (2014); "When Incest Is Not A Taboo: Desire and the Land in Eugene O'Neill's *Desire Under the Elms* and Marina Carr's *On Raftery's Hill*" from *Journal of Theater Studies* 5 (2010); "Voices from Two Theatrical Others: Labour Issues in the Theatres of Ireland and Taiwan" from *Taiwan in Comparative Perspective* 4 (2012); "Samuel Beckett in Taiwan: Cross-cultural Innovations and Challenges, and Controversies" from *Journal of Beckett Studies* 15.2 (2006). Part of "Migrant Workers on Stage: Tom Murphy's *Conversations on a Homecoming* and Jimmy Murphy's *The Kings of the Kilburn High Road* appeared in *Notes on Contemporary Literature* 44.4 (2014). Part of the critical introduction was translated from "The Irish Theatre in the Era of Post-globalization," published in Chinese in *Reflexion* 20 (2012).

Finally, I would like to extend special gratitude to my parents and sister whose gracious support and assistance gave birth to this book. Janet Hui-chuan Kao and Adam Pettit, my brother-in-law, have been great hosts whenever I visited the USA for conferences and research – on both the eastern and western coasts of the country.

Ultimately, this book is dedicated to Jihwen Wu for the most open-handed care that I have been privileged to receive.

Introduction

Migrations and cultural fusions have characterized Ireland for centuries. Before James Joyce introduced Leopold Bloom as having been born in 1866 to the mixed parentage of a Hungarian Jewish father and an Irish Protestant mother, the Emerald Isle had already accommodated generations of migrants.[1] Although it is impossible to trace in detail how the Celts, Normans, Vikings, English, Spanish, Scots and Huguenots affected the development of the island's culture, these historical newcomers probably created, over some length of time, ethnic quarters similar to what is now dubbed Little Africa in Moore Street and Parnell Street in Dublin.[2] These people became settlers and contributed to a culture that is distinctive if not positively outlandish in the eyes of outsiders.

In the second half of the twentieth century, Ireland sheltered many asylum seekers who left their home countries out of fear of being slaughtered, including many from Hungary in the 1950s, Chile and Vietnam in the 1970s, Iran in the 1980s (members of the Baha'I faith), and Bosnia and Uganda in the 1990s.[3] Regardless of whether they arrived in smaller or larger numbers, they have quietly yet significantly diversified Ireland into a multi-cultural state, and their descendants have prompted the island to reach out to many parts of the globe through mixed marriages, wars, religious missions, commerce and migration.

These factors point out how Irishness has become a multi-ethnic, multi-cultural and global concept since the turn of the twenty-first century, particularly as a result of the experiences of migrants and the returned Irish. Specifically, changes in the demographic landscape of Ireland and its economy – which has experienced many ups and downs in recent years – have given the country a brand new yet unsettling face.

---

[1] It should also be remembered that some parts of Portobello were called Little Jerusalem before the 1940s, since Jewish refugees from Lithuania started to make their way there from the 1870s.

[2] Parnell Street in Dublin and Barrack Street in Cork are also given the appellation of "Little Africa." Interestingly, some people call the Moore Street area Little Shanghai or Little Riga. This area may be seen as an epitome of a globalized Ireland with not only native Irish street vendors but "a Russian delicatessen, an Afro-Caribbean Superstore and the Talk Is Cheap International Call Shop, where a bulletin board advertizes jobs and rooms-to-let to the fast-growing Chinese" (McGuire 26).

[3] More details about the experiences of these immigrants to Ireland can be found in Jean Ryan and Michael Hayes's *Postcolonial Identities: Constructing the "New Irish"* (78-79).

However, the desire of Irish playwrights to tackle the implications of the evolving notion of what it means to be Irish has not abated. They have sought to capture them faithfully either through writing new works directly relating to those themes, by adapting foreign/classic works which are relevant to contemporary Irish experiences, or by setting their plays in overseas locations in order to appeal to a wider market. Significantly, globalization has favored the production of Irish plays in other countries, which has impacted local artists and audiences.

Although some researchers have focused on the inter-cultural, inter-ethnic and global factors found in contemporary Irish theatre, a more thorough examination of how Irish plays counteract or absorb exotic/foreign influences is called for.[4] By comparing selected historical events and Irish experiences with their counterparts in other cultural scenarios, this book aims to offer an alternative historical, yet perhaps more inspirational, perspective that projects the Irish past and present on to the world stage.

Globalization and Drama

Although the term "globalization" has increasingly been used since the mid-1980s,[5] its inception can be traced back to the Age of Exploration, in which Christopher Columbus (1451-1506) and his contemporaries

---

[4]   Although there are many individual journal articles and book chapters on Irish drama, globalization and multiculturalism, the number of monographs and collections of essays on relevant topics is still limited, in contrast to works that feature either an individual Irish playwright or issues that do not refer in particular to an international scenario. To date, notable essays exploring contemporary Irish drama in a wider European or global framework include Heinz Kosok's *The Theatre of War: The First World War in British and Irish Drama* (2007); Mária Kurdi's *Codes and Masks: Aspects of Identity in Contemporary Irish Plays in an Intercultural Context* (2000), and her *Literary and Cultural Relations: Ireland, Hungary, and Central and Eastern Europe* (2009); Patrick Lonergan's *Theatre and Globalization: Irish Drama in the Celtic Tiger Era* (2009); Victor Merriman's *'Because We Are Poor': Irish Theatre in the 1990s* (2011). Edited collections include *Druids, Dudes and Beauty Queens: The Changing Face of Irish Theatre* (ed. Dermot Bolger, 2001); *Irish Theatre on Tour* (eds. Nicholas Grene and Chris Morash, 2005); *Drama Reinvented: Theatre Adaptation in Ireland and Irish Drama* (ed. Thierry Dubost, 2007); *Cultural Perspectives on Globalisation and Ireland* (ed. Eamon Maher, 2009); *Irish Drama: Local and Global Perspectives* (eds. Nicholas Grene and Patrick Lonergan, 2012), among others.

[5]   Although the term Global Village was popularized after Marshall McLuhan, a Canadian cultural critic, described its genesis in his book, *The Gutenberg Galaxy: The Making of Typographic Man* (1962), the word globalization did not become a frequently used word until the mid-1980s. According to the Google Ngram Viewer, which charts the frequency of certain words used in over 5.2 million books digitized in its database up to 2012, the use of "globalization" has rated statistically high only since the mid-1980s. See https://books.google.com/ngrams.

set out to prove that the earth was a globe, so as to obtain spices and other commodities from the East by sailing west. Although Columbus and his crew never reached the East, his voyages opened up not only flows of capital and population but began a new era in Europe's colonial development.

European territorial expansion, from the late fourteenth century onward, facilitated constant cultural and economic exchanges from one country/continent to another, with controversies arising over how it "facilitate[d] new forms of agency" and brought forth "oppressively homogenizing effects of cultural globalization … [which] can blind us to the nature of local circumstances, practices, and needs" (Jay 2). This is doubtless true to some extent, as the phenomenon of globalization has assimilated "the surface appearance and institutions of modern social life across the globe" (McGrew 74).

In other words, globalization has been even more influential than colonization in promoting not only the exchange of commodities (recent examples include the iPhone, MacDonald's and Louise Vuitton) but also information/values through the operation of transnational media (e.g. Facebook, Twitter, Whatsapp). While the protection of human rights and the practice of democracy, for instance, have become almost universal as values to be striven for, globalization also strengthens "an increasing concentration of power, knowledge, information, wealth and decision-making authority" (McGrew 75). Few countries can effectively resist the subjugation of this new world order, in which the flow of capital triggered by transnational corporations and global financial institutions can easily cross national boundaries.

Nevertheless, globalization also enables cross-cultural dialogues in the arts on a wide scale, given that such dialogues used to be silenced by former colonial empires through "established narrations of cultural practice" (qtd in Hall 558). Notably, by embracing "mutually opposed tendencies," globalization has been "a contingent and dialectical process" that invigorates "contradictory dynamics" (Gidden 64).

In contrast to commodities that can be appraised and traded between one country and another, the stage can be both a mirror of relevant phenomena and a platform of resistance that "simultaneously encourages particularization by relativizing both 'local' and 'place'" (McGrew 74). By particularizing selected fragments of life or incidents, the performative nature of drama boldly tackles the problematic nature of the power structure of a center/periphery model in an age of globalization, by unveiling the uneven rate of development between the first and the third worlds. In addition, drama, as a cultural artefact pertaining rather "to a hybridization than a homogenization," showcases a platform on which the audience can witness or experience "the plurality of centres from which globally diffused cultural elements emanate and point to the great variety of their local adaptations" (Robertson 26-27).

Taking Ireland as its departure point, this book will therefore demonstrate how one culture can transform another or hybridize it. Such process entails profound consequences that alter the perception of Irish drama in an intercultural context.

Globalization and the Migration of Irish Drama

Ireland, having been affected by all the gains and losses to which globalization has given rise since the last few decades of the twentieth century, offers a privileged vantage point to examine how a country can be transformed by such a radical force in human history. Because of globalization, not only was the demographical landscape changed rapidly within a short period of time but Irish popular culture was diluted by foreign influences – partly due to immigration.

Statistically, in 1997 only one foreign student – a boy from Angola – was enrolled in a Dublin secondary school, whereas in 2003, the peak of the Celtic Tiger economy, 25% of the student population across the country was foreign-born.[6] It was the moment when "the country of 4 million people [was] absorbing nearly 50,000 immigrants a year" despite the high deportation rate of asylum seekers (McGuire 26). The large and fast-growing number of immigrants even made the country find it "hard … to catch its breath," as observed by Piaras MacEinri, an Irish immigration expert (qtd in McGuire 26).

Interestingly, the global economic storm of 2008 significantly reversed the migration trend. Between April 2010 and March 2013, according to the Central Statistics Office of Ireland, "nearly 20,000 people moved from Ireland to the US … more than double the figure for the three previous years" (Lewis para. 13). Presumably, these people left due to disappointment with the Celtic Tiger and its sagging economy; moreover, the emigration included the foreign capital that used to guarantee prosperity and job opportunities in Ireland.

Nevertheless, the migration to Ireland has caused irreversible repercussions to Irish culture and identity. The latter are undergoing constant (re)creation and (re)construction. Honor Fagan once argued that if "Ireland did not already exist, globalization theory would have to invent it" (133). That is, if Irishness is an invented concept, it has to be redefined alongside the changing notion of the "imagined community" in

---

[6]   For details, see McGuire's "Ireland's New Face: A Surge In Non-EU Immigration Has Transformed A Once Homogenous Nation."

Ireland.[7] In the era of globalization, Ireland can no longer cling securely to the ideal of a fabricated, isolated Gaelic Eden nor embrace a Catholic nationalism that has implicitly underscored racial divides and discounted political and religious dissenters.

The new essence of Irishness in the global community should be openly recognized. For Terry Eagleton, Ireland is a signifier that highlights "roots, belonging, tradition," while it also spells "exile, diffusion, globality [*sic*], diaspora" as markers of Irish identity (11). Consequently, when attempting to define Irish cultural identity in post-Celtic Tiger Ireland, diasporic experiences, including those of people moving in and those moving out, should be taken into account. This would constructively reflect a multifaceted, if not imagined, community with "all of the hybridity, syncretism, and even arguably the post-modernism typical of the cultural political economy of globalization" (Fagan 137).

It is equally important to examine Irish migration from a broader perspective. Ostensibly, the experience of the emigrant has been to transport Irish customs and traditions to a foreign country to satisfy one's nostalgia and reconfirm one's Irish roots. Of more profound interest is the fact that artistic/theatrical innovations also migrate – not necessarily taken abroad by a migrant artist but often through works that inspire a creative mind somewhere else in the world.

One of the most notable examples of this phenomenon is J.M. Synge's *The Playboy of the Western World* (1907), a canonical Irish comic masterpiece that has been translated and performed in many languages and adapted as films, operas, and musicals.[8] Recognized by Declan Kiberd as a work corresponding to Franz Fanon's ideal of a decolonizing text, this play has also inspired Mustapha Matura, a Trinidadian playwright. He translated it into a Caribbean version, *The Playboy of the West Indies*,

---

[7]   Benedict Anderson defines a nation as "an imagined political community – and imagined as both inherently limited and sovereign" (224). The "inherently limited" imagination of an Irish identity unfortunately forbids the emergence of an authentic, yet not always pleasant Irishness. However, it allows the dissemination of "soft-focus commercials selling mythical Ireland-of-the-welcomes" to tourists (Lanters 44).

[8]   In 1912 it was translated into German as *Der Held des Westerlands* and performed in Berlin, Vienna and Münster. It was made into a film in 1962 and shot in County Kerry. A 1994 television adaptation by Lee Gowan, *Paris or Somewhere*, set in rural Saskatchewan in Canada, is about an American young man's killing of the daughter of a local store owner. Two operatic adaptions were based on this play, these being Giselher Klebe's *Ein wahrer Held* (A True Hero) in German in 1975, and Mark Alburger's English adaptation in 2007. There have been two musicals in English, namely Kate Hancock and Richard B. Evans's version in 2005, and Peter Mills's *Golden Boy of the Blue Ridge*, which premiered in 2009 in New York.

in 1984.[9] This adaptation includes characters who migrate from County Mayo at the turn of the twentieth century to a small fishing village in Trinidad. This play, which was premiered at the Oxford Playhouse in the UK, was so well-received that it soon toured to major cities in the United States. Its theatrical success prompted the playwright to adapt this Trinidadian version of an Irish comedy for BBC2 television in 1985. In 1993 the adaptation was revived at the Lincoln Center in New York.

Of even greater significance, the migration of *The Playboy of the Western World* in the past few decades has started to accommodate alternative interpretations due to globalization. Two notable productions were mounted by Pan Pan Theatre in 2006 and by Bisi Adigun and Roddy Doyle at the Abbey Theatre in 2007.

Premiered in Beijing with an all Chinese cast, the former transposed the setting from a remote village on the coast of Mayo to a whorehouse/ massage parlor on the outskirts of modern Beijing.[10] The audience was unsettled not so much by the story *per se* but by the shortness of the miniskirt worn by Sha Sha, who played the character of Sarah Tansey: the male audience reacted strongly during the performance. Two policemen were therefore called in for security reasons on the following nights. Although this play aimed to challenge the boundaries of decency and caused the "Playboy Riots" in Dublin in 1907, the Chinese audience's emotional reaction towards the visibility of female bodies and undergarments illustrated the clash between modernity and tradition. It revealed concerns about womanhood in a communist society under the clout of capitalism. The adaptation also proves that globalization has contributed to intercultural processes by integrating contemporary urban Chinese subculture and an Irish classic, and redefining a typically Irish experience in a multi-cultural and multi-ethnic setting.

Another example of this intercultural mechanism operating through a dramatic text is Bisi Adigun and Roddy Doyle's adaptation of *The Playboy of the Western World*, in which an African actor plays the part of Christy Mohan. Mounted by the Dublin-based theatre company Arambe Productions in 2007, this adaptation is set in a suburb of west Dublin

---

[9]   Kiberd's postcolonial reading of this play can be found in his *Inventing Ireland: The Literature of the Modern Nation* (185-188).

[10] According to Emer O'Toole, Director Gavin Quinn at first preferred Xin-Jiang, China's troubled Sino-Muslim province, to be the setting of this adaptation, but he was advised that this choice of location and the staging of Uyghur Muslims could inflame ethnic sensitivities in China and would not pass the Chinese state censorship. It can be argued that to set the adaptation in Xin-Jiang would lead to a very different yet controversial interpretation of the play. See O'Toole's "Cultural Capital in Intercultural Theatre: A study of Pan Pan Theatre Company's *The Playboy of the Western World*."

with the lead character, Christopher Malomo, being a Nigerian refugee.[11] This production reveals the implicit anxiety of Irish society over the large number of Africans travelling to Ireland either as refugees or economic migrants.[12] Christy Mohan's fake story about how he was abused by his father symbolizes the asylum seekers' desperate search for a convincing reason to gain permission to stay in Ireland. Nevertheless, the black audience found it difficult to accept the comic moments inherent in the original version, Indeed, the abuses and prejudice suffered by a black migrant would be perceived as "more of a prophecy than a comedy," according to Adigun, the Nigerian playwright/adapter (83).

These two adaptations – one meant for a Chinese audience in Beijing and the other for a mixed local/migrant Dublin audience – have the power of drawing public attention to the minorities in question and their predicament of racial and gender discrimination. Thus, *The Playboy* has become a platform on which pressing social issues can be expressed and minorities can give voice to their otherwise suppressed needs and desires.[13]

In addition, the performances by non-Irish actors pointed to the re-contextualization of a dramatic text from the regional to the global level. They lent an exotic touch to an Irish text. Moreover, they introduced perspectives testifying to the universal issues likely to interest audiences both inside and outside Ireland, even in a non-English-speaking part of the world. If intercultural adaptations of *The Playboy of the Western World* has "cultivate[d] a widest possible audience," the examples to be discussed in this book will further demonstrate how Irish drama can effectively "entertain and enlighten across the boundaries of cultural inscription" (Weitz 225).

---

[11] Arambe Productions, established in 2003, has produced many contemporary plays by African and Irish dramatists. In 2006 it staged Jimmy Murphy's *The Kings of the Kilburn High Road* (2000) with a full African cast; and in 2007, Ama Ata Aidooa's *Dilemma of a Ghost* (2007) by Ama Ata Aidooa, set in Ghana, was introduced to an Irish audience.

[12] Reportedly, "there [had been] about 30,000 Africans ... living in Ireland [in 2004], compared to a couple of thousand about three years ago.... Nigerians are in the majority" (Adigun 82).

[13] As the number of essays discussing these adaptations of *The Playboy of the Western World* is considerable, I shall explore texts that have not yet received much attention. For more information on these two adaptations, see Bisi Adigun's "Arambe Productions: An African's Response to the Recent Portrayal of the Fear Gorm in Irish Drama" and "Re-Writing Synge's Playboy – Christy's Metamorphosis, A Hundred Years On"; Emer O'Toole's "Cultural Capital in Intercultural Theatre: A Study of Pan Pan Theatre Company's *The Playboy of the Western World*"; Sarah L. Townsend's "Cosmopolitanism at Home: Ireland's Playboys from Celtic Revival to Celtic Tiger"; Nicholas Grene's "Synge in Performance"; and Patricia Byrne's "Traveling with J. M. Synge."

Contemporary Irish Theatre: Transnational Practices

To further demonstrate this phenomenon of intercultural inscription, this monograph will study a collection of Irish plays which focus either on foreign nationals in Ireland, on the experiences of immigrants or on the lives of people marginalized on the fringes of society. It will examine various Irish playwrights, both established and emerging, while identifying and comparing common themes in their works and those by playwrights of other nationalities. This monograph not only aims to document the global factors that influence the modern Irish psyche as evidenced in relevant theatrical productions, but also to examine how Irish dramatists profoundly impact theatre practitioners of non-English speaking countries and enrich their theatrical aesthetics.

The first chapter, "When Incest Is Not A Taboo: Desire and the Land in Eugene O'Neill's *Desire Under the Elms* and Marina Carr's *On Raftery's Hill*" will illustrate the intertextual links between two plays inspired by Greek tragedy. O'Neill, the American playwright, whose Irish father immigrated to the U.S., can be studied alongside Carr, a contemporary Irish woman playwright. Indeed, the Irish heritage of both playwrights is manifest in their works. They also share an interest in the incestuous relationships so typical of Greek tragedies. Admittedly, their plays are far removed from the grand scale of *Phaedra* or *Oedipus*. However, O'Neill and Carr dramatize the incestuous lust of their countrymen in *Desire under the Elms* (1924) and *On Raftery's Hill* (2000). Incestuous passion, however, is not simply, as Sigmund Freud suggests, an expression of natural but suppressed sexual love between family members. It is also mixed with desire for the legitimate inheritance of land and self-recognition.

Although O'Neill and Carr both analyze these tragic family affairs from the perspective of social ethics, they introduce an unconventional, albeit not necessarily celebrated, presentation of incest, so as to challenge this taboo and the patriarchal violence which the father figures of both plays impose on their families. In other words, the incestuous love in *Desire under the Elms* between a young stepmother and her son might not have ended disastrously, if the community had been matriarchal, or had not been entirely conditioned by social class differentiation; the female protagonist, Abbie Putnam, might not have had to marry a man forty years older than herself to secure a farm. On the other hand, in *On Raftery's Hill*, Dinah Raftery's incestuous intimacy with her violent father, a widower, is portrayed as a noble act, meant to protect her younger siblings. Carr's reinterpretation of incest in an Irish setting questions the stereotypical, often male-centered depiction of resentful female victims in Greek tragedies. This chapter will therefore examine how these two playwrights – with Irish connections abroad and at home – dramatize the

Oedipus and Electra complexes of the characters. Attention will also be paid to the playwrights' interrogation of the social mechanisms to which their characters are subjected. This intertextual study of the two plays – written in different social contexts of the twentieth century – offers a new understanding of this unspeakable but potentially intimate family taboo.

Noel Ignatiev, the author of *How the Irish Became White*, argues that Irish immigrants, although suffering a marked degree of ethnic discrimination in America due to poverty, unemployment, and lack of education, gradually received social privileges like other Caucasian immigrants from Europe, by distancing themselves from African Americans. Although Irish immigrants, like their African peers resided in slums, only the Irish slowly gained the upper hand in merging with mainstream society. The success of the alliance, however, was not entirely due to the color of their skin but also to the tactics which the Irish developed, sometimes unconsciously but unavoidably with a condescending attitude, in sharing the social devaluation of their colored siblings. What has been ignored is the exact process through which the Irish – mostly through their own efforts – unsettled the stereotype of the "stage Irishman" ridiculed in the theatre and other public media: they acquired the colonial mentality of earlier settlers against colored peoples. A series of plays discussed in the second chapter – Dion Boucicault's *The Shaughraun* (1874), Edward Harrigan's *The Mulligan Guard Ball* (1879), Sebastian Barry's *White Woman Street* (1992) – written over a span of nearly one century, depict the neglected poor Irish immigrants in New York in the late nineteenth century and in the countryside of Ohio in 1916. By contrast, Irish republicans in the motherland were advocating the Home Rule and were later overwhelmed by the consequences of the Easter Rising. The experiences of the Irish diaspora are largely disregarded by most historians, whereas these plays present their real-life dilemmas in terms of interracial conflicts, class struggle, political profiteering, and gang violence in the new world. The three plays recall the deep-rooted prejudice that the overseas Irish suffered at the turn of the twentieth century, which may significantly provide food for thoughts as, in the era of globalization, the Irish are trying to accommodate racial minorities, refugees from Africa and Eastern Europe, as well as economic immigrants.

To more closely observe the changing faces of Ireland and the new challenges it is confronted with, the third chapter will compare and analyze Tom Murphy's *Conversations on a Homecoming* (1985) and Jimmy Murphy's *The Kings of the Kilburn High Road* (2000). Notably, Ireland, as an "emigrant nursery" from which, in the nineteenth century, the Irish departed in the hope of helping their families, or to fulfill their dreams by seeking foreign employment, has left its people with an "unhealable rift" that Edward W. Said characterizes as one "forced between a human being and a native place, between the self and its true home" (49). This metaphorical "rift" is not unique to those who moved abroad, but is also felt by those existing on the fringes of society, and those whose lives were perturbed by political turbulences in Ireland, economic austerities and the more recent transformations of the ethnic landscape. While both plays portray the trials and tribulations of Irish migrant workers, the former focuses on a returned emigrant whose American dream has been destroyed. The latter play, centering on five Irish laborers in London, shows the extent to which their Irish roots have withered. The intertextuality of these two plays can be examined through their critical and significantly different depictions of the Irish Diaspora and its frustrations in two dream-like locations of world powers.

The fourth chapter, "A Russian Mirror to Ireland: Migration in Tom Murphy's *The House* and Anton Chekhov's *The Cherry Orchard*," aims to examine Chekhov's work and Murphy's adaptation in an Irish context. *The House* (2000), using the recurring theme of the search for home, reflects not only the identity crisis but also the fractured sense of belonging that people from the Emerald Isle experience under the impact of immigration and rapid globalization. Colonial history has also turned the immigration in/to/from Ireland into a shift within social strata and their political powers. The forced episodes of migration in Irish history – the result of several man-made and natural causes, and the rapid globalization of the past few decades, have inspired the playwright, Tom Murphy, to use overtly humanistic themes in order to dramatize the class struggles and the economic deprivation related to Irish immigration. The nomadic experiences enacted in the two plays could be regarded as illustrations of how Chekhov reconsidered the serious nature of comedy as the traditional centers of power, lifestyles, and social conventions of his times were being challenged. Not only is each individual forced to accommodate a new, mentally or geographically nomadic lifestyle, but dramatic conventions are also critically revised. To explore the soothing comical effects of *The Cherry Orchard* and *The House*, this chapter will also focus in depth on how the nomadic elements of the plays are presented through an unconventional approach in cross-cultural contexts.

Playwrights have been quite sensitive to the changing landscape of ethnicity in an Ireland characterized by an increasing number of immigrants and asylum seekers. They have therefore been prompted to examine the bitter sectarian violence which South Africa has gone through in the past few decades as an instance of cross-national experience. The traumas of South Africa under apartheid can be examined alongside the similar experiences of partition in Ireland and *vice versa*, opening up new understandings of human conflicts, bigotry, and insularity in our global village. By analyzing two Irish plays in reference to the period of apartheid and to the Anglo-Boer War in South Africa respectively, the fifth chapter, "South Africa, Racism and Irish Sectarianism in Dolores Walshe's *In the Talking Dark* and Damian Smyth's *Soldiers of the Queen*," intends to examine racism and political sectarianism in Ireland from an inter-cultural perspective. Dolores Walshe's *In the Talking Dark* (1989), set against the backdrop of the end of apartheid in the 1990s, reminds audiences of sectarian violence in Ireland and the erasure of female subjectivity in a highly militant and divided society similar to that of South Africa in the last century. Damian Smyth's *Soldiers of the Queen* (2002), contrasting the identity crises of Irish soldiers enlisted in the British army overseas against the similar predicament of those serving as Volunteers for the Boers, recalls the antagonism between the communities of different political and religious persuasions in Ireland. The racial conflicts of South Africa, the ambivalent and difficult position of the Irish under British imperial control, and the traumas suffered by both Black and White communities, thus provide Irish audiences with the critical distance necessary to understand their own troubled history, and most significantly, the changing face of Irish ethnicity in the twentieth-first century.

British imperialism had once channeled Ireland into becoming not only a subjugator of non-white colonies while itself subjugated, but also a transnational agent that nestled exceedingly well between cultural homogenization and differentiation. The sixth chapter, "Transnational Ireland on Stage: America to Middle East in Three Texts," will deal with Sebastian Barry's *White Woman Street* (1992), Frank McGuinness's *Someone Who'll Watch Over Me* (1992), and Colin Teevan's *How Many Miles to Basra?* (2006). This chapter will put into an ethical conversation these dramatic texts that either question the ambiguity of the Irish role in international politics or unveil the ignored experiences of Irish exiles and their interactions with ethnic Others in a distant land. To differing degrees, these Irish plays resist the normative impositions of a globalized world-view, and present a hybridized yet unsettling facet of Irish diasporic life in America, France, and the Middle-East, mediated with the difficulties of changing concepts of space and time in a transnational landscape. The discussion of the three works will illuminate not only the commonality of ethical problems in general, but also how the individual playwrights reflect on the emerging ethical crises through Irish people's own historical experiences and the contemporary Middle-East conflict.

The seventh chapter, "Peace and Beyond in the Middle East: Colin Teevan's War Trilogy," will illustrate a notable breakthrough in Irish theatre in recent decades. Indeed, many playwrights are now keen to expand the "moral compass" of Irish drama. Their works deal not only with domestic matters but also with subjects of global interest. Some of these playwrights are even directly engaged with ongoing international crises. Colin Teevan, born in Dublin in 1968, belongs to the generation that has witnessed rapid social and economic changes and has enriched Irish theatre with new material on the global stage. His war trilogy comprises *How Many Miles to Basra?* (2004), *The Lion of Kabul* (2009) and *There Was A Man, There Was No Man* (2011), set respectively in Iraq, Afghanistan and Jordan (all premiered in the UK). It mirrors the improved status of Ireland in international politics: from a state struggling on the political margin to one that casts doubts on the anti-terrorist policies of the United Nations and other world powers. Based on the tradition of the critique of social phenomena, Teevan's war trilogy exemplifies how the Irish theatre has evolved from an exclusive focus on national border and identity issues to a consideration of crises beyond Ireland's confines or within borderless non-governmental organizations. Apart from human rights issues in the Islamic world, the concerns dramatized in these three plays can be listed as follows: justice under different circumstances, authenticity of war news, religious and cultural clashes between Islam and Christianity, historiography and racism. More significantly, Teevan, although not always writing explicitly about Irish concerns in Middle-East troubles, offers a retrospective view based on the tangled relationships between Ireland and Great Britain now and in the past, in an attempt to induce more effective dialogues between East and West and to move beyond ideologies.

The similarities between Ireland and Taiwan as two island nations are striking in terms of their political and economic relationship with their respective mainlands. The former is proud of being a "Celtic Tiger," while the latter is a member of "four little dragons in Asia," along with Korea, Singapore, and Japan. Nevertheless, their rapid economic growth, to a significant extent, stems from the contribution of the working class, while the voices of this social stratum are often silenced, due to the attention mass media on more captivating global and national issues. The subject of how these lower-status people identify themselves politically and culturally, justify ethnic conflicts, and heal historical scars, has therefore suffered much neglect. Under the influence of globalization and trans-national capitalism, it could be argued that the working class, as a social Other, is still, or even more, exploited and marginalised by large or giant enterprises. This remains true despite the fact that within their own sphere, the blue-collared share a kinship derived from their subjugation by economic powers. The eighth chapter, "Voices from Two Theatrical Others: Labor Issues in the Theatres of Ireland and Taiwan," will therefore study contemporary Irish plays that address labour issues, in an attempt to show how playwrights, such as Fred Ryan, Sean O'Casey, Brendan Behan, John Arden, Margaretta D'Arcy, and Frank McGuinness, use the theatre as a medium to counteract the domination of these exploitative powers. This chapter will also compare these playwrights with their Taiwanese counterparts, for instance, Jian Guo-xian, Song Fei-wo, Peng Ya-ling, Chung Chiao, who deal with power struggle not only among different classes but within minority communities. Across national boundaries, then, these playwrights concern themselves with those at the very bottom of society, those who are most easily manipulated, least able to resist exploitation, and who experience the most knotty and intractable of human predicaments.

The ninth chapter, "Samuel Beckett in Taiwan: Cross-cultural Innovations, Challenges, and Controversies," is a study of how Beckett and his (post-)modern legacies have *migrated* across the globe and have inspired a number of Asian playwrights. This chapter will explore one of the major controversies in Beckettian studies, i.e. whether the dramatist's Irishness can be discerned in his plays, many of which were first written in French. Although the debate remains unsolved, scholars such as Vivian Mercier, Sighle Kennedy, and Eoin O'Brien have argued that the playwright used a kind of humor and satire dear to the Anglo-Irish mind. The help of these aesthetic devices had previously been enlisted by Jonathan Swift and Oscar Wilde to introduce cynical comments on Irish and British issues. Moreover, like James Joyce and many of his Irish contemporary, Becket had lived in exile on the European mainland. In the view of the critics cited above, Beckett, following in the wake of this satirical tradition, renovated it in a minimalist and absurdist fashion. Accordingly, a number of scholars have endeavored to point out the playwright's disillusion with, or criticism of, religion, life, and politics. More specifically, his sense of Irishness in his works was re-conceptualized in such a way that no longer confined it to the highly politicized and insular definition favored by local activists. In order to accurately delineate how Beckett's Irishness has created a dialogic platform both for Irish and world theatre, this chapter will exemplify the way in which Taiwan's theatre groups have adapted and contextualized his plays in a post-modern Asian society, which is not less politically divided than the Emerald Isle. Beckett's drama, consequently, provides Asian directors with an ideal way to approach not only issues of identity and language but also the complex predicament that triggers Gogo and Didi's despair in *Waiting for Godot*. The intertextuality of Beckett's drama and its re-adaptations for Taiwan's audiences thus illustrate how the notion of Irishness can be made significant from a cross-cultural perspective. The skepticism and obscurity of Beckett's works becomes more apparent by observing how Asian directors, often trained in Western institutions of higher learning, have produced these plays as vehicles of their own cultural and political agenda. These directors have also considered these works as a means to connect Taiwan's modern theatres with European ones in an age of globalization. Their productions demonstrate the extent to which

UNIVERSITY OF WINCHESTER LIBRARY

Beckett has maintained a far-reaching influence on his counterparts in world theatre. Materials to be examined include theatrical reviews of Beckettian productions in Taiwan, interviews with directors, journalistic reportage, and translations of the scripts. Beckett's plays that have been staged in Taiwan since 1988 include *Waiting for Godot, Endgame, Play, What Where, Come and Go, Footfalls, Act without Words I, Act without Words II,* and *Ohio Impromptu.*

Globalization, visibly and invisibly, radically and moderately, has altered our perception of the world, eliciting a new understanding of social developments in cross-cultural contexts. It also becomes a source of inspiration for writers, artists, and historians, prompting them to develop critical perspectives which fundamentally challenge our sense of morality, race, gender, class, and religion in a world with extended cultural boundaries. At the turn of this century, following in the critical tradition of Irish theatre, many playwrights use the stage as a "nicely polished looking-glass," in James Joyce's phrase, to scrutinize social, gender, and sectarian injustice.

The final chapter will examine what constitutes "Home" for people in or outside of the Emerald Isle – using additional texts that could not be considered in previous chapters. On the one hand, Ireland has long struggled for its territorial integrity and sovereignty. As Luke Gibbon describes, Ireland is "a first-world country [which possesses] a third-world memory" (27), due to the traumatizing experiences of famine and mass emigration which still haunt it today. On the other hand, the nation's rapid development in this age of globalization has earned it the titles of "Pride of Europe" and "Celtic Tiger," at least before the global economic crisis of 2008. However, returning Irish descendants, colored refugees, and non-European immigrants have prompted many native Irish to feel their homeland had become "as unfamiliar as abroad," leading to the perception of globalization as "a process of social estrangement" (O'Toole 173). It should also be noted that globalization has irreversibly changed the way the Irish perceive themselves and has profoundly affected their worldview. Many have also become increasingly "diasporic," a mind-set not necessarily linked with a physical exile.

While globalization has united many major economic bodies in the world, it cannot easily erase the core differences of each nation's people: their ethnicities, cultures, traditions, and historical experiences. In recent decades, Ireland has had to deal with the pain of accepting and understanding the differences of the Other. To illustrate Ireland's particular "process of social estrangement" (O'Toole 173), this final chapter will use dramatic analysis to suggest ways in which the Irish could accommodate to the new world order and could accept newcomers more comfortably in the near future.

Contemporary Irish theatre, following in its long tradition as a critical forum of political and social issues, mirrors the transformation of Ireland in recent years. However, this transformation occurs in so rapid a manner that asylum seekers from Africa, economic immigrants from Eastern Europe, and returning citizens from North America, are unable to make themselves at home in Ireland. The dramatic representation of this phenomenon has not received the critical attention it deserves. Likewise, the way in which contemporary Irish dramatists engage with international affairs and crises involving peoples surviving on the margins of international politics has not attracted significant scholarly examination. An in-depth analysis of how canonical Irish dramatists are perceived in an Asian context still await full documentation. This book therefore attempts to remedy this situation, studying Irish playwrights and their works from a cross-sectarian, cross-cultural, and international perspective at the dawn of the twentieth-first century.

I. When Incest Is Not A Taboo: Desire and the Land in Eugene O'Neill's *Desire Under the Elms* and Marina Carr's *On Raftery's Hill*

The American playwright Eugene O'Neill, who had an Irish-born father, can be studied with profit alongside Marina Carr, a contemporary Irish woman dramatist, in that both of them present not only a distinct Irish heritage in their works but also a shared interest in the theme of incest in Greek tragedies and mythology. Although their plays do not possess the grand scale of *Phaedra*, *Oedipus*, or *Electra*, all of which touch on incestuous desire, O'Neill and Carr both dramatize this lust respectively in *Desire Under the Elms* (1924) and *On Raftery's Hill* (2000).[1] The difference is that the two playwrights, across decades and of different genders, challenge this taboo by critically examining the puritanical ethos to which their protagonists are subject, particularly in relation to the land. Specifically, O'Neill and Carr, to differing degrees, penetrate the forbidden desires of their characters in distress, reassessing how human complexities are conditioned by a mixture of external forces, in an attempt to ignite a new understanding of taboos.[2]

By adapting Greek tragedies and featuring the lust of women characters in New England and the Irish midlands, in a religious setting, the two playwrights have, to differing degrees, questioned the Freudian qualification of the Oedipus and Electra complexes, theatrically liberating human desires from puritanical, patriarchal, and/or colonial conditions. Rather than reinforcing accepted ethical values, their plays, as Cathy Leeney suggests, contribute to "the power to disrupt, overthrow and

---

[1] Carr has written over thirty adaptations of Greek tragedies. For details, see Marianne McDonald's "Classics as Celtic Firebrand: Greek Tragedy, Irish Playwrights, and Colonialism."

[2] The premiere of *Desire Under the Elms*, in particular, irritated the audience, and had the whole cast arrested and convicted for performing a play that was "mere smut, and filth [...], morbid, lewd and obscene" (qtd in Winther, 326). *On Raftery's Hill*, though not banned as was its earlier American counterpart, was no less controversial for having redrawn the line between affection and sex within blood relationships: "Should the incestuous abuser be regarded as mentally ill, morally reprehensible and/ or a criminal?" (Jordan 138). I would like express gratitude to Prof. Eamonn Jordan for his generosity of sending his article on Carr to me.

overwhelm narrative or story," which would "impress upon an audience not defeat, silence or obliteration but thrilling, moving, exhilarating life" (92). What should not be ignored is that both O'Neill and Carr, having a familial connection with Ireland, distant or close, have manifestly explored those desires castrated by the given morality, examining whether the forbidden desires as portrayed are imperative and "necessary for historical progress" for an immigrant/emigrant community (Younger 152). Both communities inevitably reinforce patriarchal authority which, in their works, is often either too weak or too powerful, and thus demanding to be interrogated.

Before this chapter illustrates the intertextuality of the two plays, providing an alternative reading of the shared plot concerning incestuous desire, it should be noted that O'Neill and Carr can be placed in a long writing tradition in which morally forbidden desire has been one of the repeated themes from early oral culture and mythology onwards, and continues to be a subject of interest in world literatures.[3] For instance, Homer's *Odyssey* and *Iliad* both mention the myth of Oedipus, who marries his own mother after killing his father by accident, and later dies in exile. Aeschylus's Oedipus trilogy, Sophocles's *Oedipus the King,* John Dryden's *Oedipus* (1678), and a modern opera by Jean Cocteau and Igor Stravinsky, are examples that are often discussed. The Greek myth of Electra, in which a daughter intends to avenge the death of her father, Agamemnon, by killing her mother, also inspired Aeschylus, Sophocles and Euripides in (re-)writing her tragic story. Some modern psychoanalysts believe that the affection between Electra and Agamemnon is, ambiguously, incestuous.[4]

The theme of incest is not usually accepted as allowable, and is most often regarded as taboo or prohibited in religious scriptures,[5] with fear of castration, condemnation, or death. It is a desire which, interestingly, draws

---

[3]   A survey of the presentations of incestuous desire in world literatures can be found in the entry for "incest" in Jean-Charles Seigneuret, eds., *Dictionary of Literary Themes and Motifs A-J.*

[4]   Although Electra does not openly develop an incestuous relationship with Agamemnon in the myth, modern psychoanalysts, including Carl Jung, have argued that her hidden sexual attraction for her father was one of the causes of her mother being murdered. To illustrate how women had similar emotional attachments for their fathers as men, according to Freud's Oedipus Complex, had for their mothers, Jung used the myth of Electra as a metaphor, however, Freud did not exactly agree with this analogy. See details in Michale Mikos and David Mulroy's "Reymont's *The Peasants*: A Probable Influence on *Desire Under the Elms.*"

[5]   Noted passages about incest in the Bible, for instance, include Genesis 19:15, 19:32-36, 39:1-23; Leviticus 18:6, 20:11-12, 14, and Peter 2:7-8. Incest is condemned as an act of wickedness, lewdness, unlawfulness, and would cause "the iniquity of the city" (Gen 19:15). If not for biological and genetic concerns, this is a much forbidden human desire in all other societies. The Egyptian "Tale of Two Brothers," the story

the attention of modern psychoanalysts when diagnosing undeveloped or suppressed mental syndromes. Sigmund Freud, Carl Jung, Jacques Lacan, Gilles Deleuze and Félix Guattari, for instance, have openly dissected this particular desire but with disparate interpretations.[6] By cross-examining O'Neill's *Desire Under the Elms* and Carr's *On Raftery's Hill*, this chapter will argue for a non-Freudian reading of the Oedipus and Electra complexes in these two modern adaptations, exploring how the two playwrights' Irish connections have made their works significantly intricate, and demonstrating how suppressed passion, to a certain extent, helps to operate the "desiring machine," as Deleuze and Guattari observed in their *Anti-Oedipus: Capitalism and Schizophrenia*. Specifically, the numerous adaptations of this incestuous myth, and psychoanalysts' attempts to decipher its impacts, have suggested an imaginative solution to, or escape from, the protagonists' dilemmas in these highly puritanical communities – in the Old and New Worlds on either side of the Atlantic Ocean. Although the playwrights did not portray the lust, guilt, and pleasure of the characters explicitly, the hidden consequences of incest will be deciphered more delicately in this chapter, so as to reveal how unspeakable desire can prompt the desiring machine to operate in a manner more complex than Freudian critics might have assumed.

O'Neill's *Desire* has been considered the "first important tragedy to be written in America" (Bogard 200), and won him the Nobel Prize in Literature in 1936, along with his other works, for its successful attempt at portraying a New England farming community, "hardened by the passing of generations into a type of Puritanism that had gradually come to forfeit its idealistic inspiration" (Frenz 332). Although O'Neill did not demonstrate Irishness very visibly in his works, his characters have often been analyzed and compared with the playwright's own family upbringing.[7] That is, given a middle name, Gladstone, by his father, in honor of the British Prime Minister, W E Gladstone, for his support of Irish Home Rule at around the time of O'Neill's birth, and bestowing two on his own son, Sean Rudriaghe, O'Neill illustrated his Irishness in an interview: "One thing that explains more than anything about me is

---

of Bellerophon and Stheneboea, and the tale of Peleus, the father of Achilles, from Apollodorus's *Library* II.3 and III.13, all suggested incestuous passion.

6   These interpretations, not always congruous, have contributed to an in-depth understanding of the human psyche, and have led to new explorations of its subtlety.

7   To name a few, works which discuss the implicit Irishness of Eugene O'Neill include Albert Bermel's "Art and life in Apposition"; John Henry Raleigh's "O'Neill's *Long Day's Journey into Night* and New England Irish-Catholicism"; Dorothy MacArdle's "The Dual Nature of Man"; Charles A. Merrill's "Eugene O'Neill, World-Famous Dramatist, and Family Live in Abandoned Coast Guard Station on Cape Cod"; Kristin Pfefferkorn's "Searching for Home in O'Neill's America" and Louis Sheaffer's *O'Neill: Son and Playwright*.

the fact that I'm Irish. And, strangely enough, it is something that all the writers who have attempted to explain me and my work have overlooked" (Merrill 40).

In discussion of O'Neill's dramas and his Irish connection, critics have also stressed that the playwright's unfailing interest in familial subjects has a cultural connotation as shared by most Irish Americans. They are known to have maintained strong familial and communal commitments, and continued their Irish traditional practices in the foreign land (Pfefferkorn 123). The strong family-oriented culture thus prescribed the emigrants' perception of the New World, and might have prompted O'Neill to compare the attitudes taken by his community with those found in Greek tragedies, for the joys and agonies of both seemed to be more self-contained than those of other foreign groups which merged more quickly with one another in America. These Irish Americans did "not so much leave Ireland as bring Ireland to America" (Raleigh 126). The poverty of, and prejudice against, Irish Americans gave O'Neill an outsider's perspective of the troubles and impulses of his American fellow-countrymen,[8] which has given many of his works a more autobiographical than simply imaginative nature.[9] His style of observation was also applicable to his Catholic community, earning him the name of the "Black Irishman," who "has lost his Faith and [...] [is] searching for [...] a philosophy in which he can believe again as fervently as he once believed in the simple answers of the Catholic Catechism" (Bowen 204). His skepticism about religion is, presumably, mixed with his adaptations of Greek tragedies in the context of the immigrant community of New England in the first half of the twentieth century.

That Carr's drama can be intertextual with O'Neill's, apart from both being modern adaptations of a classic theme, lies in their shared highlighting of familial subject matters. The former, specifically, focuses more on the experiences of would-be Irish emigrants and their struggles for family fortune and land, whereas the latter deals with the forbidden desires in a family of Irish immigrants surviving the harshness of New

---

[8]   Due to the poverty and religious issues, Irish immigrants in America suffered from "anti-Irish racism," which placed them on the margin of the job market. The signs which read "HELP WANTED - NO IRISH NEED APPLY" traumatized the Irish community in the early days. For details, see Maureen Murphy's "From Scapegrace to Grasta: Popular Attitudes and Stereotypes in Irish American Drama," p. 27, and Noel Ignatiev's *How the Irish Became White*.

[9]   More specifically, O'Neill's father, James O'Neill, was born in Kilkenny, Ireland, in 1849, and emigrated to America in 1854. The obsession of the Tyrone family with penury and hunger in *Long Day's Journey into Night* (1956) was part of the upbringing which O'Neill received.

England.[10] Both rural communities, one in the Irish midlands and the other in New England, are factually self-contained. The "close-knit" landscape, as described by Carr, does not simply serve as a background but as a character that interacts with other protagonists in her works (Murphy 45). Metaphorically, the landscape foreshadows the unnamable and inescapable destiny that the hero(ine)s have to strike against, and by which their sense of individuality, desires, and futures are dominated. In other words, the Irish midlands suffocate the characters, so that most of their desires and emotions become the source of physical, mental, and sexual torment. Incest, mental breakdown, and broken marriages fall into a cycle from one generation to another, and a series of family scandals is the underlying cause of current tragedies. As Carr's play presents, escaping from this suffocation, though not to be encouraged, would only be possible under the surveillance of family members and villagers. In *Raftery's*, the wish of Shalome, the grandmother ill in bed, to return to Kinneygar, India, where her parents emigrated and where she spent a happy childhood, is prohibited by her family. Barred from leaving the house, she is "like an auld record that's stuck in the groove" (12). With a son who "put stop to all […] [and] never liked to see people enjoy themselves" (11), most of the other characters in *Raftery's* are trapped in the household, with the exception of the deceased daughter-in-law (who is also Dinah's mother and Ded's wife).

Before the chapter dwells upon the different ways in which the two playwrights have approached the forbidden desires differently, it might be necessary to review briefly how desire has long been a topic of interest for modern psychoanalysts. Sigmund Freud, Jacques Lacan, R.D. Laing, Wilhelm Reich, Michel Foucault, Gilles Deleuze, Félix Guattari, among others, have all attempted to dissect the development and distortion of

---

[10] A conventional reading of O'Neill's *Desire* often includes a cross-reference to the Hippolytus-Phaedra-Theseus legend in Greek mythology. Comparative studies of the intertextuality of O'Neill's play, Euripides's *Hippolytus* and *Medea*, Seneca the Younger's *Phaedra*, and Sophocles's *Oedipus Trilogy*, also demonstrate the canonity of these tragedies in classic and modern literatures. King David in the Bible has also been a subject of comparison with Ephraim in *Desire*, both of whom incur sexual competition with their sons for women who are considerably younger than themselves. See 1 Kings 1-6. The names in *Desire Under the Elms* also bear biblical references which reincarnate "the rural New England setting of 1850, but resonate well with the legalistic, Old Testament ethos" (Bowles 11). To name a few, Eben is a shortened form of "Ebenezer," which means "stone of help" in commemoration of the divine assistance to Israel in its battle against the Philistines (See 1 Sam. 7:3-12; John 11:32-44). The name Ephraim suggests the progenitor of the Israelites. Abbie is a diminutive of Abishag the Shunhamite, a young virgin brought to King David as "nurse, lover, and, symbolically, mother, to an aging ruler" (Bowles 12).

human mentality by unearthing desires in conflict.[11] Freud, for instance, argues that the cause of neuroses resides in either suppressed and unfulfilled sexual desire or an unsolved castration complex that originates during the formation of selfhood in childhood.[12] However, this assumption has drawn its share of attackers, among whom the radical French Marxist critics, Deleuze and Guattari, explicate a "Desiring Machine" in their *Anti-Oedipus* monograph. This "Desiring Machine" invalidates the existence of a family triangle as the ground of the Freudian Oedipal complex, contending that human desires actually operate collectively as a machine, but at the same time "interrupt or partially drain off" another mechanism in this machine (5). Deleuze and Guattari also claim that desires should not be circumscribed within the family. As they observe, the overemphasis on the influence of family on individuals has inappropriately separated people with psychological problems from a larger social sphere, and deterritorialized them from the community.[13] In their observation, Freud's Oedipal model of human desires can only be a derivative, rather than an alternative, of the multidimensional and multivalent desiring machine.[14] This chapter, while not negating Freud's psychoanalytic assumptions, will present a non-Freudian reading of the two plays in wider social and economic contexts, as they relate to hidden desires in Irish emigrant/immigrant communities.

It should be noted that studies of O'Neill's *Desire* often refer to the Hippolytus-Phaedra-Theseus legend in Greek mythology for their similar storylines. What overwhelms the protagonists in these works, however, is the forbidden desire to which they are committed and which makes them behave rather eccentrically. However, it can be argued that Freud's Oedipus complex might have inappropriately convinced the critics and audiences that *Desire* is *no more than* a modern family tragedy. O'Neill,

---

[11] Freud's Oedipus Complex and Lacan's Mirror Stage, for instance, illustrate that our selfhood is formulated with sexual desire – suppressed during infancy and early childhood. Laing and Reich take a Freudo-Marxist approach by arguing that the social-economic structure is underlaid with all forms of sexual repression, which thus reinforce bourgeois morality and consciousness.

[12] For details, see Freud's *Introductory Lectures on Psychoanalysis*, vol. 1, 27, 245, 359-360.

[13] To replace the familalism which Freudian psychoanalysis promotes, Deleuze and Guattari propose a new paradigm, "Body with Organs," or *BwO*, arguing that desire resembles an "amorphous, undifferentiated fluid," which is "smooth, slippery, opaque, taut" (Deleuze and Guattari 9). Foucault, in support of Deleuze and Guattari, recognizes that desires are, by nature, nomadic, and the Oedipus complex, having been overemphasized, "subjugate[s] the multiplicity of desire to the twofold law of structure and lack" (xiii).

[14] Deleuze and Guattari's desiring machine does not necessarily supersede that of Freud's. Lacan, however, expands his Oedipal model to all social dimensions that contribute to the desiring machine. I would like to credit the reviewers of this essay for this reminder.

at the beginning of the play, in fact illuminates the social network wherein all forms of desire are interlocked under the enormous shadow of the elms. That is, the two "enormous elms [which] brood oppressively over the house" have "a sinister maternity" that makes life "appalling," "sagging," and "monotonous" (2). The elms act more than as shadows, or props, but as a powerful character that predetermines the flow of desire which either expels the characters far to the west for gold, or prompts them to be lustful and greedy for property as a token of patriarchal authority and legacy. If the maternity of the shadow is "sinister," as O'Neill presents it, what makes the maternity bitter can be not only "a crushing, jealous absorption" between lovers or intimate family members, but proprietorship over the farm (2). More specifically, the fight between Ephraim Cabot and the family of "Eben's Maw [...] [for] [h]er folks was contestin' me at law over my deeds t' the farm – my farm!" (32), and the failed wish of her relatives for claiming back the farm, is apparently a breakdown within the desiring machine, which insistently torments every member of the Cabot family.

What is noteworthy is that this farm is located on infertile land with limited financial prospects: "We been slaves t' stone walls here" (15). The reason for claiming the farm for both sides is, presumably, not for capitalistic profits but to fulfill an implicit sense of attachment to the land, which was part of the essential cultural convention for Irish immigrants. Although O'Neill did not particularly specify the Cabots as being an Irish immigrant family, Eben and Ephraim, like most newcomers to New England in the mid-nineteenth century, have both endeavored to bring wasteland under cultivation.[15] The reason why their attachment to the land may reflect an implicit but deep-seated Irish rural convention, "where farmers farmed on their own behalf with the help of relatives [...] [and were] engaged in raising cattle, sheep and pigs" (Brown 22-23), is because the traditional inheritance system in rural Ireland had been a factor determining success, status, and security. The inherent values of the land and the family were thus brought to the New World with Irish immigrants. That is, the sons who were not entitled to any land nor got a job elsewhere would be forced into emigration, with famine being another impulse.

Fear of losing proprietorship of the land to their colonial lords had also contributed to the immigrants' attachment to the land, even though it was never a profitable commodity.[16] It can thus be posited that O'Neill's

---

[15]   *Desire Under the Elms* is set "in the Cabot farmhouse in New England, in the year of 1850" (2).

[16]   The anxiety about, or grieve for, the loss of the land to colonial (land)lords is also reflected in many Irish dramas and novels. W.B. Yeats' *The Countess Cathleen* (1892), *Cathleen ni Houlihan* (1902, coauthored with Lady Gregory), *The Hour Glass* (1904), *The Land of Heart's Desire* (1904), and *Deirdre* (1907), exemplified the retrieval of

portrait of Eben and Ephraim's struggle for the lawful inheritance of the land derives from his observations of the practice and sentiments of his Irish-American countrymen in the New World. In other words, Eben's insistent claim to the land, and refusal to share it with his own father and siblings, are not entirely because of his unsolved Oedipus complex, but because the land, as a crucial element of the food chain, would bring forth all kinds of social interactions in the future – with promising fringe benefits. That is to say, in *Desire* the land is a prerequisite for the unfailing operation of the "Desiring Machine," in which all social networks are interlocked but antagonistic at the same time. For instance, the tension and lust between Eben and Abbie have ignited physical and emotional rivalries that pertain to two American social networks: one from the east and the other from the west.

The desire for land (and its adjunct properties) draws these figures together, attracting and fighting against one another, even though Abbie and Eben originate from different immigrant communities. Eben's half brothers, Simeon and Peter, leave home to seek gold in California, because the land is too meager to assure any success. Although O'Neill did not specify whether Simeon and Peter earn what they wish for with the six hundred dollars they get from Eben, the money represents their desire for land in the hope of finding more promising wealth in the west. It can be noted that Simeon and Peter, after leaving home, would still have to deal with immigrants who – with their own dreams – join this collective "desiring machine" from all parts of the world. The social and cultural networks which the Cabots belong to would continue forming a melting pot in which mingle the different prospects of this state of settlers.

The desire for land also troubles the characters in Carr's *Raftery's*, despite the fact that the female Oedipus complex, or Electra complex in Jung's term, inevitably causes them great distress and leads to bitter consequences.[17] Unlike the newcomers to America and Irish immigrants'

---

the land in either realistic or mythic manners. What is worth attention is that major Irish writers and orators who lived through the fervent political upheavals during the nineteenth and early twentieth century all expressed opinions on the land issues. To name a few of these figures, James Clarence Mangan, Herald Griffin, Isaac Butt, Sean O'Casey, Padraic Colum, J.M. Synge, R.C. Murray, George Sigerson, George Russell, Thomas MacDonagh, John O'Leary, Michael Davitt, Patrick Kavanagh. Popular novels on the Irish Famine and the decline of Big Houses suggest how insecure the Irish felt about their power over their native land. What I would like to argue is that Irish immigrants' strong attachment to the land was a prevalent cultural phenomenon in which the land serves as the basic element of a coherent identity to be claimed.

17   Jung coined the term, the Electra complex, to explain female psycho-sexual develop-ment. The idea largely derives from Freud's Oedipus complex but refers more to female libidinal attachment to the father figure and hostility towards the mother, after the girl realizes her lack of a penis and develops "penis envy." Freud, however, explicitly rejected

strong attachment to the land, the female characters in *Raftery's* appear more resentful towards the claustrophobic Irish midlands, and would like to escape from them. The land, also not promising any fertility, imprisons the female protagonists who fail to accept any gentleman suitors but, sexually and emotionally, identify with the father who deflowered them at a young age. Dinah Raftery, for instance, lost her virginity to her father after the death of her mother, assuming the wifely role and giving birth to her sister/daughter, Sorrel. Red Raftery, the father, however, was also born from an incestuous relationship between his grandfather and his mother, Shalome (Shalome is therefore the grandmother of Dinah).

The home "land" therefore initiates a cycle of sexual violation which is acquiesced in and re-enacted through different generations of the Raftery family. Although critics may argue that it was the Oedipus complex that prompts Dinah and Shalome to fall in love with their own fathers, the land itself and the inheritance system encourage the enactment of this unspeakable desire. In particular, Shalome's affair with her own father confirms the inheritance of the farm to Red, their son/grandson. Dinah's incestuous relationship with Red also reflects a similar case, because Dinah's mother, who died young, did not give birth to a son who was fit enough to inherit the farm. Ded Raftery, the only son of Red and his deceased wife, is not eligible for heirship due to being under medication for his mental problems, and has been forced to live on his own in a cowshed with "cowdung all over his clothes" (7). He is prevented from inheriting the farm, as his father observes:

> Any other father'd have him in an asylum. Not me though, whah am I to do wud the farm, Isaac? There hundred acre a the finest land this side a the Shannon and west a the Pale. And me only son and heir can't tell night from day, oak from ash, he'd milk a bull and drink ud in his tay and never know the differ. (17)

It can be put forward that the claustrophobic, or self-centered, Irish midlands are the background cause of these incestuous relationships in relation to the legitimate inheritance of the land, in that inheritance, as a social mechanism, is operated in order to fulfill personal and/or communal desires, and *vice versa*. Conflicting but prohibited desires in both plays can be deduced as initiating a cycle of mental and sexual violence hidden in the "most sordid and mean blind alleys of life," whereas both playwrights dramatize the forbidden incestuous desires through an examination that is more poetic than moral (O'Neill 450). The authority over, or desire for, the land serves as an imperative for those involved in the "desiring machine."

---

this term, for it "seeks to emphasize the analogy between the attitude of the two sexes" (3), and simplifies the complex relations between children and their parents and siblings. Freud insisted on using the phrase "feminine Oedipus attitude" in his own writing.

Freud's interests in boys' and girls' identification with their mothers or fathers, therefore, cannot always be tenable, as the proprietorship is most likely confirmed or to be confirmed when one is born and regardless of gender differences. My argument is that, since most newborns have an instinctive claim of a "territory" by engaging themselves with a nipple, the Oedipus complex is activated *after* they realize the existence of their fathers as potential competitors.

More specifically, in *Desire*, Eben tenaciously "maks stone walls [...] to fence us in" (4), and his insistence on sole inheritance of the farm, and Ephraim's denial of his lawful right, suggests their strong sense of territoriality, but in conflict. Ephraim's attachment to the land as an instinct can be understood from his contentment at spending many hours with the livestock: "I slept good – down with the cows. They know how t' sleep. They're teachin' me" (38). Apparently, his sense of security about the land is always reconfirmed by contact with the domesticated livestock, which produce no threats against his ownership of the farm.

In *Raftery's*, although the land has been much contaminated by human "carnage," none of the family members would ever consider disowning it: "We were big loose monsters [...] hurlin through the air, wud carnage in our hearts and blood under our nails" (30). It is no longer a farm as "purty/ pretty" as the New World described in *Desire* and as praised by those having recently arrived in America. The famine-racked Irish midlands, though they carry bitter memories as well as hopes, are desirable for every member of the Raftery family.

The issue of inheritance of the land becomes more insistent when Sorrel plans to get married to Dara Mood: "Why doesn't he sell ud? I've enough saved to buy half ud is and the banks'd give me the rest. Wan day I'll own all this, Sorrel, you'll see" (31). Regardless of whether Sorrel and Dara plan to settle down on the land they are about to inherit, or to sell it for immediate income, the land is the basis upon which most human desires can be fulfilled, and which will (re-)confirm their social standing as the local gentry. What is more interesting is that Red, the father, akin to Ephraim in *Desire*, is very resistant to letting the farm go to an outsider, namely Sorrel's fiancé. His instinct of territoriality is manifest in his argument with Sorrel: "I heard you and Dara Mood scheming again me, tryin to stale me farm, next thing yees'll pisin me" (34). With reluctance, Red still grants the couple "fifty acre(s) and a cheque for twenty grands," in case his daughter would be "peg[ged] [...] into the world like a broken cup," and on condition that they "don't come lookin for more when they put me bones down" (51).

What should be pointed out is that Red's incestuous relationship with Dinah, his daughter, is not necessarily due to the Electra complex, as Freud and Jung presumed, or because of their love for Sorrel: "For eigheen years I watched you and minded you and kept ya safe!" (57). It is, initially, her mother's demand that she sleep with the husband: "she comes in behind me and says ouh a nowhere, you're to sleep in wud your father tonigh [...] I was twelve [...] we don't aither buh we want ud to stop. Ud's just like children playin in a field ah some awful game" (57). Although Dinah and Red do feel tormented by their guilt, the Electra complex is not evidently an instinct between Dinah and Red. The intimate relationship – which lasted for a couple of years – eventually started when Dinah was too young to find her own lovers in the culturally closed Irish midlands.

The incestuous relationship, though morally unacceptable, can nonetheless be examined in a broader scope as a social mechanism, rather than from only a Freudian perspective. In Deleuze and Guattari's view, the land, or territory, is the basis of capitalism which may bring forth a schizophrenic social system. This system prompts the individual to subvert or deterritorialize, and then re-territorialize, social groupings, so as to confirm one's own standing. That is, the church, the family, or any communities which occupy a practical or theoretical "territory," are liable to be restructured or re-territorialized in this desiring social machine at some point of history: "what they deterritorialize with one hand, they reterritorialize with the other" (Deleuze and Guattari 257).

The inheritance or division of the farm in both plays could, therefore, facilitate the operation of a capitalistic society, and fulfill desires at both personal and public levels. In *Desire*, Eben's incestuous affair with his stepmother is ignited partially by lust and attraction, but also partially in expectation of securing the farm for their shared benefit, by means of the heirship of their *own* son. Nonetheless, Ephraim, resisting any manner of re-territorialization through marriage, insists that Eben "ought t' be marrin' [someone else] [...] [to] 'arn a share o' a farm that way" (45-6). Ephraim's attachment to the land is further reinforced by his own twisted interpretation of Abbie's wishes about driving Eben away:

> she says yew'n me ought t' have a son – I know we kin, she says – an' I says, if we do, ye kin have anythin' I've got ye've a mind t'. An' she says, I wants Eben cut off so's this farm'll be mine when ye die!" (46)

Ephraim's interpretation may be partially true but not at all defensible, especially after Abbie and Eben, falling in love, assume they could secure their rights over the farm with a newborn son. Apparently, their desire to re-territorialize the farm has to be censored by the community, as the neighbors have suspected their honesty. The gossip and jeers that are flying about, and the interference of the police, function to keep the social desiring machine running. In Deleuze and Guattari's words, the social mechanisms usually function simultaneously with "[d]ecoded desires and desires for decoding [which] have always existed," and thus capitalism and its breakdown can be operated universally by "the conjunction of deterritorialized flows" over centuries (224). The infanticide which Abbie commits is thus an embodiment of decoded desire – subject to the puritanical sense of morality in New England.

In *Raftery's*, the land is also securable with an incestuous affair between Red and Dinah, while the forbidden relationship is immorally encouraged by the deceased mother/wife. Similarly to Ephraim in *Desire*, Red is also very reluctant to part with *his* farm, proposing to give a substitute for the land – as part of the dowry for Sorrel – in the shape of a check for twenty pounds. Red's parsimony lies in the fact that the land, capitalistically speaking, could earn him pecuniary profits for the foreseeable future. Put another way, if he lost the land to Sorrel and her fiancé, he could never easily retrieve it, but the twenty pounds is easily recoverable. As a result, the land is the capital which Red, Sorrel, and Dara all want to (re-)territorialize, or hold on to, so as to maintain or create the maximum benefits.

The Rafterys' sole tie with the farm is further confirmed by the incestuous behavior between Red and Dinah, even though their mutual attachment is mixed with guilt and pleasure. This tie is further recognized after they give birth to Sorrel as both their daughter and sister. Although both Dinah and Red would like to quit this immoral relationship, Dinah, having been deflowered by her own father, knows well that she should expect no other suitor, having such a familial scandal behind her.[18] The imperative of re-territorializing the farm is therefore postponed almost infinitely due to this ongoing incestuous relationship. Not until Sorrel and Dara plan to get married is the desire for the land raised again, so that this incestuous affair has to fall under the social or moral supervision of the desiring machine – which interlocks the desires of all its members in one way or another. It can thus be judged that what the father contributes to the Raftery family, after the passing of his wife, is that he successfully secures the land for as long as he can, unlike Ephraim in *Desire*, who makes the land immediately available to the new wife. The price Red pays, which is hard to justify, is Dinah's virginity and her chances of getting married.

It is also evident that, having been, respectively, an editor of an anthology of Greek tragedies and a writer of over thirty adaptations

---

[18]   In her youth, Dinah did have a love affair with Dara Mood's brother, Jimmy, whereas the incestuous relationship with her own father deeply troubled her, so "I brok id off wud Jimmy fierce sudden and fierce hard […] things was rickety for me thah time. Ud's allas the wans you're fondest of ya drop the axe on" (55). Apparently, Dinah was so tormented about the socially forbidden relationship that she could not, and would not, feel mentally free to date any gentleman caller.

of Greek dramas,[19] O'Neill and Carr demonstrated their interest in contextualizing the Oedipus and Electra themes in a modern framework, incorporating elements of Greek mythology despite the different perspectives and endings that they introduced. What drew them to the re-dramatization of human complexities in a modern context, as O'Neill noted in the introduction to his edition of *Seven Famous Greek Plays*, is the universality of these human emotions: "Equally astonishing is the pervading obscenity, so abundant and so varied that it cannot be ignored or excised. It is so closely interwoven into almost every part of these plays that to expurgate is to destroy" (xxiii). What differentiates the plays of O'Neill and Carr from those of their Greek predecessors, however, is the way in which they provided an alternative understanding of the forbidden desire, which, in different cultural scenarios, might not have had to end so tragically, giving a new perspective for their contemporary audiences.

In *Desire*, the infanticide which Abbie commits, Eben's call for police investigation and his falsely admitted complicity, Ephraim's curse on the couple that they be hanged, and Eben's admittance of his moral sin, indeed characterize Eben as a hero with tragic flaws. Ostensibly, Eben resembles Hippolytus in the myth of Phaedra, who blackens her stepson for raping her due to her unrequited love for him. Eben and Hippolytus are both cursed by their fathers and die tragically, Phaedra commits suicide, and Abbie is about to be executed for infanticide. Nonetheless, the ending in *Desire*, though also tragic with the foreseeable death of the couple, can be seen as profoundly redirecting the desiring machine to some positive results. That is, Ephraim, at the end of the play, albeit much disillusioned but somehow illumined by the disastrous love affair, decides to free all the cows and burn down the farm to which he has been so insistently attached:

> T' hell with the farm! I'm leavin' it! I've turned the cows an' other stock loose! I've druv 'em into the woods whar they kin be free! By freein' 'em, I'm freein' myself; I'm quittin' here today! I'll set fire t' house an' barn an' watch 'em burn [...] an' I'll will the fields back t' God, so that nothin' human kin never touch 'em. (57)

As elaborated earlier, the land has been an object of desire for all the parties intending to lay a firm social foundation in the desiring machine.

---

[19] As stated earlier, O'Neill had a scholarly interest in Greek drama, editing *Seven Famous Greek Plays* with Whitney J. Oates in 1938. Marianne McDonald surveyed Irish playwrights' interests in Greek mythology, among whom Carr has written over thirty adaptations of Greek mythology for different occasions. Frank McGuinness observed that Carr "knows what the Greeks know [...] I am certain [...] she writes in Greek." See McDonald's "Classics as Celtic Firebrand: Greek Tragedy, Irish Playwrights, and Colonialism," and M.K. Martinovich's "The Mythical and the Macabre: The Study of Greeks and Ghosts in the Shaping of the American premiere of By the Bog of Cats...."

The idea of claiming territory, as an instinct, can be the origin of desires and emotions that are unlikely to be erased but indeed sustained, even if they are not morally approved. Ephraim's disclaimer to the land and talk of "freein' myself" suggests his extended resistance to the subjugation of the land, which has initiated his animosity toward his sons, lust for women, and uncertain belief in God. Realizing that Eben has already "swapped it t' Sim an' Peter fur their share o' the farm – t' pay their passage t' Californi-a" (57), Ephraim, who seems to be indefatigable, finally recognizes his own weakness: "I kin see [God's] hand usin' Eben t' steal t' keep me from weakness" (57).[20] The farm in flames and Ephraim's recognition of his own weakness imply the purification of the desiring machine after all the relevant parties have admitted their own sins: greed, lust, incest, dishonesty, ambition, and betrayal.

Unlike the myth of Phaedra, the ending of *Desire* sheds positive light on characters in suffering, given that all of them lose their right to the land after the infanticide. They are freed from the burden of the land as capital, and the lesson of compassion is manifest after Abbie and Eben are arrested and are about to be sent under guard to different places: "They kiss [...] Eben takes Abbie's hand. They go out the door in rear [...] They both stand for a moment looking up raptly in attitudes strangely aloof and devout" (58). The couple are reconciled and learn to appreciate the goodness of life: "Sun's a rizin'/ Purty, hain't it?" says Eben as his last words to Abbie (58). What is most profound, however, is that O'Neill does not negate the cycle of de-territorialization and re-territorializaion in human history. The farm will probably be taken over by the sheriff as an external force who is "looking around at the farm enviously [...] Wished I owned it!" (58). The reclaiming of the free land may therefore bring forth a new cycle of sins and pleasure, so that the desiring machine will continue to function, regardless of the presence of the Cabot family.

The ending of *Raftery's* is unconventional, with a rather philosophical insight into forbidden desire and the issue of love. The division of the land to create a dowry for Sorrel is dismissed after Dara realizes that he will not get a substantial portion of the land, but only a check for twenty pounds from his future father-in-law. He argues with Sorrel, for his current social status as "a scrubber from the Valley" will not be improved, should he not be gifted with the profitable land (54). Unable to bear with Dara's pride, and knowing that her fiancé was more interested in the land than in herself, she calls off the wedding without much hesitation. Regarding Dinah's incestuous relationship with her father, the playwright, not following the

---

[20]   The overwhelming elms, justifiably, contribute a counterforce to the strong ego of the aging father, Ephraim, who constantly refers to the God of the Old Testament for uncompromising moral guidance.

traditional characterization of Phaedra as a tragic heroine, reconsiders the significance of love in a modern context. Specifically, Carr does not particularly victimize Dinah, as most sociologists and psychiatrists might have done, but presents her as a mature woman who is brave in the face of her own forbidden desire and its consequences. That she and Sorrel can consider their incestuous family with humor, instead of being ashamed or judgmental, implies a new insight which the playwright would like to introduce:[21]

> Dinah [...] We're a respectable family, we love wan another and whahever happened ya happened ya be accident. D'ya honestly think we'd harm wan another?
> Sorrel Spare me your Legion a' Mary canter. We're a band a gorillas swingin from the trees. (58)

Sorrel's humor about her family as a band of gorillas may be taken to show how the playwright justifies the issues of human desire and sense of territory. Put another way, the sense of territory by which human desires are driven can be strengthened either through marriage or an incestuous relationship. Shalome's undying motivation in leaving home in search of her deceased father, who has behaved incestuously with her daughter, suggests desire for the home land, or instinct of claiming the territory, even though she is portrayed as being mentally disordered. As to the former, the territory can usually be enlarged if one marries into a family with land. Dara in *Raftery's* and Ephraim's expectation of Eben's marriage with some other woman in the town in *Desire* both suggest the intention of creating or enlarging one's territory as an instinct – which is applicable to most creatures. As to the latter, an incestuous affair, if not to be judged moralistically, would not necessarily break down the operation of the desiring machine, but would at least secure the given size of the territory. The loving human relationships – with mixed desires and affection, as Shalome/her father, Dinah/Red, and Abbie/Eben have experienced heartily – therefore contribute to social stability, rather than creating an ethical crisis, to some extent, provided that morality does not have to be forced upon them and confine the natural course of desire.

In particular, Sorrel's humor about humans being not much different from gorillas, and Ephraim's contentment at being with the cows in his barn, disclose their ignorance of human nature, as well as their human fear of desire if not under social control. The negation of desire on the part of ourselves and others has not only ostracized and condemned those

---

[21] Dinah and Sorrel's father, Red, was given birth by their grandmother, Shalome, who committed incest with their great grandfather. Sorrel is both Dinah's daughter and sister, with Red as the biological father of both of them.

in socially unfavorable relationships and sexual activities, but has also created walls, visible and invisible, among people of different ethnicities, sexual orientations, or/and classes. Wars between nations and religions, or fights within a family and community, can thus break out, and are followed by more hatred and resentment.

What O'Neill and Carr were attempting to achieve by rewriting the classical myths was, justifiably, to rebuild universal understanding of tragic heroes and heroines from a more humane perspective, leading the audiences to approach human complexities with compassion. By appreciating how both Carr and O'Neill re-interpreted classical myth, we can see how the former was the inheritor of the latter, as she specified in an interview in which she talked about exploring the conflict of human desires: "It's hard to beat [...] Eugene O'Neill's *The Iceman Cometh* and *Long Day's Journey into Night*" (Murphy 56)".[22] Following O'Neill's representation of Abbie as a self-determined and compassionate woman, rather than a sinner, Carr rewrote the experiences of women in the Irish midlands, "inverting the actions of the Poor Old Woman in the earlier drama and refusing the myth of an idealized Mother Ireland" (Sihra 19).

In other words, both playwrights individualize these mythical characters by exploring their desires in conflict and redefining their significance for contemporary audiences. It can also be understood that both playwrights, writing in the contexts of emigrant/immigrant societies in connection with Ireland, were more interested in the relation "between man and God, [than] between man and man," as the puritanical ambiance serves to reinforce emotional taboos (Krutch 450). Carr's realistic approach to women in the Irish midlands therefore interrogates the patriotic nature of Cathleen ni Houlihan, who was dispossessed of her farmhouse and "four beautiful green fields," as dramatized in the 1902 play by Lady Gregory and W.B. Yeats (81).

O'Neill's portrait of Ephraim as a harsh and hypocritical father (about his lust) also questions the fatherly authority of Puritanism in New England. What O'Neill and Carr have brought forth is a form of deconstruction of the given desiring machine whereby men and women of chastity do not always meet but are maneuvered, often indefinitely. The resistance of the Cabots and Red to re-territorialization can also be seen symbolically as being against patriarchal, patriotic power, or the entire

---

[22] Carr is a well-read playwright. In her interview with Mike Murphy, she mentioned Sean O'Casey, Samuel Beckett, and J.M. Synge, from all of whom she received positive influence. She also mentioned Anton Chechov, Henrik Ibsen, Tennessee Williams, and O'Neill, whose observations on human nature might have deepened and/or renewed Carr's understanding of delicate human complexities which her predecessors had not unearthed so carefully.

social structure, as these immigrants and emigrants have to either claim a piece of land from the natives or give it up to the colonizers. Implications such as these may be more complicated than those defined by the Oedipus or Electra complexes.

Part of the shared significance of the two plays lies in the fact that some of the protagonists, for example Ephraim and Ded, can retrieve a sense of security when retreating to the barns. The intention which O'Neill and Carr shared in depicting this seeming congeniality between humans and domestic animals may have been to remind the audience of an ignored perspective whereby humans should act as part of the natural world, rather than as dominant social or political beings. Satirically, that humans can interact with farm animals more peacefully than between themselves is because animals cannot produce real threats against people, whose superior position is thus reinforced, whereas interpersonal interrelations are always frustrating and fragile.

What should also be noted is that both playwrights, through presenting a more agreeable interaction between humans and nature at the end of their dramas, suggest how human expectation of, or desire for, the companionship of domesticated animals is actually more subject to the natural temperament of the latter. Therefore, human desire can hardly be freed from external forces, or the human-centered desiring machine, as Deleuze and Guattari phrased it. Religion, for instance, does not alleviate the sufferings of the protagonists, nor is it able to stand in a position beyond the far-reaching desiring machine. Having said this, what subjugates the desires of members of the emigrant and immigrant communities unceasingly, however, is the silent but forceful land – which haunts the background. Only love and compassion, as presented by O'Neill and Carr through Abbie and Dinah, can strategically countervail the domination of the land – *who* has been playing the role of a demanding operator of the desiring machine – for peace and justice.

II. Remaking the Stage Irishman in the New World: Dion Boucicault's *The Shaughraun*, Edward Harrigan's *The Mulligan Guard Ball*, and Sebastian Barry's *White Woman Street*

Introduction: The Stage Irishman at Stake

Modern Irish playwrights are internationally recognized for their talent at dramatizing the "troubles" of their nation, be they cultural, political, religious, or sectarian, with attention being paid to the insightful controversies contained in their works. However, what prompts the (re-) creations of the Irish nation, or Irishness in general, on stage is the anxiety that implicitly but incessantly irritates Irish playwrights and audiences about the public perceptions of their homeland. The underlying anxiety, arguably, emanates from a lingering colonial condition where the Irish had often been caricatured and smeared by their rulers, or the English print media, especially in the age of Fenian rebellions and the Land League, as simians, buffoons or beggars, or stereotyped as "slothful," "feckless," "devious," "violent," and "ungrateful" (Meagher 71-72).[1] These unfriendly, almost spiteful, presentations of the Irish motivated a number of playwrights, critics, and those of the Irish diaspora, to propose a different theatrical image of their people, claiming to be more authentic in their first-hand observations, in order to redress those caricatures that had socially categorized them as the Other, or on the lower rung of the social ladder.

Although these playwrights – to be discussed in this chapter – succeeded in revamping Irish characters in realistic ways, in contrast to the existing stage Irishman as a figure to be ridiculed, what should be noted is that their re-creations of the Irish can still be implicitly problematic in the "truths" they represent as evidence of existing political preferences. A study of

---

[1] Specifically, newspaper and magazine cartoonists in Victorian Britain, partially under the influence of distorted Darwinism, tended to caricature Irishmen as inhuman apes or monkeys with "red wigs, red noses, green whiskers, or little beards" (Wittke 260). Irish-Americans were often depicted as bestial and violent simians with "squarer jaws, stronger chins, and higher facial angles" by the cartoonists of the mainstream media, for example, the New York Times, according to Perry Curtis (59). The line which emphasized "NINA" (No Irish Need Apply) in the recruitment section of newspapers also suggests this collective prejudice against the Irish as the Other, so as to maintain the dominance of the privileged class.

these Irish dramas, particularly those set in America, may illustrate not only an ignored picture of the Irish diaspora struggling on the breadline yet solidifying their cultural identity, but also suggest how they wished to be seen and how they saw other ethnic communities, including African Americans, with whom they often shared urban tenements or slums. The reexamination of these relevant plays – featuring Irish-American experiences – will supplement both Irish and American histories in which the interactions of the Irish diaspora with immigrants of other ethnicities have not been sufficiently documented, particularly their bitter power struggles for limited economic and political resources. The "true" faces of Irish-Americans which the playwrights invent may, although they are sometimes contradictory, disclose the process of "how the Irish became white," in Noel Ignatiev's term, by using different types of violence to consolidate their hard-won status or strategically "whiten" themselves through assimilation into the legal, economic and political landscape of American society.[2]

The process for Irish immigrants to become "white" was evidently painful, for they had been undemocratically categorized by the socially privileged as a deprived, unwelcome class, sharing the non-white status given to Mexican-Americans, Cuban-Americans, Colombians, Latinos and Chinese; not based on the color of their skin but their country of origin. According to Ignatiev, the Irish, among these "non-white" immigrants, gradually managed to distance themselves, often violently, from people of these colored ethnicities by taking up odd, mostly dangerous, jobs which the owners of colored slaves would not accept for fear of losing "properties." On the other hand, the Irish, prior to emigrating to America, were experienced in organizing labor unions to request better wages and social benefits from their English employers, so they were able to use these skills to earn an improved status in the more promising land of the New World. What is profoundly interesting is that the Irish and the Blacks, having been categorized as the Others, were "antagonists and doubles" on the social and economic margin but both demanded a greater pace of social mobility (Onkey 9).

---

[2]   In *How the Irish Became White*, Noel Ignatiev argues that Irish immigrants, though mostly famine refugees, were not necessarily victims of class oppression in the New World, but gradually embraced racism to subjugate their Black brothers in the tenements/slums where they cohabited and competed in the labor market. Despite the fact that Irish nationalists often claimed themselves to be dominated by the colonizer, Ignatiev argues that the Irish were no less racist than other Caucasian immigrants and had "learn[ed] to subordinate country, religious, or national animosities, [...] to a new solidarity based on color – a bond which, it must be remembered, was contradicted by their experience in Ireland" (96).

What I would like to propose, not necessarily in contradiction to Ignatiev's sociological assumptions, is a more nuanced observation of the interactions between the Irish and other ethnic communities, and an examination of the changing faces of the stage Irishman in the late nineteenth-century American theatre. The plays which this chapter will investigate will reveal neglected facets of the Irish immigrants' lives, dreams, ambitions, aspirations, frustrations, struggles, and pleasures in the political and economic contexts of their times. Put another way, the three playwrights to be discussed, differently from sociologists such as Ignatiev, tend to present a more romantic but not necessarily untrue delineation of their nation, and also comment critically on the ambiguous position that the Irish held as victims and victimizers in the immigrant community. The three dramas to be discussed, listed chronologically, are Dion Boucicault's *The Shaughraun* (1874), Edward Harrigan's *The Mulligan Guard Ball* (1879), and Sebastian Barry's *White Woman Street* (1992). These three plays, written over a span of more than a century but all portraying Irish-Americans between the late nineteenth and early twentieth centuries, may provide audiences with an intertextual and cross-cultural understanding of the Irish diaspora in the New World, and how they neutralized their Otherness by, for instance, imposing violence on their African brothers.

Dion Boucicault's *The Shaughraun* (1874): A "Subversively Fenian" or Melodramatic Drama?

Before this chapter investigates how Boucicault re-characterized the stage Irishman, who usually appeared on American stages as "a blundering, ignorant, comic peasant" and "a staple of the American theater [...] magazine and newspaper stories and popular literature" (Meagher 50), it may first be necessary to elaborate the cultural and colonial determinants that defined the American middle-class theatregoers' perception of the Irish in the nineteenth century. These determinants may be no less difficult to remove than the racial ideology that Ignatiev outlines in terms of the "whitening" process of the Irish from the sociological viewpoint. Notably, the stage Irishman was not an American theatrical invention but had been fabricated by English and some Irish dramatists since the mid-eighteenth century, along with Scottish and Welsh stage characters.[3]

---

[3]   *The Committee* (1662), by Sir Robert Howard (1626-1698), was the first drama with a stage Irishman named Teague, being Irish for Timothy. His *The Twin Rival* (1702) also has a footman with this name. According to Christopher Murray, "Teague the servant was immensely popular on the English stage in the eighteenth century, often found in plays not by Irish authors at all and acted by men who had never set foot in Ireland in their lives" (504). English playwrights who produced such a character include Thomas D'Urfey, George Powell, John Durant Brevel, and Moses Mendez. Captain Macmorris

Their plays were mostly premiered in London before they were brought to Philadelphia and New York, and many English playwrights had never been to Ireland but caricatured local people through a collective colonial imagination of the Irish Other. The stage Irishman, by contrast to the English gentleman on stage, was usually a character who was either in the role of an uneducated footman, or was stigmatized as a savage or a traitor, speaking in a Hiberno-English dialect or brogue. They were made, if comic, to amuse audiences with their verbal and logical blunders; if crude, to impress theatregoers with their savagery or dishonesty.[4] It can be argued that the colonial mentality that exploited the stage Irishman lay partially in twisted Darwinism, and partially reflected the expectations of the ruler in regard to how the Irish should behave as part of the British Empire. As Christopher Murray suggests, the English in the eighteenth century were always cautious of possible alliances between the native Irish and the French, as both peoples were Catholic. The Irish were thus often presented at English theatres as traitors to the country, or as conspirators with Jacobites. The "bungling, innocent, and loyal" Irishman, understandably, became the favorite character who could temporarily ease the English audiences' sense of insecurity about their given superiority over the Irish whom they ruled. Boucicault's *The Shaughraun*, which he subtitled "an original Irish drama in three acts," is however controversial in the way in which he featured an over-idealized Irish-British reciprocal relationship, designed to appeal to middle-class audiences in New York, London, and Dublin, despite the fact that it much displeased the radical wing of Irish nationalism – an issue to be discussed later.

One very peculiar thing about *The Shaughraun*, although it is "an original Irish drama" premiered in New York in 1874, is its revival in 2004 as the centerpiece of the Abbey Theatre's centenary celebration, along

---

in *Henry V* (1599), by William Shakespeare, is a typical stage Irishman demeaned as such: "he is an ass, as in the world [...] [with] no more directions in the true disciplines of the wars, [...] than a puppy-dog" (3.3.15-18). Playwrights from Ireland also joined in the making of this either comic or savage stage Irishman, so as to ingratiate London audiences; to name a few, Isaac Bickerstaffe, Hugh Kelly, John O'Keeffe, and Richard Brinsley Sheridan. Nineteenth-century Irish novelists, Charles Lever and Somerville and Ross, also recurrently sketched the stage Irish in their works. George Bernard Shaw's *John Bull's Other Island* (1904) is critical of these caricatures of the Irish, and indirectly prompted the vehement attacks on J.M. Synge's *The Playboy of the Western World* (1907) for its offensive presentation of the Irish peasant woman.

[4]   Thomas Forrest's *The Disappointment* (1767) was the first play written by an American playwright with an Irish character. As Wittke says, there had been at least a score of American plays with stage Irishman characters before 1828 (253). For details of Irish characters on stage in early American theaters, see Kent G. Gallagher's *The Foreigner in Early American Drama: A Study in Attitudes*, pp. 115-134, and Annelise Truniger's *Paddy and the Paycock: A Study of the Stage Irishman from Shakespeare to O'Casey*.

with J.M. Synge's *The Playboy of the Western World* and Stewart Parker's *Heavenly Bodies*.[5] These three plays, not exactly with similar agendas, are critical of the hierarchy of social powers that had restrained playwrights from presenting more realistic Irishmen on stage but instead required them to follow a theatrical convention that was based on colonial sentiments. For instance, *The Shaughraun*, although it broke the box office record by running for one hundred and eighteen evening performances and twenty-five matinees within six months in New York (Odell 522), is probably an outcome of political compromises. That is, its happy ending was in part to suit public taste, and in part to fulfill Irish-Americans' nostalgia for their homeland, despite its portrayal of Fenians who are set free by Queen Victoria.[6] The ending, in which the Irish and the English are reconciled, also ensured its successful later production in London. What I would like to argue is that the play, although it was commercially celebrated in contrast to *Playboy*, which provoked open protests, may have been overrated by the public, in that *The Shaughraun* was candidly in line with the expectations of Irish-American theatregoers, who were mainly middle-class, for a reciprocal relationship with England as a possible but romantic solution to the Irish troubles of the time.[7] In other words, although some believed that this play was "Boucicault's most political work: set in the immediate aftermath of the Fenian atrocities in England in 1867" (McFeely 54), this view may not be tenable, as *The Shaughraun* did not evoke radical reactions that had the potential of altering the political inferiority of the Irish in their homeland, and neither did it offend mainstream audiences in New York, London, and Dublin. The problematic nature of this play may be more evident if it is studied alongside Harrigan's and Barry's later

---

[5] Parker's *Heavenly Bodies* was produced at the Peacock Theatre as a double bill with *The Shaughraun* in 2004. *Heavenly Bodies* is a stage biography of Boucicault, dramatizing the playwright's ambition for fame, his creativity, and his struggle and compromises between the arts and the political forces of his time.

[6] The Fenians, deriving their name from Fianna, a band of Irish warriors in the second and third centuries, were a nationalist revolutionary movement for an Irish republic independent from Great Britain. The Fenian Brotherhood in America was established in 1858, supplying their Irish counterparts, for instance, the Irish Republican Brotherhood, with money and arms for revolts against the English administration. The Fenian movement which Boucicault portrays in this play was well known about by Irish-American audiences.

[7] The performances of *Playboy* during the *Abbey Theater's American tour* aroused violent protests by various Irish-American Catholic organizations because of Synge's portrayal of an assertive, independent Irishwoman and an Irish patricide. This play enraged the Catholic and Irish nationalist public because it undermined conservative Catholic values and the paternalism of Irish patriotism. The controversy led to full houses, especially in New York and Philadelphia, although the significance of this box office success is not the same as that of *The Shaughraun*, which was well-received, for it conformed with public taste.

plays – which provide a more close-up observation of the ignored realities of the deprived Irish-Americans who were often excluded from theatrical entertainments and might have held sentiments that were different from Boucicault's.

What makes *The Shaughraun* an *original* Irish play is rather a comparative question, in that most of the plays produced at American theatres at the time – particularly those with comic, sly or savage Irish buffoons – tended to stigmatize or exaggerate Irish qualities. The negative portraits of the Irish inevitably irritated Irish-American immigrants and their next generation descendants, who desired social mobility and respectability.[8] The "originality" of this Irish play, as the playwright claimed, reflects the changing status of Irish-Americans at the time of its production, because of the characterization of an *Irish* peasant, Paddy Conn, who is the Shaughraun of the title.[9] He is portrayed as an agile, sympathetic, loyal wanderer with a sense of justice, rather than a stage Irishman who is "ignorant, lazy, unreliable, emotionally unstable, hard drinking, often violent, improvident" (McCaffrey 28). Specifically, Conn is not only a hero who rescues a Fenian prisoner, Robert Ffolliott, but a lovable Irish gentleman in love with a village girl, Moya. His admirable qualities, and their wedding with which the plays ends, were the key that brought success to this romantic melodrama in the first place. What fascinated American audiences, however, was the notion of anti-hegemony with which the nation struggled to be independent from European domination. The condescension of an English officer, Captain Molineux, is humorously illustrated in the play but was convincing enough to prompt the audiences' sympathy towards the oppressed Irish. That is, the success of the play stemmed from the fact that American audiences, even those not of Irish ancestry, could easily see their relationship with Irish Fenianism, in terms of their shared efforts at nation formation.

It should be noted that Boucicault's *The Shaughraun*, well-received, and Synge's *The Playboy of the Western World*, severely protested against, both reverse the usual power relationship by presenting women who are significantly more dominant and confident than their gentleman suitors.

---

[8]   The beginning of the modern Irish diaspora dates from the potato famine of the 1840s. It is estimated that, by the early 1920s, there were 1,037,234 Irish people, including second and third generation descendants of immigrants, living in the United States (Brown 20). Compared with the African immigrants, their experiences in dealing with political matters – before emigrating to the US – contributed to their rising political influence. Irish singers, dancers, composers, playwrights, and actors had a large and growing influence on American popular culture, and the effects of this are still evident.

[9]   The Gaelic word, "shaughraun," or seachrán, means wanderer or vagabond, or describes the state of traveling or wandering. It is probably a fitting description of the condition of deprived Irish emigrants in America.

Nevertheless, *Playboy* received more critical attention, for its power reversal between protagonists was explicitly akin to that between Ireland and England in a colonial framework, whereas *The Shaughraun*, the commercial hit, avoided severe criticism by being moderate in dealing with nationalistic matters – with Robert Ffolliott set free by Queen Victoria as a celebrated gesture of mercy. What made the public receive the two plays differently is thus the strategies which the playwrights employed in counteracting artistic expressions, political leanings, and public taste. The rather less offensive strategy used by Boucicault is the open-ended device of giving only Conn and Moya a chance of getting married. The other two relationships, between the English Captain Molineux and Claire Ffolliott (a Sligo lady), and between Arte O'Neal and Robert Ffolliott (the Fenian), do not end up with a proposal or engagement. There is no hint as to why these two couples could not tie the knot, but it can be assumed that the audiences would thus refrain from making the political analogy of an Irish-English marriage, rejoicing only in the engagement of Conn and Moya, the two Irish people, in this melodrama. The reason why the playwright did not have Robert and Arte get married might be because of the Fenian identity of the former, which it would have been unwise to celebrate openly or give political encouragement to at the time of the production.

However, the key reason why *The Shaughraun* could be a commercial hit was not merely because of the open ending which caused limited political sensation but suited the general expectations of the audiences. It was, however, its anti-English undercurrent and the pursuit of democracy that fascinated audiences and incurred their empathy for the oppressed Irish. That is, *The Shaughraun*, an original *Irish* play as Boucicault intended, strategically altered the audiences' perception of Ireland by putting the Irish in the foreground and giving the English a secondary, supporting role throughout the play. For instance, the initial contact of Captain Molineux with Claire Ffolliott, the Fenian prisoner's sister, reversed the English-centered convention by having Claire accept the apologies of the English officer for his mispronunciations of Gaelic place names: "I remarked your misfortune [of being English]; poor creature, you couldn't help it" (*Shaughraun* 173). As he is romantically attracted to Claire, his understanding of the Irish locale, Suil-a-beg (pronounced Shoolabeg), becomes wider after he gets more involved with the villagers' daily activities, for instance helping Claire with the churning. The audiences' perception of Ireland was also broadened with Captain Molineux's encounters with other locals who talk in witticisms and behave on friendly terms with the English.

What is also noteworthy about the play is its implicit nationalistic nature that prompted the audiences' sympathy for Robert Ffolliott, the Fenian on the run, whereas the arrest warrant issued by the English government forces him to part with his girlfriend, Arte O'Neal, whom Robert cannot protect when she is abducted by Corry Kinchela, a local landlord, to be his wife without her consent. Captain Molineux's mission – which is resented locally for enforcing colonial control over the villagers – is a failure, as the Irish villagers collaborate with each other, trusting no English officers, and want to rescue the Fenians by themselves. What is more intriguing is that, perhaps to ease the political sensitivity of the play, a decree of special pardon for the Fenians is issued by Queen Victoria. The local conflict is thus avoided, and the villagers' enmities are directed towards the notorious landlord who abducts Arte O'Neal, and Harvey Duff, a police agent disguised as an Irish peasant who informs against the locals. Perhaps either to avoid offending theatregoers with diverse political leanings, or to suggest tacit cooperation between the Irish and the English, the landlord is arrested and social order is quickly restored by Captain Molineux and his English soldiers before the curtain falls. It can be claimed that the commercial success of this play, significantly, lay in its even-handed treatment of the Irish-English relationship, so as not to arouse discontent from influential groups during its tours in the US and England.

Although *The Shaughraun* had impressive success at the box office, a number of theatrical criticisms still centered on its political (in)correctness. Some praised it for being the "most subversively Fenian play" (Cullingford 27); others attacked Boucicault for being "a greedy palm – ready to work for the British Government, the devil,"[10] and the playwright should have "advocated a 'no surrender' approach" (qtd in McFeely 65). One critic gave a rather fair comment by suggesting that this play offered "an assertion of integrity as a form of nationalism […] [There] is an integrity that cannot struggle free of imperial assumptions but is still a reflection of them" (Cave 72). These statements may be true to some extent, but these critics have seemingly overlooked one profound piece of irony which Boucicault devised in regard to the French surname of the English captain, namely Molineux.[11] Specifically, Captain Molineux, who was relocated to Ireland on a mission on behalf of the British Empire, is presumably of French descent, as his name suggests. Although the play does not mention his family background, his presence in Ireland suggests his "otherness" in the realm of imperial politics, and his difficulty in retrieving the cultural identity of his forefathers. He

---

[10]   The quote appeared in *Irish World*, 13 February 1875, p. 6.

[11]   Molineux, also spelled as Molyneux, Molineaux, Molines, Mullineaux, and Mollyneux, originated in the Seine-Maritime area of the province of Normandy. The name, meaning a miller, was introduced into England by the Normans in 1066 and then the Protestant Huguenots in the seventeenth century. Mulliner, an Anglicized version, is widely recorded as a surname in the north-west of England.

may have been intended as a role model for the colonized, for he holds a privileged official position, and the ruled may therefore agree willingly to integrate with the British Empire. Interestingly, his "otherness" allows him to act more humanely and to identify with the locals, for instance, in his keen pursuit of the village beauty, Claire, and his willingness to join in with farming activities. The issue therefore resides in the fact that these Others can never be fairly integrated with the British administration but will be in league with each other – directly or indirectly – in resisting the oppression of colonial hierarchy. That the playwright did not produce a happy ending, with all three couples getting married, might suggest the unerasable "otherness" of the Irish and those of French descent, so that the play became less melodramatic but more political.

Edward Harrigan's *The Mulligan Guard Ball* (1879): Enemies or Doubles?

As mentioned earlier in this chapter, the commercial success of *The Shaughraun* did not eventually serve to guarantee Irish Catholic fundamentalists' faith in Boucicault's efforts at invalidating the stage Irishman, in that many of them insisted that the only presentable type of Irishman must quit "whiskey [...] [and act with] the chivalry, the patriotism, and the generous impulses brought in to set off the unmistakable humor of [Ireland]" (qtd in McFeely 55).[12] Their shared resentment against *The Shaughraun*, although it did have much effect on the play's box office takings, nonetheless created another ideological stage Irishman who should "register dissent against Britain [...] [to be] culturally different from both the British and Anglo-Americans" (McFeely 59), and he had to be a practicing Catholic, an abstainer from alcohol, and an unmistakable nationalist. Both Conn, the Shaughraun who is always drunk, and Robert Ffolliott, as an Anglo-Irish Fenian, could hardly be tolerated by these deep-seated nationalistic commentators, despite their expectations of Irishmen on stage being no less ideological.[13]

Harrigan's *The Mulligan Guard Ball*, which premiered in New York on 13 January 1879, presents Irish characters via an approach that is somewhat different from Boucicault's *The Shaughraun* and how Boucicault expected Irish people to be.[14] This play demonstrates what

---

[12] In *Irish World*, 19 Dec. 1874, p. 3.

[13] It may thus be contended that there is no surprise that the Abbey's American tour of Synge's *Playboy* met with a strong wave of criticism in the 1910s – almost thirty years after *The Shaughraun* premiered.

[14] "The Mulligan Guard" is the name of an Irish-American social group in the ethnic community of the lower east side of New York. "The Skidmore Guard" was a Black group, among other unofficial ethnic groups.

Harrigan, born in New York of Irish lineage, observed from everyday life on the streets of the lower east side of Manhattan. He presents, in a journalistic manner, his deprived neighborhood where the "militias" of different ethnicities clashed. In spite of the fact that the play portrays little about Irish nationalism in America, unlike *The Shaughraun*, its box office sales were impressive with "Irish military organizations [taking] whole blocks of seats, [leading] the applause, and listen[ing] eagerly for songs which would become popular favorites" (Wittke 258); "[t]he auditorium was crowded in every part, and many persons were turned away, being unable to obtain even standing room" (Finson 89). Popular as a celebrated musical drama, *The Mulligan Guard Ball* ran for more than one hundred performances in New York, and was followed by six other "Mulligan Guard" plays by Harrigan in a series over the next two years.[15] The play attracted a wide range of audiences, not only of middle-class theatregoers but also of second and third generation descendants of Irish immigrants, and people of other ethnic origins. The popularity of Harrigan's plays was partially because his characters were not limited to those of an Irish origin but included members of other ethnicities among his grocery men, butchers, barbers, dock workers, street-cleaners, contractors, pawnbrokers, tailors, shysters, washer-women, servant-girls, truck men, policemen, and "an assortment of lovable bums and waifs," of contemporary New York (Moody 535). Unlike audiences and critics who paid to see Boucicault's *The Shaughraun*, those who flocked to Harrigan's plays, including the Irish, were not particularly concerned about whether his Irish characters were patriotic and not alcoholic, but whether these plays closely mirrored the daily experiences of the tenement dwellers of New York. The study of his plays therefore allows us to examine the ignored experiences of working-class Irish-Americans and their relationship with those who were also struggling in the "vilest place in town" (Moody 535), and to explore the Americanization of the Irish through Harrigan's theatrical but no less authentic characters.

Significantly, what made *The Mulligan Guard Ball* (and other musical plays) enormously popular was that the songs – created by Harrigan's theatrical partner, Tony Hart, were lyrical and "sung throughout the country" (Meagher 105).[16] However, the cultural hybridity with which the playwright grew up inspired him to write an Irish play as *original* as

---

[15]   The other six plays in the Mulligan Guard series were *The Mulligan Guard Chowder* (1879), *The Mulligan Guards' Christmas* (1879), *The Mulligan Guards' Surprise* (1880), *The Mulligan Guard Picnic* (1880), *The Mulligan Guard Nominee* (1880), and *The Mulligan Guard's Silver Wedding* (1880).

[16]   Edward Harrigan and Tony Hart, known as "Harrigan & Hart," became the most famous comic team in America in the late nineteenth century. They remained partners until 1885.

it could be, so as to reflect the currents of his ethnic community where Germans, Italians, Irish, and Africans competed for job opportunities and other limited resources. Specifically, as a Protestant living in a Catholic Irish area with a father from Ireland and a mother from New England, and working with Hart whose parents were both from County Mayo in Ireland, Harrigan's life experiences could hardly conform to those of any ethnic group that would be politically dominant but also involved in the process of cultural and racial coalescence in America. However, it was certainly the case that Harrigan, alongside other playwrights who wrote musical plays or vaudeville shows for urban audiences towards the end of the nineteenth century, contributed to the assimilation of different ethnicities, and thus the process of Americanization, with his plays' widely popular songs. The over-booked theatres therefore suggest the making of such a cultural and political identity – together with the efforts of second or third generation descendants of Irish immigrants – even though its progress was not always as comic as in *The Mulligan Guard Ball* but was involved with racial conflicts and prejudice, as the next section of this chapter on Barry's *White Woman Street* will reveal.

It can be argued that *The Mulligan Guard Ball*, although it presents a farcical event, namely a failed ball organized for urban Irish dwellers, closely mirrors the everyday racial clashes that involved the Irish, the Blacks, and other minorities. However, the play prioritizes the interests of the Irish, at a time when they were trying to "whiten" themselves. It is also worth noticing that Harrigan did express his concerns relating to the social prejudice that forced the Irish and the Blacks, both of which groups were socially and politically marginalized, to fight a bitter battle not only for opportunities to make a living but also for racial recognition. The ethnic contradistinctions, although they contributed to self-discovery, self-assertion, and a sense of dignity on the part of the ethnicities involved, also added fuel to the fire by incurring a series of conceptually and physically violent events that were suffered by the unprivileged minorities. The conceptual violence was actualized in the form of ethnic segregation. For instance, in *The Mulligan Guard Ball*, the Blacks are barred from entering any restaurants run by the Irish, and those that they can enter serve "very bad victuals" (Harrigan 554). Likewise, the Blacks refuse to take Irish passengers in their carriages: the "Colored Secret Society [...] Prevent de Irish from Riding on Horse Cars" (Harrigan 554). Violating these social "laws," tacit though their nature is, could easily lead to physical violence. In other words, although the two communities both survive with limited social resources, the denial of each other seems imperative for retrieving their own self-esteem and identity. The clashes of the two communities also imply how the ethnic dwellers in the urban tenements assume or imitate the power hierarchy by which they have been victimized, in order to fulfill their own desire for power. More notably, Harrigan, as an Irish descendent, in fact portrayed these racial conflicts from an Irish perspective that denigrated the Blacks. As it happened, the Black characters in Harrigan's plays were acted by Caucasian performers with black make-up, which suggests that the playwright did not intend to challenge the convention of a white-centered dramaturgy. Thus the Blacks were still seen by "white" playwrights as figures of fun who could be portrayed as caricatures and stereotyped as being uncultured and unsophisticated.

In *The Mulligan Guard Ball* the issue that causes dissent between the Irish and the Black tenement dwellers is a scheduling conflict over a ballroom which both parties have booked for the same date.[17] The reason why this conflict is difficult to resolve is not really because no other venue is available in town, but that neither group wants to concede to the other. Forcing the other party to give up the ballroom thus becomes a display of power, which is as unresolvable as the racial segregation mentioned earlier. In the play, the ball does take place as planned, with the Black guests arriving earlier accompanied by the Skidmore Guards, carrying weapons, who are assigned to keep the Irish out of the ballroom. As the tension builds, it is quickly settled by the venue coordinator who apologizes and admits his mistake in having double booked the ballroom. He then opens the other venue on the top floor for the exclusive use of the Blacks. The Blacks, satisfied at being placed on top of the Irish, accept the offer: "Dat's de first time we made de Irish stand from under" (Harrigan 562). Everything ends in farce when the ceiling of the lower ballroom collapses just as the Blacks are about to dance, so no ball is held on either floor and many people are injured.

The interest of the play comes less from the Blacks and the Irish co-inhabiting the same ghetto/tenement area and sharing the limited resources of the lower east side of New York, but the playwright's simplistic depiction of the Blacks as having no uplifting qualities. In *The Mulligan Guard Ball*, they are portrayed not only as supporting characters but as always being antagonistic. They are demeaned by being subjugated to the Irish in the ghetto: "After I licked the nagurs – I engaged them to wait on the supper table. Ha – ha – the devil a cent will they get at all" (Harrigan 563). Harrigan's negative depictions of colored minorities also applies to Brother Palestine Puter, a native American Indian, who is shown as demeaning himself by doing anything only for money and does not mind

---

[17] Another storyline is Tommy and Katy's elopement on account of their desired marriage being opposed by their fathers, who are Irish and German respectively. Since the couple has foreseen the chaos due to the scheduling conflict, they plan to elope in the middle of the ball, but their plan is overheard by Tommy's father, Dan.

waiting on the Irish in humiliating conditions: "I'm gwine to wait on table at de Mulligan Guard supper to-night for 15 dollars – No matter about color or enmity. Come with me – just think 7 1/2 for [negroes] for waiting on table" (562). It may thus be observed that the caricature of the Colored/Blacks, or "the Comical Negro," was a brutal but effective counterbalance for Irish-American playwrights when re-portraying the Irishman on stage – by either keeping a distance from them or belittling them. More specifically, the theatrical degradation of the Blacks probably stemmed from the inferiority complex of Irish-Americans for often being called "white niggers" or "white buckra," – not by "white" Americans but originally by some of the Blacks, who used these terms to justify their prejudice against poor Irish immigrants who were often seen in rags in the ghettos: "My [White American] Master is a great tyrant […] he treats me badly as if I was a common Irishman" (qtd in Gibson 15); "to be called an 'Irishman' had come to be almost as great an insult as to be called a 'nigger'" (Nolan 228). The antipathy of the Blacks to the Irish, incidentally, accelerated the Americanization of the former, so this should be regarded as one of the contributions of the Irish.

It is thus fair to say that *The Mulligan Guard Ball* should not be viewed simply as a farcical musical drama but one that mirrored the anxiety of Irish-Americans over their debased social status, so that Harrigan tended to depict the Blacks in an unfavorable manner but the Irish as being fairly humane and superior. The positive depiction of the Irish is undoubtedly the key for them to be gradually accepted by, although not really assimilated into, mainstream American society. Put another way, by smearing the Colored Others as threats, the talents of the Irish in dancing, acting, and music in this melodrama are placed in the foreground and are thus easily noticed. The intention was therefore to do the Blacks an injustice in order to celebrate Irishness on stage, despite the images of the Blacks always being fragmented or stereotypical: "Not all the Irish are good Irish, but all the colored people [in the Mulligan series] are bad colored people" (Howells 316). It can also be judged that, although Harrigan was acclaimed to be "the first [who] recognize[d] that within the crowded tenements of New York, something like community could exist in spite of the poverty and ethnic tensions" (Onkey 164), his picture of working-class Americans was biased, for failing to portray the Blacks as being as diverse as the "white," respectable Irish, who always appear as being loyal, responsible, trustworthy, and devoted to their friends and neighbors. One may argue that Harrigan's contribution to the American theatre is his dramatization of different "Englishes" in the New World (Murphy 27), whereas *The Mulligan Guard Ball* is a cruel example of how the Blacks were differentiated from their Irish counterparts by means

UNIVERSITY OF WINCHESTER
LIBRARY

of mainstream biases against the Coloreds, in order to claim to forge an Irish-American identity.

Last but not least, Harrigan's preference for Irish-American interests is implied in the title of the play. That is, if the title was changed to "The Skidmore Guard Ball," this would probably lead audiences to make different observations on the intruders, or the Irish "Mulligan Guards." This title reversal might not be applicable if Harrigan intended to continue what Boucicault and other Irish-American dramatists had been doing in confronting the traditional comic stage Irishman. The theatre which temporarily fulfilled the aspirations of Irish-Americans, by covering up their destitution, successfully allowed their anxiety at being on the social margin to be relaxed, with Harrigan's plays implying that the Irish were running the ghettos.

Sebastian Barry's *White Woman Street* (1992): The Redemption of the Cycle of Imperial Violence

It is apparent that Boucicault's and Harrigan's plays did not portray the Irish from the same approach, although they both created more humane or down-to-earth Irishmen on stage – by contrast to the earlier stage Irishman as a figure to be ridiculed. As this chapter suggested earlier, Boucicault's *The Shaughraun* was implicitly but skillfully in line with moderate Irish nationalism with its anticipation of an Irish reconciliation with the English. Harrigan's *The Mulligan Guard Ball* employed stern realism about Irish-Black conflicts in ethnic ghettos, implying the prospect of the Irish moving on to a higher rung of the social ladder. One similarity between the two plays, however, is their shared agenda of giving the deprived Irish-Americans a gloss with which the audiences could enjoy a more affirmative image of the Irish, leading to their desired improved status.

What should be noted is that this shared motive was tinted with the political preferences of the 1870s, when the second and third generations of Irish-American immigrants began to redefine and distinguish their cultural identities and traits from those of other ethnicities. There was a lack of retrospect in Irish-American history *per se*, particularly as regards their ambiguous position as a ruled/subjugated object in the hierarchy of American society. What was even worse is that they were often employed as mercenaries to carry out tasks that the "Whites" would not want to perform. "Do you suppose a German would fight mit a nigger?", as a German butcher says to an Irishman in *The Mulligan Guard Ball* (556). There was also a lack of documentation about how the Irish outcasts – who did not belong to the urban community which Harrigan depicted – interacted with people who were much less socially favored and survived by robbery, thievery, and prostitution. Moreover, there was little close observation of the mental conflicts, or sense of guilt, of the Irish-Americans who victimized native American women who were doubly or triply marginalized, and at the very bottom of the social ladder. Although the two plays discussed above did manage to celebrate some kind of (American) Irishness and idealize it, the most unpleasant aspects of their attitudes and behavior are still under-represented.

Despite Barry's *White Woman Street*, first produced in 1992, seeming to be anachronistic when seen alongside the two plays discussed above, and not sharing the same motive in presenting a soothing or positive image of Irish people, the play is concerned about the prime years of an Irish protagonist in the 1880s in the wilds of Ohio. It is noteworthy that *White Woman Street* is, to a certain extent, biographical rather than invented, in that Barry's grandfather (and also his uncles), having served in British colonies overseas during World War II, "regretted the colonial attitudes he had put on with his uniform, the contempt for 'natives'" (Kurdi 44). In *White Woman Street*, Trooper O'Hara is a native of Sligo in his fifties, planning, alongside a multinational group of gangsters, to rob a train loaded with "glistening gold" in 1916 (Barry 131). Critical of the master-narrative of nationalistic dramaturgy, this play focuses on those "do not fit with the way we want to imagine our history" (Grene 169). What is also interesting about the play is that the Easter Rising of 1916, during which period *White Woman Street* is set, is only mentioned in passing without attaching any significance to it. This event, however, is not really missing as it is bound to create a strategically strong resonance among Irish audiences, who are reminded of this very year at the beginning of the play. By introducing a revisionist look at this crucial year in modern Irish history, the play eventually discloses an ignored but unsettling facet of Irish-American life that had continued to trouble their forefathers down the years. In other words, the Easter Rising rings its bell in a manner that is invisible but not silent, by having the audience return to a historical time other than that of Easter Rising, which Irish historians have tended to spotlight unreservedly. This strategy allows the audience to observe more distantly how the Irish Famine and the Indian Wars (of Britain) had caused the Irish to be both victims and oppressors in the New World. The ignored experiences of the Irish diaspora in Ohio, as Barry illustrates and as will be discussed in this section, may help awake, or create, a new social conscience by unearthing a dark side of Irish-American history.

White Woman Street is the drama of six male protagonists who are culturally displaced outlaws on the run – with conflicting ethnic backgrounds and religious sentiments. The main protagonist, Trooper, who came to America from Ireland with other immigrant workers to build canals and railroads, is the one who claims to have witnessed, or probably joined, the mass slaughter of native Indians as "a proper employment" in his youth (Barry 144). James Miranda, a thirty-year-old Black who escaped from a slave farm in Tennessee, is a former serf who saw his peers killed and dumped in a ditch by their owner, and had a brother whose head was cut off by his master. Nathaniel Yeshov, a young man in his thirties from Brooklyn, constantly feels alienated for being the product of the intermarriage of his Russian father and Chinese mother, a woman who thought herself "a wingless bird in the Land of Fire" (Barry 143). Being brought up as a Christian by his father but unable to pray in either the Russian or Chinese language, and not feeling recognized as an American, he thinks "it was prison the way I be in the head" (Barry 158). Clarke, in his seventies, a native American Indian from Virginia, experienced the mass slaughter of his people and watched women being raped by Whites. He survived by becoming a pimp for colonial officers, and speaking "dame good English [...] [as] easy as white man" (Barry 155). Mo Mason, also in his seventies, an Amish in Ohio, has never returned to his puritanical community in the past fifty years, but is still mentally trapped by its teaching that is in conflict with his desire for whores. Blakeley, an Englishman from Lincolnshire, is no less alienated than other "poor robbermen without no homes" (Barry 130). What draws together these people on the run for the past five years, except for their common experience of having been in prison and wishing "to forget such places" (Barry 158), is the longing to be "a true man with gold [...] Gold can turn a human creature any colour" (Barry 141).

Their yearning for gold as an attempt to assist their social mobility is not really a matter of criticism, as American west had attracted not only characters like these six but also a great number of fortune-hunters from across states and continents since the Gold Rush in late 1840s. The Gold Rush did create fringe benefits that could produce men of wealth in one night. The six robbers, unable to afford the passage to the West but harboring this wish of being rich, joined the Gold Rush – still lingering – in 1916 by planning to rob a "through-going train" that carried gold and their opportunities (Barry 131). Apart from the planned crime, it is Trooper's sense of guilt, for having caused the suicide of a girl after being deflowered (by him) in a whorehouse, that takes them to the town and "White Woman Street". As an old man, Trooper's revisit to White Woman Street is for symbolic redemption: "I thought, if I was in that room again, I could say something to her, I could do something kinder" (Barry 163). However, there is another motivation for retracing his steps here, which is to fulfil his nostalgia for Ireland, the motherland. This is because the young Trooper, among a group of Irish soldiers "sullied up by [Indian] wars" (Barry 149), saw the visit to an Irish whore – from Listowel in Ireland as was claimed – as "a sight of home, a goddess of my own countrymen" (149). The visit is therefore a ritual that is worth Trooper's traveling through "five hundred miles of wilderness" (Barry 147), to redeem his sense of homelessness. Arguably, the metaphor which associates an Irish whore with a "goddess" presents a powerful challenge to the nationalistic myth about Cathleen ni Houlihan, sustained by W.B. Yeats and Lady Gregory, as "a young woman [...] [with] the walk of a queen" whom the Irish should die for without hesitation (11). What comforted these Irish exiles is presumably not the stage Irishman, nor its revised version, but their physical contact with an Irish woman, her smell and touch: "Weren't she like a saint to those men, a place for pilgrimage [...] a holy well, a shrine, St. Bridget, some powerful class of folk that would bring you luck and ease your longing" (Barry 147-8). That is, the Easter Rising of 1916, an event whose importance was always celebrated by Irish nationalists and historians, cannot compete against the physical warmth of an Irish whore that can immediately fulfill the Irish exiles' longing for home, or a Mother Ireland.

However, the whore from Listowel turned out to be an illusion because, when young Trooper arrived at the town, she no longer worked there. Instead, he found a colored Indian girl, literally a virgin, who was "pretty as the dawn with emerald eyes [...] [but had] things worse than tears, that dry and fearful look. A lost look" after being raped by young Trooper. Trooper's long-awaited ritual of spiritual sanitization through fornication with an Irish whore/goddess turned out to be a scene of death where the girl "dip[ped] down to take my cold English blade [...] dragged it flashing like a kingfisher across her throat. She dragged it with force" (Barry 163). His nostalgia for Ireland becomes a lifelong nightmare, which has prompted him to run away from White Woman Street for the past thirty years. What he does not fully realize is that his domination over the body of the Indian girl, as a matter of fact, derived from the power granted to him by the "English blade" he carried. Despite being in the same boat as the Indian prostitute, his fellow Irish people never enjoyed an equal footing with native Indians in America, nor were they respected by the colonial administration: "I seen Irish [...] holed up in the crevices of America just as cockroaches do, or the very lice on my body, I never saw an Indian as bad as an Irish" (Barry 144-145). More specifically, Trooper (and the other Irish laborers) had been so physically and ethnically subjugated to the given social/colonial hierarchy that his rape of the young Indian girl, or "that furrow" (Barry 148), allowed them to receive a temporary, improved status as White dominators. Nonetheless, outside the whorehouses, both native Indians and the Irish were given little respect but survived on the social margin in brutal and inhuman conditions: "That time Indian weren't said to be even just a human person, but a kind of running hare or dor[mouse]" (Barry 148). Arguably, this kind of ethnic clash is a result of the jungle laws by which the weak are the prey of the strong; the weakest in *White Woman Street* are thus the Indian women who were not slaughtered by the Whites but kept as sexual objects for men's pleasure, and tools that allowed the Irish to feel "whitened," or politically upgraded. The interesting thing here is that these jungle laws are signified early in the play with Mo, who has gunned down a female wild boar as food for the day. Mo does feel sorry for killing a "fair-looker of a sow. A nice shapely girl" (Barry 136), but has no means of escape from these survival rules.

Ironically, this cycle of violence between wild animals and humans was not less severe in the lower rung of this society. The value of the Indian virgin, for instance, is no higher than that of the boar, and she could not express her anger except by slashing her throat with force. On the other hand, the lives of the six homeless protagonists mean little to the gunmen on the "through-going train" (Barry 131), and they are shot without mercy. Even though the gunmen might have a sense of guilt about shooting human beings, they have no choice, no more than Mo has when shooting the boar for food. The Indian Wars, in which native Indians fought against the English/European intruders, were not much different from the Easter Rising in Dublin, in which the Irish and the English also battled against each other causing bloodshed, whereas the Irish famine refugees became the victims and the forced victimizers in this cycle of imperial violence in America. The Englishman, Blakely, and many others who also left his home town of Grimsby in England, having no food to eat, have suffered the same ethnic violence that guarantees them no privileges – as obtained by most of the English officers – but forces them to remain on the social margin. Their lowlife experiences have been neglected by historians on both sides of the Atlantic. They were so uprooted that they couldn't "recall [their] own first name[s]" – by which they were called at home (Barry 166), but were shot dead in a foreign land.

Conclusion: Unchangeable Ethnicities and the Changing World

The endings of the three plays are all very different on the surface. They are either open, in Boucicault's *The Shaughraun*; farcical, in Harrigan's *The Mulligan Guard Ball*; or tragic, in Barry's *White Woman Street*. They are all, however, thought-provoking in the ways in which the playwrights present the possibility of rethinking Irish-American history, the remaking of Irishmen on stage, and the retrospective view of colonial violence and its devastating impacts across the Atlantic. The three plays, to a differing degree, all illustrate Irish facts. They are authentic but not necessarily politically correct with their subject matter, either by breaking through the convention of the stage Irishman or presenting the neglected experience of the Irish diaspora. The three plays, incidentally, document the development and collapse of the stage Irishman, and how audiences perceived (American) Irishness in the late nineteenth century, without accommodating the ethnic Others in the melting pot. Written in the late 1870s, Boucicault's *The Shaughraun* and Harrigan's *The Mulligan Guard Ball* reflect to a significant degree the social anxiety about the public perception of the Irish at a time when they were struggling for fair recognition by moving themselves from the political margin to the center. Barry's *White Woman Street*, portraying the Irish diaspora during the same period of time, looks far beyond the struggles of urban Irish tenement dwellers, unearthing more openly and steadily the unpleasant, colonial history in which the Irish were the Other, and not the admirable heroes created by Boucicault and Harrigan. The changing perspectives, as portrayed by the three plays, suggest a running tradition, which many Irish playwrights have employed consistently to invent, transform and/or criticize Irish social conventions.[18]

It can also be noted that, although Boucicault's and Harrigan's plays were meant for performance in the popular theatres in the late nineteenth century – with lyrical songs and farcical scenes – the endings of the three plays are all sophisticated in different ways. As Boucicault's *The Shaughraun* shows, of the three couples, only the Irish villagers, Conn and Moya, tie the knot after many hardships. Neither the English officer, Captain Molineux, who is desperate for the Irish lady, Claire Ffolliott, nor Arte O'Neal and Robert Ffolliott, the Irish couple, get married at the end. The reason why the playwright did not devise a happier ending may be because the play would thus appear too farcical or melodramatic. It could also have been because Boucicault wanted the audience to focus its attention on Conn, the shaughraun of the title, in contrast to the comic but degraded stage Irishman. More importantly, the playwright might have preferred to avoid the suggestion that England and Ireland could share a metaphorical "marriage" relationship, as the London audiences had probably expected. As to Harrigan's play, its ending is rather farcical with all the creditors and "six butchers with cleavers" running after the Mulligans for payment of debts (565) before the curtain falls. The way this play ends may be seen by some as entertaining, or trivial, whereas

---

[18] Arguably, the Abbey Theatre acted as the collective force of this tradition, despite its agenda of rejecting propagandistic nationalism being severely criticized at the time. The three plays, incidentally, present the changing notions of Irish nationhood – both directly and indirectly. The fact that Ireland was politically subjugated to England was doubtless the impulse with which overseas Irish playwrights, including Oscar Wilde and George Bernard Shaw among others, had expressed concern for Irish status in their dramas.

it actually serves to demonstrate the ethnic conflicts and oppression that involved Irish immigrants on a daily basis. The flying "cleavers" symbolize, to a significant extent, the different types of violence that would likely incur a scene of bloodshed similar to that in Barry's *White Woman Street*, although Harrigan suggested this outcome rather implicitly. The ending of Barry's play is intense, with Trooper's death seen as the redemption of his rape of an Indian virgin. His death also signifies the forced sacrifices of the Irish diaspora under British and American colonial control, due to which "Jees Christ don't walk in these woods" (Barry 167), as Blakely states hopelessly as he stands by the dead body of Trooper.

One contribution which theatres can make, as Jeffery H. Richards argues, is to allow "the making and remaking of appearances [to] occur nightly […] [In theatres] identities are roles and roles change as plays change" (7). Significantly, these three plays all reveal the volatility of identities. Being an oppressor can be seen as a matter of shame and regret, and the plight of the ruled can become an issue for rethinking and criticism. Those who do not fit the nationalistic imagination may become the sources of celebration. Not subject to volatility, however, are the diverse ethnicities *per se*, in that they are to be respected rather than being confined to stereotypes. The agenda which the three plays share is, understandably, the quest for a new interpersonal and interethnic relationship in a society that is evolving into a multinational community. This is a global village that does not constantly mark one's otherness or foreignness but confirms the peculiarities of an individual in competing yet supporting ways. The violence within the melting pot in America in the late nineteenth century provides an important lesson that can still be learned in this current era of globalization.

III. Migrant Workers on Stage:
Tom Murphy's *Conversations on a Homecoming* and Jimmy Murphy's *The Kings of the Kilburn High Road*

Introduction: From Home to Unhomely

Not long before the Celtic Tiger emerged in the mid-1990s the Irish were still depicted by Roddy Doyle, who perhaps intended something more than a humorous expression, as "the blacks of Europe" in his 1991 novel (7), *The Commitments*, given that poverty, widely known to the outside world, had been so inscribed as a nightmare on the Irish psyche that young people were prompted to seek foreign employment and emigrate. Nevertheless, behind the façade of the Celtic Tiger is a little-seen "unhealable rift" of which Irish exiles were formerly unaware but which now prompts Irish people – at home and overseas – to recognize their homeland as containing new and unfamiliar faces (Said, "The Mind of Winter" 49). According to Edward W. Said, this rift is "forced [to open] between a human being and a native place, between the self and its true home" ("The Mind of Winter" 49). Thus it can only with difficulty be healed and forgotten, regardless of whether Ireland has become a new destination for migrants due to its remarkable prosperity in the Celtic Tiger era. To explore their ignored voices that are largely left out of the official histories of Ireland and the countries where they arrived, this chapter will examine how social injustice and alienation confined Irish migrant workers to the margins of written histories.

In his "Interculturalism and Irish Theatre," Jason King maintains that "Irish theatre, in particular, has served to delineate the contours of [an] imaginative space" through an increasing number of plays about Irish migrants (25). Specifically, contemporary playwrights have begun to be concerned about (returned) migrants' experiences at home and overseas, although these have yet to be fully discussed and they have not had the same attention on stage as topics derived from Irish history. The insufficient level of detail in research on Irish migrants may be because this is a potential Achilles heel in the Irish consciousness, in that the mass emigrations since the mid-nineteenth century are not regarded as a pleasant chapter in history; many people left due to poverty with only low-level work skills, and many were never able to return. This has traumatized Irish families and embarrassed Irish governments ever since Independence for their economic protectionism and impotence in stopping the youth of Ireland from departing. It could therefore be claimed that the increasingly large quantity of Irish plays written since the mid-twentieth century on migrants' experiences reveals implicit but deep-rooted anxieties over this historical trauma, thus urging an examination of this neglected community that has been on the margin of Irish media and demographic studies.

Before this chapter looks in detail at two migrant plays which illustrate contrasting experiences, it might be useful to review the writing of plays about migration in the Irish theatre. That is, Irish playwrights since the 1960s had started to reflect – long before post-colonial critics voiced their critiques in the late 1980s – on the problems of the Irish being culturally subjugated by their former British rulers or romanticizing about life on the other side of the Atlantic. Notable works include John B. Keane's *Many Young Men of Twenty* (1961), Tom Murphy's *A Whistle in the Dark* (1961), *A Crucial Week in the Life of a Grocer's Assistant* (1969), and *Conversations on a Homecoming* (1985), Brian Friel's *The Enemy Within* (1962), *Philadelphia, Here I Come!* (1964), *The Loves of Cass McGuire* (1966), and *Faith Healer* (1979), Hugh Leonard's *Da* (1978), Christina Reid's *My Name, Shall I Tell You My Name?* (1989), and so forth. They all explicitly or implicitly illuminate how foreign cultures, either being brought back by returned migrants or imagined by those who are desperate to leave, shatter a person's self-identity and question the over-dominance of the Catholic Church. Even more migrant plays were pushed out in the 1990s with playwrights exploring a wider spectrum of ignored experiences at home and overseas, such as Dermot Bolger's *In High Germany* (1990), Gavin Kostick's *The Ash Fire* (1992), Frank McGuinness's *Someone Who'll Watch Over Me* (1992), Jimmy Murphy's *Brothers of the Brush* (1993), Donal O'Kelly's *Asylum! Asylum! (*1994) and *Farawayan* (1998), Anne Devlin's *After Easter* (1994), Martin McDonagh's *The Cripple of Inismaan* (1996), and Sebastian Barry's *White Woman Street* (1997). After the millennium, as the spectacular economic revival of the Celtic Tiger gave rise to a reversal of the migrant flow from being outward to inward, racism and cultural clashes captured public attention in a multinational Ireland – with Roddy Doyle's *Guess Who's Coming for the Dinner* (2002), Jim O'Hanlon's *The Buddhist of Castleknock* (2002), and Dermot Bolger's *The Townlands of Brazil* (2007) and *The Parting Glass* (2010). That said, Irish theatre has served as a space where Irish audiences can learn to face those parts of their national history that have been neglected, often because they cause distress when recollected.[1]

This chapter does not aim to survey all Irish plays that touch on migration but to consider Irish overseas workers whose experiences are worth greater attention from historians and sociologists, because their blood, toil, tears and sweat have changed significantly both Ireland and their destinations. It is also noteworthy that these returned workers have often felt themselves to be "familiar stranger[s]" at home after their lengthy stay outside Ireland (Hall 492), in that they have suffered a "sense of betrayal by their homeland and [...] violence that often surrounded them" in Irish ghettos (Billington, "Which Side"). As "exile is indeed the cradle of nationality" (Higgins and Kiberd 9), a close observation – not from within but external – can engender a new understanding of this globalized state, especially when it is being hybridized with ethnic cultures.

The two plays to be discussed are Tom Murphy's *Conversations on a Homecoming* (1985), which centers on a visiting emigrant whose return from the United States disrupts the serene life of the townsfolk in east Galway in the early 1970s, and Jimmy Murphy's *The Kings of the Kilburn High Road* (2000), portraying five Irish migrant laborers in London and their sense of being "unhomed" (Bhabha, *Location* 9).[2] These plays present two different angles from which to see Ireland: from the inside and the outside respectively, while both document the mixed sentiments of Irish migrants and the transformations of Ireland with which they are distantly engaged.

One common feature of the two plays is that the exile/emigration of their protagonists all started during the 1960s and 1970s, before and during which a large-scale movement of Irish emigrants to Britain had taken place. Specifically, more than fifty thousand people left Ireland between 1945 and 1960, and 75% of them ended up in the United Kingdom

---

[1]   Interestingly, contemporary Irish playwrights do not concern themselves only with Irish migrants but often shift their attention to other ethnicities who have suffered forced migration and racial conflicts. For example, John Barrett's *Borrowed Robes* (1998) features Jews suffering anti-Semitism in Cork in 1904; John Banville's *Conversation in the Mountains* (2008) concerns the Jewish poet Paul Celan and his visit to Martin Heidegger who was once a supporter of Nazism; Dolores Walshe's *In the Talking Dark* (2001) and Damian Smyth's *Soldiers of the Queen* (2002) depict the identity crisis of the Irish in South Africa during apartheid and the second Anglo-Boer War (1899-1902) respectively; Colin Teevan's *How Many Miles to Basra* (2006) criticizes the roles of the US and UK during the Iraq War (2003-2011).

[2]   The meaning of being "unhomed," as Homi K. Bhabha argues, is not the same as homelessness but is a sense of alienation that mentally and culturally uproots people, no matter where they stay – whether at home or in exile. This will be further explicated in the plays to be discussed.

(Delaney, "Emigration" 440).[3] It should be noted that the two plays illustrate Said's argument about migration as a postcolonial phenomenon, in that migration has become part of "our age – with its modern warfare, imperialism and the quasi-theological ambitions of totalitarian rulers – [an] age of the refugee, the displaced person, mass immigration" (*Reflections* 174). The emigrations to the United Kingdom and its former territories may thus implicitly counteract the lingering colonial effects and the unceasing economic subjugation of an emigrant-sending country.[4] On the other hand, although Irish migrants tend to accommodate themselves quickly in a foreign land and create their own communities to counteract the uncanny (in Freud's meaning of the word) in their new home, this cannot remove the fact that they are in an "unhomely" place. For migrants, home can no longer retain its traditional meaning or function, while, as Bhabha describes, the sense of being "unhomed" may "creep up on you stealthily as your own shadow [...] [in] *the* house of darkness, the house of dumbness, the house of suffocation" (*Location* 9).[5] This could be a common and always present truth in any community of exiles. When the boundaries of home are remapped in the global era, it may be that the trauma of being "unhomed" can only be healed in relative terms.

Internal Exile in Tom Murphy's *Conversations on a Homecoming*

In contrast to other works in his repertoire, Tom Murphy's *Conversations on a Homecoming* has not been the subject of much in-depth discussion, although the play demonstrates a variety of ignored perspectives on Irish migration in the mid-twentieth century.[6] It should

---

3   According to Delaney, 12.5% of the Irish emigrants arrived in the United States, and the rest in Canada, Australia, and New Zealand. Most of their destinations are English-speaking countries and former British territories.

4   How Irish immigrants are treated with prejudice in the UK is dramatized in Tom Murphy's *A Whistle in the Dark* (1961), Christina Reid's *My Name, Shall I Tell You My Name?* (1989), and Anne Devlin's *After Easter* (1994), among others.

5   To specify what "the unhomely" is, Bhabha refers to Isabel Archer's own description of her isolation in a manor house in Henry James's *The Portrait of a Lady*. For details, see Bhabah's "Unhomely Lives: The Literature of Recognition" in *The Location of Culture*. The above quotes from Bhabha are taken from James's *The Portrait of a Lady*, pp. 360-1.

6   For centuries Irish migration had never been inward until 1963, when, coincidentally, John F. Kennedy paid a state visit to Ireland (Ellis 125). Statistics show that between 1956 and 1961 the percentage of young Irish men and women who opted for emigration had once reached as high as 31.7% (Delaney, *Demography* 232). An inflow of migration was seen in the 1970s with a recorded number of more than 100,000 former emigrants returning from Britain and the United States (Delaney, "Emigration" 442). However, the mass emigration of the young Irish resumed in the 1980s, which "came as a shock,

be noted that Tom Murphy's focus on the neglected experiences of Irish migrants reflects, to a large degree, a personal rupture between himself and his home: "My times of greatest expectation and despair were spent at the railway station in Tuam seeing a father, brother or sister off, or waiting for one of them to return;" his father and eight older siblings all left Ireland in the prime of their lives ("Interview" 175). The "unhomeliness," regardless of whether it is experienced by those left behind at home or those going away, has its roots in dark recesses of the Irish memory, as depicted in his migrant plays.

This play features the unsettling effects on the return of his old friend, Michael Ridge, from America, but what really distresses the townsfolk who gather in a run-down pub in a "forgotten-looking place" in east Galway (*Conversations* 3) is the suffocation of a "Gaelic Eden," or "a genuinely independent, self-sufficient rural Ireland," as defended by the government of Éamon de Valera (Brown 159, 142). The cultural conservatism has not only kept Ireland "suffer[ing] for a time-lag, or at any rate [run] on a different time-table from other countries" (Mercier 86), but has made it more "uncanny" than "homely," by contrast to the new countries to which the emigrants have traveled. Although the play centers on rural experiences, it makes little appeal to nostalgia but presents, in unfavorable terms, a parochial Ireland that has nurtured economic and cultural anachronisms. In contradiction to the propaganda of a pastoral Ireland, what Murphy presents is "the grim reality of Ireland in the second half of the twentieth century without redeeming features" (Csikai 203). Arguably, being "unhomed" is not simply a byword for homesickness, but an expression describing the mental state when a migrant realizes how his/her personal experiences in exile contradict existing propagandas about home.

The play is set in The White House, a local pub, where Michael meets his old friends after being ten years abroad in America. His home visit, nevertheless, produces a variety of reactions among his friends, since he was the first one of his group to seek self-realization in the New World and this led to them dropping their plan to co-run this pub. Their greetings of Michael are initially warm and enthusiastic. However, while their friendship is being renewed through recollections of their youthful times and aspirations, alcohol prompts these "angry young men" to give vent to what has been weighing on their minds over the past ten years, particularly their unresolved grudges against each other and the domination of the

---

and to many as a disappointment" (Lee 44). Although the number of Irish emigrants since independence has been staggeringly large and many of them were unskilled or half-skilled workers, their overseas experiences have rarely been addressed in detail.

Catholic Church.[7] Although this play does not contain much physical action but consists of "conversations" within this circle of friends, the more alcohol they consume, the more angry or sarcastic are their remarks about their homeland.

Despite the fact that the past events they reminisce about may well be twisted in the telling, the play provides the audience with a critical distance from which to examine a shared experience that once haunted this emigrant-sending country, and its anachronistic mode of life. Specifically, not only is the on-stage clock not working, but the off-stage town clock and church clock never chime together. The picture of John F. Kennedy, as placed on the shelf, suggests how this President has been over-worshiped as an icon, or is an imaginary guardian who, ironically, could not even protect himself when assassinated in 1963. Although the songs they sing are a combination of American popular songs, religious hymns, and Irish folk songs, none of the songs are *about* and *of* the present. To name a few, "I'll Sing A Hymn to Mary" and "All in the April Evening," are classic Christian songs that are timeless.[8] Both "Bridle on the Wall" and "Sierra Sue" are American country and western songs featuring the loss of favorite ponies; the former was a popular song released in 1936 and the latter in 1941.[9] The American country song, "Blanket on the Ground," as well as the Irish pop song, "A Bunch of Violets Blue," are about a past love and Irish migrants' homesickness respectively, although both were released in the 1970s.[10] It can be argued that the broken clock, the picture of a late Irish-American president, and songs about loss reflect the anachronistic divides

---

[7]   The term "angry young man" was first coined in the 1950s to describe young British people who were disappointed and held anti-establishment attitudes during the cold war period. John Osborne's play, *Look Back in Anger* (1956), was a key text in the style of social realism. It can be contended that the five protagonists in *Conversations on a Homecoming*, all in their early and late 30s, are part of this angry generation which was caught up not only by the stiff ambiance of cold war society but also by the puritanical domination of the Irish Catholic Church.

[8]   For the hymn, "I'll Sing A Hymn To Mary," see p. 78; for "All in the April Evening," see pp. 39, 43, 69. Interestingly, Junior is the one who leads most of the songs or invites others to sing in the play.

[9]   "Sierra Sue" and "Bridle on the Wall" are American cowboy songs, featuring the regret of cowboys who have lost their favorite ponies, see p. 67 and p. 69. It can be argued that these cowboy songs provide the characters with imaginary impressions of the "western" world.

[10]   "A Bunch of Violets Blue" and "Blanket on the Ground" are sung or mentioned respectively on p. 6 and p. 39. Although the former is a contemporary song from the 1970s, it features the homesickness of Irish migrants: "But I'll not forget old Ireland / Far from the old folks at home" (p. 6). Billie Jo Spears's "Blanket on the Ground" was once a number one song in the American country music chart in 1975. Interestingly, the name of this American song is only mentioned once by Liam but none of the characters seems able to sing it at all.

between Ireland and the outside world, or within itself. More specifically, the self-cognition of Irish migrants had always been unfashionably in the past or entrusted to religious doctrines. Ironically, none of the characters seem to be strongly in favor of traditional Irish folk or rebel songs, while the old American cowboy songs give them an imaginary impression of the New World and a sense of adventure that they can hardly enjoy at home.

All the talk and singing in *Conversations on a Homecoming* take place at The White House, which Michael romanticizes as "our refuge, our wellsprings of hope and aspiration" (*Conversations* 10), whereas his country, in the locals' view, has been nothing but the "last refuge in Europe" (*Conversations* 6). For Michael, who has not been home for ten years, this pub has been sentimentalized as a place where he expects to find "the warm relaxed atmosphere that becomes a substitute for home" (Kearney 56). His sense of home in Ireland is apparently contradictory to the reality, because The White House is simply a run-down establishment that becomes a living confirmation of their false hopes for a new Ireland. More specifically, ten years ago all of them co-built The White House and had a high expectation of it becoming their new *home*, where they could realize their youthful ambitions in a "home to re-inspire us, take a look at our problems, shake us out of our lethargy, stop us vegetating, show us where we went wrong [...]" (*Conversations* 50). For them, including Michael, "selling pints [here was] a second consideration [...] [the] real purpose was to foster the arts, to give new life to broken dreams and the – horn – of immortality, nightly, to mortal men." (*Conversations* 53). Dissatisfied with de Valera's government in economic matters and assuming socialism to be an ideal approach for ending the exploitation of the working class, they turned the pub into a home base to counteract the operation of capitalism in Ireland: "the real enemy [...] that we shall overcome, is the country-and-western system itself" (*Conversations* 67). What they did not realize was that, partly due to their limited understanding of socialism and partly due to the romantization of Gaelic Eden, the proletariat in socialist regimes did not lead a better life than theirs in Ireland. The over-idealization of socialism was simply their instrument to for them to ignore their impotence about the social injustice, despite the fact that "[the] social movements of the minority's groups in the sixties, in towns, villages and cities, was the rising culture" (*Conversations* 66). It can be said that their insistence on staying at home, rather than escaping across the Atlantic as Michael did, prompts them to think and behave anachronistically and to make themselves unable to face reality.

The withering of their youthful dreams and rapid downgrading of "home" is partly because of Michael's departure for America and his betrayal of the ideal of socialism, but the straw that breaks the camel's back is the death of John F. Kennedy, the expectations of whose visit to

Ireland in 1963 were over-hyped as "an ending to the Famine, as a triumph out of the Famine [...] [and] an ending of a bad epoch, a bad century" (qtd in Ellis 125). Although these protagonists were all prone to left-wing thinking in their youth in the 1960s, and wished to give everyone an equal standing at The White House: "all one room [...] there should be no public bar, no divisions or class distinctions" (*Conversations* 38), they can never get away from the fact that The White House is by nature a capitalistic establishment and, most significantly, they cannot escape the overwhelming effect of John F. Kennedy's visit on all levels of Irish society. That is, as the first Catholic US president, of clear Irish descent, "his election to the White House [had been widely seen] as an Irish victory" and "'the greatest page' in its history as the Sunday Independent called it" (Ellis 113, 125). The naming of their new home/base/pub as "The White House" suggests the confidence being acquired from this Irish success in America.

The over-celebrated JFK myth, interestingly, was further reinforced by JJ, one of the pub's founders who "looks like John F. Kennedy [...] [and] JJ hopped up on that American-wrapped bandwagon of so-called idealism" (*Conversations* 52). Contradictorily, JJ is only a returned immigrant "limp[ing] back from England" (*Conversations* 52), while his facial resemblance to the American president gives rise to bigger American dreams and a self-deceptive pride among the townsfolk, misleading them to expect a progressive Ireland, which did not happen fast enough during the 1960s. Neither John F. Kennedy nor JJ could rescue them from a mundane and colorless life, but their sense of being unhomed, or alienated from the outside world, only deepened. In other words, the Emerald Isle remained a morbid rather than an uplifting state in that their illusions were broken.

Michael's "conversations on a homecoming" re-confirm the spiritual dispossession that overcame his countrymen. The home he returns to is no different from or perhaps even more disappointing than the one he left ten years ago. Despite that, his old friends are, on the one hand, no less resentful of the parochialism of the Catholic Church, and they have no real courage to detach themselves from its spiritual subjugation, in case, as Tom declares, "I might lose my religion" (*Conversations* 65). Put another way, they do hold strong antipathies toward the state and the Church, believing that both have led them to have false hopes about Ireland, and they are more anxious about being betrayers to their two home *masters*. They do not feel Ireland to be a homely place but have no choice but to start their "internal exile and yet be at home" (Naficy 3).

On the other hand, they are wary of the modernization or Americanization of Ireland and the fact that "strangers [are] comin' in to run the town" (*Conversations* 65), while they cannot halt the concurrent emigration due to high unemployment in Ireland. For instance, Junior, one of the co-founders of the pub, has had seven brothers go away from home to join the Palestine Police Force of the United Nations. For Junior and other Irish people who have family members scattered overseas, and for Michael who returns home with romantic and nostalgic notions, Ireland becomes "novel and unfamiliar" and to some extent "frightening," which makes their home uncanny (Freud 95). However, their frustrations about their homeland have been a traumatic experience that haunts them, no matter whether they are in internal or external exile, but they remain unspoken. Michael, in part refusing to be more traumatized and in part feeling more disappointed about the insularity of rural Ireland, still chooses to return to his other home in America on the day after he meets his friends, even though he feels rootless there and will suffer more failures in his career. His home in Ireland is not inhabitable, while he no longer holds a romantic vision of his home town and chooses somewhere freer and less uncanny.

The next play to be discussed will examine Irish overseas workers from a different angle: not judging the exiles from the perspective of those remaining or trapped at home but unearthing their ignored sentiments through the eyes of those desperate for home but unable to return. They suffer from shattered illusions and failures, and are largely engulfed not only by London streets but also by official Irish history. Their unhomed experiences may be more poignant, since they are geographically closer to home, when compared with those of Michael in *Conversations on a Homecoming*, but many of them cannot make their journey home even once in their lifetime.

Despair and Wishes in Jimmy Murphy's *The Kings of the Kilburn High Road*

If migration is a mirror that offers Irish audiences a chance to observe themselves from a distance, Tom Murphy's *Conversations on a Homecoming* and Jimmy Murphy's *The Kings of the Kilburn High Road* may be paired as the front and the back of the mirror. The former projects a returned migrant's perspective as to where he comes from; the latter reflects the pains and pleasures of Irish migrant workers who are forced into exile. Both plays are set in pubs – one is in east Galway, the other in northwest London, while their conversations reveal how attitudes towards home change with social transformations, including globalization. It is noteworthy that *The Kings of the Kilburn High Road*, produced in 2000, can be seen as a theatrical sequel to Tom Murphy's play which was first written in 1972 and revised in 1985.[11] The study of the two plays on the theme of migration will illuminate the new forces that have emerged or are being counteracted within Ireland, how the country is breaking away from parochial rule and opening its arms to multiculturalism, how Irish migrants are still being subjugated by forces within and across borders, and, most importantly, what still remains unspoken and neglected in the experience of deprived migrant workers in exile.

It is important to note that the issues relating to being a minority seem to be the impulse that kept *The Kings of the Kilburn High Road* popular as a stage play, as it was performed twice by African Voice during the St Patrick's Day Festival in 2003, and by Arambe Productions during the Dublin Fringe Festival in 2006.[12] Both Irish productions, however, were made with all-African casts. The audience was no doubt impressed by the fact that the African actors – among whom were immigrants and asylum seekers – portrayed experiences that were supposed to be predominantly Irish. That these African actors spoke lines about being dislocated in front of Irish audiences may appear "uncanny" to some extent, as they are never free of racial prejudice in Irish society. Their homelands in Africa may also be experiencing a similar situation in that Ireland has just extricated itself from being an emigrant nursery but does not open its arms to refugees who seek material fulfillment in the way that their forefathers did. More significantly, the casting of Africans may be construed as marking the transformation of Ireland from being largely a nation with a single ethnicity to a multi-cultural, globalized state during the era of the Celtic Tiger. The mixed experiences of Irish overseas workers may thus be not only regional but also echo what people of other ethnicities have been forced to go through when they have left their countries of origin.[13]

Although *The Kings of the Kilburn High Road* is set at the turn of the twenty-first century, and the action never goes beyond a pub in Camden Town in northwest London, the six Irish characters are haunted by their

---

[11]   In 1972 Tom Murphy staged *The White House* at the Abbey Theatre. The play's first act is subtitled "Conversations on a Homecoming" and the second act "Speeches of Farewell." The first act deals with the present, and the second is a flashback of JJ's life in 1963, the year when John F. Kennedy visited Ireland in June and was assassinated in November in Dallas, Texas. This play was revised in 1985 under the title *Conversations on a Homecoming* for a production by Druid Theatre Company. This revision comprises stories of the present and the past in a single act.

[12]   The play was premiered by Red Kettle Theatre Company at the Garter Lane Theatre, Waterford, Ireland on 12 June 2000.

[13]   Notably, *Mixing it on the Mountain* (2003), by Maeve Ingoldsby, a writer for RTÉ, presents an African St Patrick arriving in pre-Christian Ireland and being captured by Celtic raiders. St. Patrick was enacted by Solomon Ijigade, a Nigerian asylum seeker. This play challenges the convention by which St Patrick is generally regarded as a Caucasian.

memories of home, which they left in 1975, and their unfulfilled wishes about going home – with pride and having made enough money.[14] They came to England in their youthful prime like "six [...] matadors [with] the best of clothes [...] [and] smiles from ear to ear" (*Kings* 57), although, by being unskilled, they are constantly subjugated by those with power over them in the labor market and are always on the lowest rung of the social hierarchy. These young men at first planned to stay for two years at most, but harsh reality has prompted them to take different routes that suit them in their new home and to stay longer than they expected to do. Specifically, Joe, seeing no future in working in a sweatshop, has abandoned his mates to run his own business as a foreman and has not hired a single Irish worker as he is unable "to get a good Paddy in this town for love or money" (*Kings* 36). Because they have not been able to go home, Maurteen and Shay have settled down with English women and now have children; Jap has a black girlfriend but does not want to have babies, in case "me kids [do not] look like me" (*Kings* 21). Git is the only one who remains single. All of them, except Joe, can only take odd jobs irregularly on various building sites, and age has defeated them as their strongest foe. The only person who does not appear on stage is Jackie, a jobless man who has thrown himself under an underground train after a failed love affair, realizing that he has spent "twenty-five years over here an' only a one room flat [rented] in Hammersmith to show for it" (*Kings* 54). It can be argued that most of these Irish migrant workers are more or less in the same boat as Jackie, but they do not have the guts to put an end to themselves although they clearly know that they cannot afford to "even have [a] coffin opened" for them if they die (*Kings* 51).

The experiences delineated in this play are vividly painful. According to an RTÉ survey not long ago, "a 'wet' hostel in Camden where up to 450 men live – more than a quarter of them Irish [...] now houses men suffering from physical and mental illness, depression and chronic alcoholism [...], [some have remained] in England for more than fifty years" (Ferriter, "Paddies' Pain"). It can be stated that *Kings* documents Irish workers who have long been ignored by both English and Irish societies but remain unhomed. For them, home in Ireland is a destination that they cannot physically return to, while mentally the illusion about going home has been the source of pain and grief. It is possibly true to say that they will be more like "aliens back over there, aliens" (*Kings* 46), if they do go home, as Shay presumes. Jap, who has been unable to make a home visit even once in the past thirty years but is unwilling to admit

---

[14]   The play was first produced in 2000. Although the playwright does not specify the year when the story takes place, the characters are all in their late forties and constantly mention that they have not returned home to Ireland for thirty years, so it can be assumed that the play is set in the present. The play was published in 2001.

to his broken wishes, often boasts about how well-received his imagined visits have been: "My visits, my visits are the stuff of legend over there, fella," despite the fact that he has only been able to "ring home every two months, rain or shine, […] to see how everyone is" in the past thirty years (*Kings* 16).

Returning home is understandably a mission impossible for these migrant workers. Their new home, no matter whether they are living in a hostel or renting a one-bedroom flat like Jackie, can hardly provide a sense of homeliness or rootedness. In other words, because they are always moving from one building site to another, their lodgings and relationships are temporary. For Jap, the notion of home is intangible and has been regularly confirmed by his phone calls every two months and his imaginings of "how everyone is" at home (*Kings* 16), whereas there is nothing new for him in England to update people about other than his daily drudgery. Joe, however, is the only one who finds the courage to break the false hope about going home wealthy by first separating himself from his Irish mates and then firmly refusing to hire any of his Irish acquaintances, despite being named "Paddy Englishman" (*Kings* 60). His refusal to employ his Irish friends is an attempt to cut himself off from his ties to home, so as to survive better in the new land and to be more English. All his friends, including Jackie, have been given the cold shoulder by Joe, as he thinks they are despicable as "a bunch of no good, lazy drunken bastards that'd get yeh thrown off more jobs […] I'd be out a' business in a week if I were to give any of [you] a job, be bankrupt" (*Kings* 60). In order to further his chance of success, Joe disguises his Irish origin and assumes the role of oppressor by recruiting migrant workers from elsewhere rather than from home.

It can be observed that all the ageing Irish characters in the play, except Joe, are direct victims not only of racial but of class clashes, and have no means of rising from poverty but are sinking into a even lower social stratum. It is even more ironic that, if they can secure a passage to go home, they will still be the prey of other ethnic minorities, inasmuch as the owner of "a travel shop five minutes up the road" is a Pakistani who would be "only too happy to take [their] pounds, shillin's an' pence off" [them]" (*Kings* 14).

However, what home means to these Irish protagonists is subject to change, especially when they realize that there is only a remote hope of ever going home. Among them, Jap is still mentally in Ireland through his regular phone calls home, even though he has been alone in England without his family for thirty years. Although Joe is more well-to-do and able to return to Ireland once in a while, he does not find Dublin as homey as before, in that Dublin has become a "different city […] Christ, I was walkin' around an' didn't know whether to go in for a pint or a pizza" (*Kings* 46). Shay shares similar sentiments to those of Joe, admitting that actually "[England] is our home" now after "[we've] even been livin' here longer than we did in Ireland [...] A pigsty, that's what I left behind me, a fuckin' pigsty [...] all of us did" (*Kings* 47). This truth cannot be pleasant to Jap at all, when he is forced to face the fact that the home he hopes to return to now only exists in his hallucinations. In other words, being exploited in the UK, although he is now more metropolitan, has made him more unhomed and not physically Irish: "Shirt on me back's from fuckin' China. Roof over me head's owned by a German" (*Kings* 47).

Rapid globalization has also turned this Irish pub where they congregate into something similar to English ones, in that the jukebox no longer provides "rebel songs" which would potentially offend English customers: "I remember the day there'd be nothin' but rebel songs on that yoke" (*Kings* 23). As Shay frankly observes, after thirty years in England they are becoming "more English than the English themselves" (*Kings* 47), rather than being Irish. It is ironic that their wake for Jackie is held at The Lion, an English pub. That is to say, they are barely able to counteract the continuing subjugation of the former imperial ruler. Although they only meant to make money in England and go home at the first opportunity, they have gradually been assimilated into the colonial center/home and become less Irish. Specifically, what they earn from hard work is always consumed quickly through their drinking habit when they renew their Irish bonding in the pub.

In this play, all their conversations take place in an *Irish* pub which is no longer as homey as they had previously trusted it to be. To mitigate their homesickness, these migrant characters always tend to reconfirm their Irish origin by drinking with other Irishmen, so as to enjoy "a [short] reversion to a completely Irish way of life" (Kearney 56). Nonetheless, the alleviation of Jap's nostalgia gradually becomes undesirable, because globalization now confers privileges on the former imperial power that enables it to overbear those who are politically and economically disadvantaged – as a form of neocolonialism.

It can thus be judged that Jackie's suicide is a silent protest against the endlessness of the exploitation, and is ironically a quicker way for him to realize his dream of homecoming – in a coffin – even though "he never made anythin' of himself" in England (*Kings* 35). His death further affirms how diasporic they are in terms both of their new home in England and their old Irish one; both homes have become uncanny and unpleasant places to be in. They can only return home temporarily – not via Holyhead nor on a plane – but during a time of drunkenness when the alcohol takes over: "You're sayin' that now an' we full 'a drink, but don't yeh know it'll be a different story entirely in the mornin' an' the drink gone?" (*Kings* 66), as Jap remarks.

What makes them unhomed or diasporic is thus a never-to-be taken passage to their motherland from their home in England but the truth that they will forever be dangling between wishes and despair about going home: "I don't know where I am any more, who I am. All I see of meself is an old man lost" (*Kings* 65). This is not only Jap's most candid self-declaration but that of Jackie and many migrant workers who cannot see an end to their exploitation.

Conclusion

The common factor between these two plays about migration is that the new home where the protagonists have settled is not a place of hope and happiness, nor does it secure good fortune. The new home is more likely to become a purgatory where the migrants feel displaced. For Michael in *Conversations on a Homecoming*, The White House in his home town in east Galway, although it is "a bathetic version of Kennedy's Camelot/White House" (O'Toole 181), is where he thought he could be healed, or symbolically re-baptized in a homely place, after enduring various kinds of hardship overseas. For Jap in *The Kings of the Kilburn High Road*, his regular phone calls home to Ireland significantly ease his sense of alienation in the UK together with an imagined picture of home, which saves him from his everyday drudgeries.

However, Michael's physical return and Jap's spiritual homecoming do not, even slightly, change the fact that they are constantly in a state of purgatory after being uprooted from home, no matter whether their migration was voluntary or not. Notably, Michael, returning from America, does not lead the affluent life that his old friends have assumed, nor does he have a stable income. It is out of frustration that he would like to see his home again and consider resettling in Ireland. Compared with other Irish migrant workers in America, he might be more fortunate in being able to afford a passage back home, given that one of their acquaintances from Ireland was seen on the street with "no shirt, [only] an old pullover, no heels to his shoes" (*Conversations* 78). It is noteworthy that Jap and Git in *The Kings of the Kilburn High Road* and Michael in *Conversations on a Homecoming* all try to cover up the truth that they live in poverty, in case their families are disappointed at their failures. It can fairly be assumed that they are unable to improve the quality of their lives, nor can they better their social status or redress the fact of being displaced persons. Likewise, they can hardly make themselves a new home in which they feel they belong, when they have to live a lie to meet familial expectations and bolster their own pride.

Most importantly, both plays are testimonials of Ireland under the subjugation of neo-colonialism. In *Conversations*, foreign enterprises are coming on to the scene to not only make use of cheap Irish labor but also to eradicate traditional Irish life: "[All] those men of prudence and endeavor who would sell the little we have left of charm, character, kindness and madness to any old bidder with a pound, a dollar, a mark or a yen [...] [All] those honest and honourable men who are cutting down the trees for making – Easter-egg boxes!" (80). The changes which these economic powers bring forth would unavoidably make Ireland unhomey, unfamiliar, or even uncanny, in the eyes of Irish overseas workers when they return from where they emigrated to. In *Kings*, the former British Empire still continues its economic and political subjugation over the powerless people within its territories, depriving them of a home identity; as Shay claims: "This is our home. Here [...] We've even been livin' here longer than we did in Ireland" (*Kings* 47).

The two plays therefore challenge the conventional or nationalistic understanding of being Irish, and suggest how the meaning of home may be being changed alongside the advent of transnationalism. In other words, the sentiments which these non-white actors express on stage are not novel to Irish audiences, as they are being reminded of "a colonial past of shame and shared humiliation" that produced their home (Kiberd 72), and seeing home/society changing quite rapidly and almost completely with a new ethnic landscape. Last but not least, the characters in these two plays all have their conversations in a backroom behind the bar, and the audiences are seemingly eavesdropping on their lives. Put another way, the stage setting may suggest how these alienated characters have no place of their own but can somehow only be themselves when gathering in a small corner. The audiences can only engage quietly with their discussions, listen, and try to understand their ups and downs.

When migration forces Ireland to open its door wide to the outside world, home can no longer function as one's secure shelter, but instead it is a place subjugated by economic and political currents coming from outside. Home can no longer be the last resort where one renews oneself and enjoys the sense of belongingness but it is where the displacement starts, when "the borders between home and world become confused" (Bhabha, *Location* 9). What had been thought to be essential to qualify as home therefore becomes difficult to derive or is even missing, but it can still be haunting to those who feel unsettled and intimated due to migration. The rift between the lost home and the relocated one(s) would bring on a sense of "silence, solitude, [and] darkness," or "the uncanny" among migrants who are now in a frightening and unfamiliar environment (Freud 229).[15] As the ethnic landscape of Ireland has been changed significantly by globalization in recent years, this imaginative space visualizes a "contact zone" where ethnic minorities and mainstream communities "establish [...] relations [that involve] conditions of coercion, racial inequality, and intractable conflict" (Pratt 6). The "contact zone" should function now partly to accommodate ethnic minorities and partly to heal the unresolved national trauma of being an emigrant nursery. That said, Ireland should turn itself into an open, equal and multiracial forum for all ethnicities *at home*, rather than the center of mental paralysis from which James Joyce and many others desperately separated themselves.

---

[15] "The uncanny," as a Freudian concept, is from the German word "unheimlich," the opposite of "heimlich" (homely) and the Yiddish "heimish" (native). Although not everything "novel can easily become frightening and uncanny" (Freud 195), whatever is novel and unfamiliar can make the environment uncanny. Freud argues that this kind of uncanniness, as a mirror to infantile anxiety, reflects the castration complex from which "the majority of human beings have never become quite free" (Freud 229). For details, see the chapter on "The Uncanny" in Freud's *Writings on Art and Literature*, pp. 193-233.

IV. A Russian Mirror to Ireland: Migration in Tom Murphy's *The House* and Anton Chekhov's *The Cherry Orchard*

Anton Chekhov, whose career was partially inspired by Henrik Ibsen, exerted an influence on many European playwrights, a number of whom were Irish, by producing "problem plays" in the style of "unflinching, analytical realism" (Leerssen 47). Specifically, Chekhov's *Uncle Vanya* and *Three Sisters* were adapted respectively by Frank McGuinness in 1980 and by Brian Friel in 1981 for the newly-founded Field Day Theatre Company, in order to "bring quality drama to the people of rural Ireland" (Richtarik 196).[1] Thomas Kilroy, also a Field Day playwright, adapted Chekhov's *The Seagull* in 1981, not only transporting the action to "the wilds of Galway" but employing a peculiar language familiar to the Irish audience so that they would not be "lost in [the] polite vagueness" of existing English translations (Kilroy, "Seagull" 80).

Tom Murphy, having emigrated to London with his blue-collar family in 1962 and worked "on the buses or on the buildings or in pubs," gained first-hand knowledge of emigrants who were struggling in "Irish ghettos" where dwellers, in his own words, "carry a most curious guilt that they were very much inferior to the people they had left behind" (Billington 96). These Irish people, however, felt alienated or even distrusted when they returned home, which still breathed, to some extent, a xenophobic air with its religious and political sentiments. Witnessing "an extraordinary cult of violence" in these socially marginalized communities (Billington 96), Murphy has approached this ignored subject since his early plays.[2]

---

[1] Chekhov's one act play, Swan Song, directed by Thomas MacDonagh, was performed in January 1915 at Edward Martyn's Irish Theatre. *Uncle Vanya* was the first of Chekhov's full-length plays to be introduced to Ireland and was staged in June 1915. Before the 1980s there had been a long interval before Chekhov's plays were produced again in Ireland, except for a production directed by Maria Knebel in 1968. Knebel was trained under Constantin Stanislavsky. Her "traditional approach" was criticized by Seamus Kelly, for she failed to "make a greater impression [by having] the action [...] translated into an Irish idiom and context" (Dixon 78). For a list of adaptations and translations of Chekhov's plays in Ireland, see Robert Tracy's "Chekhov in Ireland."

[2] Set mostly on the model of Tuam, the small town where he lived in the 1950s, these plays include *On the Outside* (1959), *A Whistle in the Dark* (1961), *Famine* (1968), *A Crucial Week in the Life of a Grocer's Assistant* (1969), *The Morning after Optimism* (1971), and *Conversations on a Homecoming* (1985). *A Whistle in the*

This chapter aims to examine Chekhov's *The Cherry Orchard* and Murphy's *The House* which, through a recurring theme of searching for home, reflect not only the identity crisis but a fractured sense of belonging that people of the Emerald Isle bear under the impact of immigration and rapid globalization. It will consider whether the forced and voluntary migrations in the two plays can disjoin the social forces that tend to stereotype or marginalize protagonists whose alternative outlooks on human existence in a de-territorialized world can be a point to investigate in an era of globalization. It will also demonstrate how the social denial of the formerly privileged underlines their sense of being uprooted, or rootless, and defies the traditional centers of power. Their roving experiences may suggest, on the one hand, how Chekhov reconsiders the serious nature of comedy; and on the other hand, how Murphy subverts the traditional Irish attachment to home(land) and initiates a search for the self and for a type of transcultural Irishness.

Murphy as an Irish Chekhov and the Chekhovian Comicality

What may have prompted Irish playwrights to produce an Irish Chekhov were the shared scenarios of social upheavals that broke out in both Ireland and Russia at the turn of the twentieth century. That is, the Anglo-Irish Ascendency and the Russian aristocracy were both about to collapse, and the middle classes were coming into major political and economic advantages from the old authorities. The rapid social changes, however, seemed to leave most citizens paralyzed in the face of the prevalent violence used against the politically and economically privileged. These minorities were now nearly incapacitated politically, were vulnerable, and not all were able to seek shelter elsewhere. The mental paralysis concerning the political and social violence mirrors the almost numb conscience that many modern Irish writers aimed to penetrate.[3] The

---

Dark and *A Crucial Week* were rejected by Ernest Blythe and Earnan de Blaghd, members of the Abbey Board, for their unsettling depictions of Ireland and its people, despite the fact that *Whistle* and *On the Outside* had won a number of manuscript prizes. *Whistle* was premiered at the Theatre Royal in London in 1961, and *A Crucial Week* was not staged at the Abbey until 1969. The London productions of these two plays were severely criticized by Irish critics in that "No blacker picture of the Irish has been painted on the stage"; "I never saw such rubbish in all my life" (*Evening Press*, 22 March, 1962; qtd in Griffin 17). Apparently, Murphy's Ibsenian approach to Irish life as being leeched by emigration was in great disfavor from the Abbey's conservative management.

3   Although works involving surrealism, magic realism, and *stream of consciousness are not uncommon in* modern and contemporary Irish literature, realism is still a major style of writing for Irish novelists and playwrights. James Joyce's declared intention to give "the Irish people [...] one good look at themselves in my nicely polished looking-

recurring theme of home in Murphy's works corresponds, interestingly, to that in Chekhov's *The Cherry Orchard*, where the conditions that presaged the Russian Revolution offered everyone a chance to be relocated to a new place or position, although not necessarily a secure one. It can be noted that Ireland, as a globalized state in progress at the present time, may share some social features with Russia during its revolutionary era, in the sense that the divides between social classes were greatly reshuffled in Russia and the Irish ethnic landscape is currently being fundamentally revised with the arrival of non-white newcomers. Murphy's contemporary Irish adaptation of a Russian classic, *The Cherry Orchard*, in a setting that would be more familiar to Irish audiences and embracing the theme of immigration, therefore implies not only public uneasiness about the immigrant Other but also the playwright's efforts to make both new and old residents feel at home – through the theatre as a public venue.[4]

The Cherry Orchard is a groundbreaking work in the history of Western theatre. On the one hand, despite the fact that Chekhov specified that this play was "A Comedy in Four Acts," he was experimenting with a new dramaturgy which was too difficult for the then director, Constantin Stanislavski, and the actors to comprehend properly before it was premiered at the Moscow Art Theatre in 1904. Chekhov, who was ill with tuberculosis at the time and had only a few months to live, was not happy with the premiere performance, criticizing the production for being "all wrong, the play and the performance. That's not what I saw, and they couldn't understand what I wanted" (qtd in Rayfield 241). Having had a grandfather who worked as a serf whose "blood [had been squeezed] out of himself drop by drop" (Frydman 31), what Chekhov wanted was not a drama of frustration, which was what Stanislavski imposed on his audiences, but a "comedy" in which they could feel cleansed or redeemed, rather than being given a short pleasurable escape from the ongoing social and political turbulence that they were experiencing in daily life outside the theatre. In other words, redrawing the map of political and economic power in pre-revolutionary Russia and exhibiting "how bad and dreary your lives are," should not, according to Chekhov, upset audience members but, "should [they] realise that, [...] they will most certainly create another and better life

---

glass" has been firmly inherited by most of his Irish literary successors through different genres (*Letters* 2: 135). It can thus be contended that *The House*, written according to a realistic convention, aims to unveil the predicaments of a bankrupt Anglo-Irish family in the aftermath of the anti-British-rule movement, and how rapid-acting capitalism is the straw that breaks the camel's back in this play.

4   Murphy does not read Russian. His adaptation of *The Cherry Orchard*, as he specifies on the title page of the script, derives from two literal translations by Chris Heaney and Patrick Miles respectively. Miles also served as Murphy's consultant in adapting *The Cherry Orchard*.

for themselves [...] It will be quite different, quite unlike our present life!" (qtd in Magarshack 49). Specifically, in *The Cherry Orchard* and *The House* – the latter an Irish adaptation of the former with an intertextual and revised storyline – the aristocrats must relocate themselves elsewhere, which may imply the awakening of their slumbering society; more significantly, both playwrights create fresh perspectives on the past for their contemporaries. The collapse of the aristocracy may not in itself be a cause for distress, as the characters involved can somehow look forward to the changes with courage and hope, as the playwrights show.

People who are forced to leave home, emigrate, or fall into another social stratum, will most likely become roamers who have trouble claiming a physical location as home but will feel themselves to be constantly in transit: either coming or going home, or looking for one. This condition is applicable to a state in the process of globalization, such as Ireland, where migration has significantly altered or disturbed the locals' sense of neighborhood and the world, "represent[ing] a virtual invasion of the home ground, tradition and a sense of national or communal identity" (O'Malley-Younger and Herron 149). Those who are entitled to a new identity would not feel settled but bear a sense of "internal exile" which, in Ien Ang's words, makes "displaced peoples [...] cling to a primordial notion of ethnic identity [...] as a secure sense of origin and belonging, and roots" (18). Being an "internal exile" is also a common experience for those who feel intimidated by ethnic newcomers or those who have newly returned, due to which the boundaries between home, state and the world have become amorphous and the natives cannot stay as they are but have to expand the territory of their "imagined community."[5]

It should be noted that the subversive nature of *The Cherry Orchard*, the predecessor of *The House*, lies in nomadism, a type of modern life observed by Gilles Deleuze and Félix Guattari that prompts characters to migrate from one place to another. According to them, being nomadic can be a physical or mental condition, or both, and one may not have to move out of "home," or into exile, in order to feel that one's identity has been assimilated with or negated by external forces. Migration, in other words, can be mentally or geographically conditioned and proceed along different routes, having "no beginning or end; it is always in the middle, between things [...] it is alliance and conjunction which uproots the verb 'to be'" (Deleuze and Guattari 24). It is thus interesting to note that Murphy's adaptation of *The Cherry Orchard*, produced at the Abbey

---

[5]   The concept of the "imagined community" was developed by Benedict Anderson, who claimed that any community, regardless of whether it is large or small, national or provincial, is a product of the collective imagination of people who perceive themselves to be the same. Anderson's book, *Imagined Communities,* first published in 1983, addressed this concept in depth.

Theatre in 2004 (four years after *The House*, in which Murphy actually resets Chekhov's materials in 1950s Ireland), touches upon relevant issues of migration to which all the Irish, natives or newcomers, are subject in different ways. Although the characters involved all migrate, sometimes unwillingly, from one state to another or from one social class to another – usually to a lower position – they become exiles *within* their own communities.

The Cherry Orchard (1904): A Modern Comedy of Russian Aristocrats in Decline

Although there have been numerous versions in English,[6] Murphy's 2004 Irish version of *The Cherry Orchard* is largely subversive in terms of his agenda to "re-create what was alive, musical and vibrant in the original [...] [but] avoid looking like the back of the tapestry" (Murphy, Preface 2). His remark implies his reservations about other translations and his hope for an Irish version which not only keeps the "'spirit' of the original [...] [but] translate[s] that 'spirit' into a language and movement that have their own dynamic," rather than working on Chekhov's work "line by line or speech by speech" (Murphy, Preface 2). Significantly, Murphy's version testifies to Chekhov's innovative approach of creating subtexts, or inner lives for his characters, which makes translation into other languages either impossible or "interpretively open," as Murphy himself indicates (Preface 2).[7] What is extraordinary about Murphy's version, therefore, resides in the losses and gains that occur when making a Russian play "our own" with cultural and linguistic references that are closer to Irish local audiences. Specifically, the ambiguities in Chekhov's subtexts make little allowance for a definitive interpretation of the play, allowing directors, actors, and translators to render the play with an open

---

[6]　There have been numerous English translations of *The Cherry Orchard* for productions in British and American theatres and those in other languages. Translators and adapters of *The Cherry Orchard*, to name a few, include Stanley Appelbaum, Libby Appel, Hubert Butler, Curt Columbus, Elisaveta Fen, Michael Frayn, Chris Heaney, Allison Horsley, David Lan, Elisaveta Lavrova, David Mamet, Stephen Mulrine, Richard Nelson, Stuart Paterson, Martin Sherman, Tom Stoppard, Julius West and Avraham Yarmolinsky. Frayn's and Yarmolinsky's versions may be the most often anthologized to date. It can be assumed, however, that many adapters, like Murphy, have no knowledge of the Russian language but have had to rely on other literal translations.

[7]　Chekhov, dismissing the possibility of having his works translated equivalently into other languages, once made a skeptical remark as follows: "I can't stop them, can I? So, let them translate away, no sense will come of it" (Chekhov 357). However, the subtexts which he creates through silence, signs, and symbols, and broken sentences, allow open interpretations and have inspired many other dramatists to produce plays with Chekhovian elements in other languages.

approach, while many of them do not acquire any knowledge of the Russian language.[8]

That *The Cherry Orchard* can be regarded as a comedy, as Chekhov intended, has to be understood in the context of its first production in 1904, when Europe had been turning itself upside down as emerging forces were eager to claim positions of power. That is, the *fin de siècle* that marked the bridge between the nineteenth and twentieth centuries had made Europe simmer with uncertainties, depression, and moral degradation. In Russia, the ongoing industrial revolution, the emancipation of the serfs in 1861, the supply of free labor to the cities, the growing political influence of the middle class, and revolts against the rule of the tsars, including the assassination of Alexander II in 1881, had produced a state of near anarchy. These conditions are brought to light in this play in which "people are starving, sleeping in the streets, sleeping in sheds or thirty/forty to a room, with fleas, in filth and damp, and all leading to foul language, greater ignorance, obscenities, eruptions of mindless, barbaric violence, immorality," while the rich "sit around talking" and highbrows "make speeches about the eighties and the Decadent Movement and the seventies – to the poor waiters!"[9] Having lost faith, lifestyle and values, Russians in Chekhov's time could hardly be expected to have a clear sense of direction for their future, whether at the personal or national level. The collective uneasiness of society as a whole – caused by political agitations and economic problems – cannot be healed with a farce or a simple comedy which entertains audiences with nightly pleasure or a moment of escape. Although *The Cherry Orchard* is set amidst the social distress and angst of Chekhov's time, it is not a play about the uncertain future of Russia but one with hope and love shown through its seemingly trivial dialogues and subtexts.

Interestingly, few characters in *The Cherry Orchard* remain on a fixed political or economic level in their changing times, including the servants who have lived off the fringe benefits of the estate. The privileged members of the Ranyevskaya family are all about to move or have been on the move, and those who serve them or rely on their leftovers are forced

---

[8]   Take for instance the 1968 production of *The Cherry Orchard*, directed by Maria Knebel, who was trained under Stanislavsky. Knebel recollected that the Irish cast expressed empathy for the exiled characters who wished to return home. Their empathy may have been due to the fact that emigration had been a common Irish experience in the mid-twentieth century, during which "the young must abandon [their homeland] […] which remains the site of childhood memories, and to which the exile feels compelled to return. Such notions were central to Knebel's Irish production, but were not imposed on Chekhov's play" (Dixon 78).

[9]   Chekhov, *Cherry Orchard* 38, 33. Throughout, references to *The Cherry Orchard* are to Murphy's 2004 version.

to find new jobs or shelter elsewhere. It may be argued that those who intend to look for a job outside the old aristocratic realm correspond to a postmodern mode of human existence "where individuals overcome repressive modern forms of identity and stasis to become desiring nomads in a constant process of becoming and transformation" (Best and Kellner 77). What the Ranyevskaya family experiences, as do their servants, is consonant with the uncertain future that Russian civilians face, whatever their social standing.

The turmoil in Russian society therefore prompts all the characters in the play to dismiss an outdated and repressive identity so as to welcome a vibrant and newly given one. Take Anya, the seventeen-year-old daughter of Lyubov, for instance. She has been exiled with her mother since the age of twelve and has longed to come home: "I'm *home*! Tomorrow when I wake up I shall be *here* [...] I shall *run* out and into and through the orchard" (*Cherry Orchard* 10). The bankruptcy of her family, however, makes her more down-to-earth and willing to be a "career woman" – which is unprecedented in her aristocratic family: "I'll get a job – *a job*! And I'll be able to help [my mother]" (*Cherry Orchard* 69). She actually leaves the estate "laughing," as Chekhov specifies: "Goodbye, old house, goodbye, old world!" (*Cherry Orchard* 75). Varya, the adopted daughter of Lyubov, having been an experienced governess on the estate during Lyubov's five-year absence, decides to work later as a housekeeper in Ragulins. This is, however, a laborious job and she can no longer keep a high profile as before but has to take orders from a new (middle-class) employer. Gayev, Lyubov's fifty-one year old brother, takes a positive view of the sale of the estate: "Now that it's all been decided, once for all, we're calm. We're even quite cheerful, hum? [...] I've landed on my feet: banker now, financier now" (*Cherry Orchard* 68).

While they are bidding farewell to each other and to the old house, "more evidence of their happiness" is in the air that makes everyone feel "well-up within" (*Cherry Orchard* 69, 74), rather than being bitter about the decline of aristocratic traditions. Different from Lyubov's despondency about the loss of the estate, Anya's optimism is vivified when she comforts her mother by saying that leaving the homeland will bring another chance to "plant a new orchard, a better one, you'll see, you will, and like the sun in the evening it'll all make sense, and you'll smile" (*Cherry Orchard* 61). Most significantly, it is the sense of loving and being loved, as Anya talks gently to her mother, that soothes Lyubov's grief for the loss of the cherrylands and prompts everyone to embrace the changing times in higher spirits, instead of taking the loss with deep regret: "Why are you crying? Cherry orchard is gone, that's true, but your life too is out there in the future. My beautiful mother, I'm so grateful to you. I'm so grateful for you. I bless you, I love you" (*Cherry Orchard* 61).

Urban industrialization and the sale of the cherry orchard are the two main forces that tear the aristocratic family apart, but they prompt all the characters to proceed into new walks of life. Lopakhin, taking over the cherry orchard as the son of a former serf, is planning to build summer cottages there for middle-class holidaymakers, so as to make more money. He will presumably gain access to echelons of the upper-class. It can be assumed that the fortune this parvenue will make will not bring him peace of mind but he will constantly feel uprooted from the land where he shared childhood memories with the Ranyevskayas. He will no doubt experience "internal exile" within the state for being a single *individual* in an industrial mechanism (Naficy 3), moving upwards or downwards among different social classes. Pishchik, who starts to buy neighboring plots of land, piece by piece, near the cherry orchard – with loans from poppy-grower Lopakhin – soon turns into a parvenu. White clay is found on his new land by china makers who offer to rent it on a twenty-four year lease (*Cherry Orchard* 71). Joining with Lopakhin, he will supplant the Ranyevskaya family as the new landed gentry, and be subject to a new, perhaps vicious, circle of capitalistic operations. Ironically, it is the land that turns him into a *nouveau riche*, whereas the land also causes him to be an exile – metaphorically, as he can no longer make himself at home in this estate as before, while Russia is being geared for a new capitalistic and mechanistic world.

Chekhov, however, does not favor any particular party in *The Cherry Orchard* but is critical of the political ideology, namely Marxism, that has become important in pre-revolutionary Russia. He indirectly makes fun of Petya, a disciple of Marxism and a former tutor of Lyubov's son, for the intellectual paradoxes he gets himself into. That is, although Petya boldly accuses Ranyevskaya, in Marxist terms, for her "sin" of enslaving "living souls" to operate the cherry orchard, distrusting romantic love between any couple for fear that "petty illusions" will undermine "where we're headed" (*Cherry Orchard* 43), Chekhov does not endorse Petya's radical thoughts but, through the words of Lyubov, stresses the significance of loving and being loved. More specifically, Lyubov, as a mother with a lost son, a widow, and a woman who has broken her marriage vows but has also been deeply hurt by her relationships, sees Petya as "my dear *young* good philosopher [...] [who is being blown] [...] from pillar to post" (*Cherry Orchard* 51, emphasis added). In other words, Lyubov, compassionately, is distressed at seeing the *young* philosopher being manipulated by political ideologies and refusing to transcend any human suffering or understand her mixed life experiences.

The Cherry Orchard is often wrongly perceived as a tragedy, in that the Ranyevskaya family is forced to fall from its privileged position. Members of the family either go into exile or have to make ends meet at best they can. Lyubov, for instance, has no choice but to depart grudgingly for Paris to live with a dying lover who offers her shelter. Both of her daughters have to look for jobs to support themselves. Her brother, Gayev, at the age of fifty-one, finds his first job in order to earn a living. The family seems to fall to pieces and there will hardly be a foreseeable reunion during the rest of their lives. However, the comicality of this play lies in the financial and mental relief of the Ranyevskaya family upon the sale of the cherry orchard. They are now free of their ancestral burden and are not likely to be left behind during the process of modernization: "The sound of a breaking string (a metallic twang) [...] and the sound of the axe on the trees" can be heard at the end of the play. These sounds are not necessarily ominous but signify the arrival of a new life. This celebrative subtext is reinforced by Lopakhin's offer of champagne to the Ranyevskaya family upon their departure, and Petya's final speech, "hail, new life! (*He goes, cheerfully.*)" (*Cherry Orchard* 75). The air of joy is accentuated by the healthy return of Firs, a male servant who is discharged from hospital after Lyubov leaves. None of these characters suffers any devastation at the end; they are able to stand firm in their new life. This chapter will now examine how this Chekhovian "comedy" is fused with Irish migrant experiences and social change in *The House*, and the discussion will be deepened by questions about the insular social discourse as it works against returned Irish emigrants.

The House (2000): *The Cherry Orchard* in Ireland and Its Revised End

Something that often troubles producers and audiences of *The Cherry Orchard* is the understated plots and disjointed dialogues with which Chekhov turned over a fresh page of realistic dramaturgy. His theatrical experiment caused not only the failure of its premiere – in the eyes of the playwright – but that of reviewers to understand Chekhovian aesthetics. For instance, Zinaida Gippius, among other early critics, maintained that the play was "unperformable," thus launching an "anti-Chekhovian school of criticism" (Rayfield 241). Rather than reproducing popular melodramatic elements, the implicitness in Chekhov's dialogues, on the one hand, mirrors the stagnancy of "real life" in which, as the playwright observes, "after all, [...] people don't spend every moment in shooting one another, hanging themselves, or making declarations of love. They do not spend all their time saying clever things" (qtd in Valency 249). On the other hand, the indirectness of Chekhovian aesthetics allows considerable room for adaptations or translations in different cultural contexts across language barriers. The realistic dramaturgy which Chekhov accomplished therefore enriches the interpretative strategies of drama. His theatre – often instilled with subtexts – strategically allows *non*-definitive interpretations to develop, paving the way for creative adaptations or inter-texts, rather than "spell[ing] the death of invention" that would probably suffocate the theatrical arts (Dixon 97).

Based on this premise, Murphy's *The House*, set in the 1950s in an Irish ambience, may be suitable for examination as a work inter-textual with *The Cherry Orchard*. This Irish adaptation featuring an Anglo-Irish family in decline has an explicitly nostalgic atmosphere in its characterizations, dialogues and stage effects, interrogating the conventional ideal of "home" in a soon-to-be globalized Ireland. The playwright, having experienced life in Newcastle in the 1950s as a young emigrant working "on the buses or on the buildings or in pubs, [living in] predominantly Irish ghettos [...] [with] an extraordinary cult of violence," empathizes greatly with those "having a sense of being betrayed by the country of their origin [...] [and] also [feeling] that they had betrayed that country" (Billington 96). The affinity between Chekhov's Russian gentry and the Anglo-Irish Ascendency, alongside Murphy's understanding of *The Cherry Orchard*, which he went on in 2004 to adapt/translate for the Abbey Theatre, is the reason why he revamped Chekhov's play with an Irish flavor. More specifically, what is shared in both plays is that both the Russian gentry and Anglo-Irish Ascendency had been swept away politically and culturally as new states developed, being intimidated by revolutionaries and emerging political elite and, in economic terms, failing to hold on to their property – inherited from their forefathers – in the face of drastic social changes.[10]

One slight but significant difference is that the Anglo-Irish presence in *The House* implies historically a foreign, English operation in Ireland, whereas the Ranyevskayas in *The Cherry Orchard* share a coherent Russian identity with those "around and beneath them" (Kilroy, "Seagull" 82).[11] This cultural and political difference allows Murphy and other

---

[10]   F.S.L. Lyons points out that the Anglo-Irish Ascendency "lived the sort of life that landlords lived everywhere [in Europe]. Shooting, fishing and hunting, interspersed with hospitality more lavish than they could afford—this was the framework of their lives" (Lyons 19). The Ranyevskaya family in *The Cherry Orchard* shares a similar cultural milieu with that of the de Burcas in *The House*, before both of them go bankrupt and cannot even afford their daily expenses.

[11]   Murphy, however, is not the first playwright to give Chekhov's plays an Irish flavor. Thomas Kilroy, in 1981, had produced Chekhov's *The Seagull*. In this version, Kilroy reset *The Seagull* on an Anglo-Irish estate in the west of Ireland in the late nineteenth century. His producer, Max Stafford-Clark, agreed with Kilroy that "some English language productions of Chekhov tended to be lost in polite vagueness," and believed that "an Anglo-Irish setting would provide a specificity, [...] [which will make the play more] comprehensible to an English audience" (Kilroy, "Seagull" 80). They both felt that "an Irish setting would more easily allow the rawness of passion of the original to emerge" (Kilroy, "Seagull" 80). This adaptation was produced at the Royal Court,

Irish playwrights to adapt Chekhov's plays to reconstruct a lost tradition, lifestyle, and culture that was once present in their homeland. The local flavor therefore "make[s] the Russian [characters] more real" and more accessible to a wider audience by expressing emotions "in a language we can understand, both more immediate and mediated by difference" (Kavanagh 18). *The House*, as a play after Chekhov, shows how the Anglo-Irish heritage crumbles but is later preserved by the returning well-to-do Irish immigrant Christy, before globalization overrides the insularity of Irish society and fundamentally revises the cultural core of the Emerald Isle.

What makes *The House* a play after *The Cherry Orchard* is its consonant but somewhat different plot in which two classes from the extremes of a collapsed social hierarchy are about to meet and make compromises: the newly emerged *nouveau riche* and the old aristocrats who are in decline from a formerly privileged position. Christy, who is like Lopakhin in *The Cherry Orchard* in coming from a lower rung of the social ladder, has made his fortune by engaging in unsavory business practices in England. Both Christy and Lopakhin were born into working class families and both lost their mothers at a young age. Both were given special care by the matriarchs of privileged families, respectively the de Burcas and the Ranyevskayas, and both grew with mixed feelings of attachment to the motherly figures who seem to carry the "original sin" of being aristocratic figures. Unlike other Irish emigrants who worked in the mines or on building sites, Christy earned enough as a "pimp" in London (Murphy, *The House* 212) to accumulate a fortune and buy the de Burca estate with little difficulty. For Christy, the de Burca estate, where he was nurtured and educated, has always been "'home' to him – at least subconsciously" (*The House* 187), and his attachment to the "trees, landscape, air, fresh air" around the house has prompted him to "rescue" it and to save the dignity of the family from going bankrupt. The de Burcas are akin to the Ranyevskayas in that both families are (agri)culturally aloof from the land that their ancestors planted, especially the de Burcas with "Norman blood sure from way back: it never left them [...] They're – different" from the rest of Irish natives (*The House* 209).[12] In other words, both

---

London, on 8 April 1981, receiving some negative reviews, as it was seen as a new play, "not a translation, or a version" (Dixon 108). Kilroy nevertheless argues that he had dubbed it "after Chekhov" on its book cover. Notably, Brian Friel also adapted Chekhov's short story "The Yalta Game" in 2001, dubbing it "after Chekhov" as well as having an Irish landscape. This adaptation was published in 1993.

[12] De Burca, which means "fortified hill," is an Anglo-Norman surname. Although the play does not mention the family history of the de Burcas but that of their estate, established before 1839, the de Burcas originated from France, migrating through Britain and on to Ireland in the early eleventh century. This landed family produced

families have traditionally lived in a state of unity for centuries, whereas the unceasing calls for modernization and capitalization not only dissolve their traditional landed system but force the two families to enter "a fractured state of exile" (Keating 176). Notably, what makes *The House* "more real" to local audiences, compared to its Russian prototype, is the Irish characters' perception of their *reality* in a changing world (Kavanagh 18). Therefore, the "tragicomic" elements of *The House* are, perhaps as Murphy intends, more verbally effective than those of the subtexts of *The Cherry Orchard*.

In *The House*, Christy, which is short for "Christopher" meaning "Christ-bearing" in ancient Greek, seems, along with other returning Irish emigrants, to have a mission to save those in need in their home town by either sending money home or spending it in local venues during their summer visits.[13] Goldfish, for instance, who has returned from America, proudly asserts "we're bigger than here, we're – the energy" of the place (*The House* 285), and "flicks/pitches" with an air of patronage "his coin change into a corner of the floor" at a pub before he departs again for America (*The House* 282). Christy, although not as arrogant as Goldfish, harbors a similar attitude by taking pity on Mrs de Burca, a widow who "is worried about her three daughters and their futures […] and coming to a decision to sell the family home has been difficult and complex [for her]" (*The House* 235). Having no choice, as she is nearly bankrupt, Mrs de Burca is forced to sell the estate which was a dream place of "[her husband's] […] and mine," in order to make ends meet (*The House* 235).

The short summer visits of these more well-to-do Irish emigrants, giving immediate pecuniary relief to the locals, could hardly be more unsettling to their puritanical native town under the domination of the Catholic Church. Having no regard for their financial contributions to Ireland, or, more significantly, for the cultural dynamism which they bring with them, the local priest sees these returned emigrants as sources of pollution, accusing them at Mass of being ungrateful and morally suspect: "Guide all our emigrants down the right path abroad, stop them from ever straying, teach them abstinence and forbearance […] And keep them in mind of the land of their birth so that they may one day return to the bosom of thy heavenly mansions" (*The House* 219).

---

many earls, barons, scholars and poets who contributed to the diversities of Irish civilization. Variants of de Burca include de Burgh, Burgh, de Burgh, and Burke.

13 Christopher was honored as Saint Christopher, based on the legend of having carried the Christ child across a river and being martyred in the 3rd century AD. Metaphorically, Christy and other returned Irish emigrants seem to share the same mission by carrying those destitute at home over to a more stable financial state.

For these returned emigrants, home thus becomes a place of anger and disappointment, and also a place where, ironically, they feel rootless after so many years' exile and hard labor. Married to an English woman, Peter, one of the returned emigrants from England, for instance, has trouble identifying where he will be culturally accepted. His sense of exile becomes even more unmistakable in his Irish homeland, which is the subject of his dreams "about it and all" (*The House* 197): "[...] a strange thing: I wakes up this morning. Was it early? Was and all, mate, was and all. And I'm lying there like I'm drowning. Like it happens (at) times, the other side, but does you expect it at home, ay?" (sic, *The House* 224). It can be argued that Peter, Christy, Goldfish, and many others in this play, all feel rootless and betrayed by their mother country, and are insultingly mistaken as English or American by local civil servants. It is ironic that these emigrants – as saviors of some kind – have been working so hard overseas to relieve the poverty of their siblings at home.[14]

Produced in 2000 and set in an unnamed town in the 1950s, *The House* serves as a faithful mirror to the painful process through which Ireland was transformed into a globalized state from a culturally closed society that celebrated the three "Fs" of farming, faith and family in Éamon de Valera's era. These returned emigrants and the last remaining Anglo-Irish Ascendency all witness a globalized Ireland beginning to take shape, although the process is not always emotionally easy. That is to say, all the parties involved pay a price, sometimes a very difficult one, when they have to make an unwilling choice for an unknown future. One of the three daughters of Mrs de Burca, Louise, in her twenties, has trouble with her drunkard husband whose business is about to collapse. Marie, in her thirties, having recently lost her husband, is planning to emigrate along with her widowed mother – with the money from the auction of the estate. Without "an alternative plan for here," believing that the sale of the house will "settle [three daughters]," and realizing that the "old life [is] disappearing" (*The House* 235), Mrs de Burca unwillingly makes the difficult decision to auction the house for the sake of the money it will bring. However, Susanne, the youngest daughter, who feels a deep attachment to the estate where she spent her childhood, is strongly opposed to the auction, for she holds that "even if I'm away, I belong here. I'd like to have some standing" here in Ireland (*The House* 234). She resents the fact that the family never consult her for an alternative view on the issue, so that she "could have come up with" some solutions (*The House* 234),

---

[14] For instance, Goldfish, less emotionally reserved than Christy, complains of Ireland as a "fucking place [which gets] on my nerves" (*The House* 280). He was mistaken by a judge at court as being from England, whereas he "come[s] all the way back from the United States [...] [and] I am *from* this town" (*The House* 282). Put it another way, he is by birth an Irish but at home the court denies his Irishness.

and she threatens that she will not leave the house whatever happens, even if "it all fall[s] down" on her head (*The House* 235). These contradictory sentiments make the auction an emotionally difficult case.

Furthermore, the house – which has been on its current site for at least two centuries – is more than a symbol of wealth and status for established and potential dwellers, but is an active, if silent, actor in the social transformation, with its increasing market value that secures the last hope of the family for relief from financial and marital crisis, and for a new life after emigration. The house is also literally a death trap for Susanne, who drowns in an incident suspiciously involving Christy as a murderer. Significantly, her death results from her failed attempt to block, single-handedly, the ongoing social transformation by obstructing the placing of the house on the market. To put it another way, the house metaphorically plays a silent but sinister role as it will stand more firmly in the coming era of capitalism. Christy and the de Burcas, alongside other immigrants/emigrants, are not the real winners but all suffer the consequences of being uprooted forcefully both from the land and from their traditional social positions. The house seems to be a voiceless but willful character that does not need any salvation or sympathy from any party but acts as a staunch, more valued body in a modern Ireland.

Satirically, none of the emigrants can be exempt from the prejudices at home, but at least they gradually revamp the local culture with an international flavor. Goldfish, for instance, who has acquired an American accent, wears "a gold watch, and a gold ring [...] [and] his dress and vocabulary tell [his] story" (*The House* 194). Peter, returning from England, is overwhelmed by the Broadway blockbuster *The Sound of Music*, singing with pride the Irish version of its cover song: "I is for the Irish in your [heart]" (*The House* 203). Christy often tries to impress others by re-enacting lines from English films with a Spanish accent. Foreign film and singing stars, such as Bette Davis, Arthur Tracy and Paul Henreid, are often the common subjects of their chitchats. Peter, who is closely akin to Petya in *The Cherry Orchard*, acts with cynicism and hostility toward those who are suspiciously under corrupted foreign influences.[15] These people, unable to be religiously and culturally assimilated by the locals, form their own small community in the town, whereas their practice of mixing different cultural elements testifies to the process by which Ireland was about to open its doors to the outside

---

[15]   "Petya" is a pet form of the English, Scandinavian and German "Peter." It has different variations, including the Dutch and German "Piet," the Spanish "Piti," the English "Pat," "Pate," "Payatt," "Peto," and the Czech "Pét'a." Murphy's choice of the name, "Peter," may, on the one hand, correspond to "Petya" in *The Cherry Orchard*. On the other hand, Peter, the person, behaves like an Irish "paddy" circumscribed by insular ideology.

world and the forces of modernization, despite many locals, such as Jimmy, holding a "supercilious [...] and envious" attitude towards the returned "foreign" Irish (*The House* 194). To exhibit these complex and rapid social changes, the scenes of the play therefore switch between a local pub where emigrants make themselves at home, and the estate where the de Burcas manage to survive their last minutes together before the home is dissolved.

Conclusion: One Story, Two Spirits

It may be contended that *The House* and *The Cherry Orchard* both vivify the impact of migration on all walks of society, and allow audiences to see how intercultural exchange and modernization unsettled a xenophobic Ireland and Russia, and how local people resisted the cultural and economic dynamism brought about by social upheavals. However, in contrast to *The Cherry Orchard*, *The House* seems more explicit in portraying the critical roles that these Irish returned workers play during the modernization of Ireland in face of the prejudices against them. Specifically, by largely relying on background noises, such as the sounds of cables snapping and axe blows falling, *The Cherry Orchard* does not pinpoint so outspokenly how provincialism can uproot people from their beloved country and force them into unsympathetic exile. Venturing farther afield than those in *The Cherry Orchard*, the characters in *The House* are physically and mentally more rootless and restless, even though they have broadened the horizons of the locals and "the rolls of money they flash" give their motherland the chance of modernization (194). What modernity means to these returned emigrants in *The House* is not necessarily a high quality of life but a series of moves from one location to another, and an unending search for home. What makes the two plays similar, nevertheless, is the possibility of reconciliation between the new rich/middle class and the uprooted Ascendancy. In *The House*, Christy, the buyer of the de Burca estate, and Marie, one of the former owners, shake hands at the end of the play – with mixed emotions. Lopakhin in *The Cherry Orchard* offers champagne to the Ranyevskayas before they depart. Probably not feeling amenable to this gesture under the circumstances, none of them accepts his offer, apart from Yasha, the manservant, who drinks one glass after another. In both plays, the sense of reconciliation is apparently mixed with hope and implicit resentment before the curtain falls.

Some critiques of Chekhov's *The Cherry Orchard* are often either complaints about the nothingness of the play, or accusations that the play is a nostalgic defense of the old regime. Some criticize the play for being only "an imitation of an action in the strictest sense" without much creativity (Fergusson 31).[16] Nevertheless, it may be justifiable to argue that Chekhov's creativity lies in his challenge to the notions of home and exile, and his empathy with what is now, after the 1970s, dubbed diasporic by cultural critics. That is to say, *The Cherry Orchard* and its Irish counterpart, *The House*, depict the experiences of human migration at times when society was evolving under the influences of industrialization and modernity; the direction of home, or a metaphorical homecoming, is no longer one way or linear.

As the two plays demonstrate, home is a motif much contested in *The Cherry Orchard* and *The House*. However, despite the similar storylines, the playwrights' approaches to home are different. Chekhov's approach focuses more on the impact of industrialization on the landed gentry and their optimism, whereas Murphy's concern is the losses and gains of the middle or lower middle class. The backgrounds of Murphy's characters are also more diverse, and their emotions toward social change are more straightforward than those in *The Cherry Orchard*, which are expressed through Chekhovian subtexts. The common feature of the two plays, presented in different cultural scenarios and historical eras, is the march of people toward "avowedly 'global' times" (Bhabha, "Arrivals and Departures" viii). A home, in the era of globalization, can no longer be simply defined as a place where a family resides, nor is it an abode to which everyone returns regularly. It can be a place that people visit infrequently or say farewell to, like that in *The House*. In other words, Home functions as a "powerful cultural signifier" by which one looks for more than just an existential shelter but a sense of cultural belonging (O'Malley-Younger and Herron 149). This sense of belonging does not have to be the same as that of one's siblings or fellow countrymen, but it is unique to any individual when defining who (s)he is or hopes to be, according to personal experiences.

It can thus be contended that, in *The Cherry Orchard*, Paris is where Lyubov feels at home and is loved by her many admirers, rather than the gloomy and bleak Russian hometown. Yasha, her servant, feels that he is more "made for Paris" than the cherrylands (*Cherry Orchard* 68). Lopakhin, though he has never been to Paris, "dress[es] like a Parisian" (*Cherry Orchard* 16). The returned emigrants in *The House* feel betrayed and alienated by Ireland for not only having been smeared as the bringers of evil influences but intentionally mis-identified as being English or American. These reverse immigrants all ultimately return to their *new* homes, where they probably feel more culturally settled and less emotionally intimidated. Ironically, Goldfish in *The House* seemingly

---

[16] The above is Francis Fergusson's paraphrase of negative criticism against *The Cherry Orchard*, not his personal opinion.

cannot wait to return to America, and "reverts to his American accent" (286) long before he gets on board.

These reactions toward one's homeland and hopes for a new world suggest that modernization has deprived the home of its traditional power, and home is no longer a carrier of a definite cultural hegemony or nationalism availing of a grounded identity. Home becomes a location where many people stay temporarily, take a rest, and depart as roamers. Home is a destination – not a final but a mobile one – and a temporary shelter for people, especially those who break away from the traditional hierarchy that takes home as a basic unit. Nevertheless, although it ends tragically with Susanne's suspected murder, *The House* seems to re-interpret more elaborately the central motif of home which *The Cherry Orchard* fails fully to illuminate. In other words, *The House* illustrates more explicitly the contradictions between freedom and social discipline, deepening what Chekhov means about being an artist who is critically free of all ideological or cultural shackles: "I am not a liberal, not a conservative, not a believer in gradual progress, not a monk, not an indifferentist. I should like to be a free artist and nothing more" (Chekhov, *Letters* 63).

The ambiguities in Chekhovian language have prompted many successors in theatres across cultural and national boundaries to interpret the unsaid between his lines. The social phenomena he depicts from his own time, ranging from migration and class struggle to inter-culturalism, are common themes in a later, globalized world and nurture a power of subversion that helps create a space "nomadic, limitless, labile and in process, as opposed to primordial, essential and fixed" (O'Malley-Younger and Herron 150). This is a space where artists can meander inside a theatre – metaphorically – but start their journey toward a new home and search for a unique individuality. With the open endings of both texts, what Chekhov and Murphy embrace is the sense of liberation that, rather than constricted by an existing, old social order, prospers by constantly moving and repositioning in the global village.

V. South Africa, Racism, and Irish Sectarianism in Dolores Walshe's *In the Talking Dark* and Damian Smyth's *Soldiers of the Queen*

> Dark mirrors multiply the soul's unease;
> the self's other side remains unmapped
> despite riotously spent images chronicling
> the idiocies of my odyssey.
>
> (Robert E. Fox, "Ulysses in Africa.")

Introduction: The Irish Diaspora in South Africa in Retrospect

What makes Irish theatre a unique form of expression, despite its long tradition of being a forum for different political and religious persuasions in Ireland, is its nature as a production of linguistic, cultural, and political coalescence, especially after English became the major language of performance in Ireland. This language enabled Irish tradesmen, Catholic missionaries, civil servants and soldiers to perform their duties; it allowed anti-colonial campaigners to befriend their peers in the United States and former colonies; and it somehow eased the difficulties of unskilled or semi-skilled emigrants when they first arrived in a foreign land. The consequences of being competent in the settler's language have lingered from the early nineteenth century to the twenty-first century.[1] One particular consequence is that, aside from the growing influence of the Irish diaspora on the Irish economy and politics, contemporary Irish playwrights are gradually shifting their attention towards international affairs and people of mixed origins and their pressing issues, and re-exploring the overlooked adventures of the overseas Irish. Performers of

---

[1] The British government set up a large number of national schools in Ireland from 1831. One aim of these national schools was to bring "culture and civilization to lower classes and more remote regions" (Coleman 36). However, they were severely criticized by Irish nationalists for being a means of anglicizing Irish children, as they did not teach any Irish history or literature but sought to have the children acquire the colonizer's mentality. English was the only language used in classrooms. By 1900 more than 700,000 pupils had attended the 8,674 national schools in Ireland (Coleman 36).

color are not absent from the theatrical scene, and the Irish stage is being transformed from an insular to a multicultural medium.[2]

Though geographically far removed from each other, the fact that South Africa and Ireland shared a regrettable history of rule by the British has been a matter of interest in Irish writing since the early twentieth century. The ambiguous role of the Irish presence – as both the ruled in their own country and the ruling in the British administration of South Africa – is often a popular topic for Irish writers and critics. The most remarkable example is James Joyce's *Ulysses*, in which 11 episodes refer directly to South African affairs, and others "evoke its presence through metaphorical parallels established elsewhere in the text" (Temple-Thurston 249). It has also long been appreciated that to properly dissect both *Ulysses* and *Finnegans Wake* it is necessary to keep in mind the Anglo-Boer War of 1899-1902, given that Joyce's extensive and consistent references to South Africa imply the nature of his political views about his home town and its ties with England. Moreover, what prompts contemporary Irish writers to delineate racial divides in Ireland, or similar phenomena in South Africa is that Ireland experienced a similar transformation to South Africa when asylum seekers and refugees flooded into Ireland from Eastern Europe and Africa. Racist attacks on black communities and individuals are no longer headline news, with Northern Ireland having been tagged the "race hate capital of Europe" and Belfast the "most racist city in the world" by the European media (McVeigh 402). Incidentally, graffiti which express explicit racist attitudes are no less obtrusive in the Republic of Ireland. The increase of serious racist incidents in Dublin has prompted critics to comment that "racism [has] moved from the margins of Irish political life to the centre" (Lentin and McVeigh 3).

This chapter therefore aims to scrutinize two less discussed dramas that unearth the neglected experiences of the Irish diaspora in South Africa in particular, examining how a country under apartheid may be a mirror, albeit not necessarily a faithful one, to the Northern Ireland Troubles and alarming racial conflicts across the Emerald Isle. Most interestingly, the

---

[2]   Casts of black actors and actresses have not been uncommon on the Irish stage in recent years, nor have plays addressing multicultural conflicts. For instance, Jimmy Murphy's *The Kings of the Kilburn High Road*, which features the disregarded experiences of Irish workers in London, was produced by Arambe Theatre with five black actors. Arambe, founded in 2003 by Bisi Adigun, a Nigerian director and immigrant, has produced a number of African plays dealing particularly with themes of cultural and racial conflict, including Ama Ata Adioo's *The Dilemma of a Ghost*. It also staged a production, in 2007, of J.M. Synge's *The Playboy of the Western World* with a Nigerian actor taking the leading role of Christy Mahon. In the same year, this play was restaged by Pan Pan Theatre Company, directed by Gavin Quinn with an entire Chinese cast, after receiving high critical acclaim in 2006 in Beijing. These instances explain the growing transformation of the Irish theatre in the era of globalism.

two plays concerning South Africa – written by two Irish playwrights – observe the racially split nation from two different angles, if studied alongside each other. The two plays are Dolores Walshe's *In the Talking Dark* and Damian Smyth's *Soldiers of the Queen*. Walshe's play exhibits how people of mixed races were negated and mistreated in South Africa under apartheid in the late 1980s; Smyth's portrays a former Irish soldier whose mental breakdown stems from racial conflicts in Southern Africa in the late nineteenth century, and his troubled identities by antagonism between England and Ireland.

Before delineating the significance of the two Irish plays, it may be necessary to explore the reasons why the study of the Irish diaspora in South Africa has been insufficient, and why there has been little detailed research on their interactions with other European settlers and natives. Examinations of their far-reaching influence on the politics and economy of the Irish homeland also remain deficient. Despite the fact that the number of Irish people in South Africa reached 60,000 in 1904 (Akenson 9), the reason for the inadequate study of Irish emigration to this part of the world is partially because the Irish migrants were mostly middle-class skilled or semi-skilled male workers who, unlike those unskilled refugees from famine who mostly fled to the New World (the United States and Canada), they saw this passage to South Africa "more like going for a long sojourn" (Colum 32), as stated in the biography of Arthur Griffith.[3] More specifically, many male Irish workers at this time – whose number was almost two thirds of the whole Irish population migrating to South Africa – presumed that they would return to Ireland or transfer to other British colonies, regardless of whether they settled alongside local Afrikaners or black natives (McCracken, "Irish Settlement," 145).[4] That

---

[3] Although the census report of the time did not show such a remarkable number of immigrants from Ireland, Akenson proposed a "multiplier" to estimate the size of the "entire ethnic cohort," which includes those who were Irish born, Irish born outside South Africa, and those who declared their parentage as being Irish ("Irish Identity," 9). The 1904 census of the Irish population was 18,000; the multiplier, as Akenson proposed, was 3.375. No matter whether Akenson's estimate is the most accurate, it can be assumed that the Irish population, was much more economically and politically stable in South Africa than in the New World.

[4] Both the Irish and Afrikaners belonged to a "superior class" in South African society. The Afrikaners were mostly descendents of Dutch colonists who first settled in the Cape of Good Hope in the late seventeenth century, arriving in a larger numbers with the Dutch East India Company. They lost their Dutch citizenship in 1795 when the Prince of Orange surrendered control of the Cape Colony to British rule. This incurred Afrikaners' anxiety to establish a separate national identity other than being British. Their resentment against British rule engendered a series of conflicts and two Anglo-Boer Wars in 1880 and 1899 respectively. Many Irish radical nationalists, such as Arthur Griffith and Michael Collins, had visited and/or expressed admiration for the leaders of the Boers. See Patricia A. McCracken's *"Arthur Griffith's South African*

is, these Irish, who were more economically privileged and involved in the British administration, journalism, the railways, commerce, and the police force, were in a position to mingle more quickly with the locals due to their colonial presence in commercial or official functions; "[i]t is ironic that it was the British Army ... that did most to bring these exotic ... individuals to southern Africa" (van Onselen 2). Given the enormous number of Irish people who sailed to northern America between 1841 and 1925 – approximately 4.82 million (Lyons 45), and the strong Irish-American communities operating there, it is not surprising that historians have paid much less attention to this rather small circle of Irish immigrants who ventured into the "dark continent."[5] Moreover, their ambiguous role in the British army also leads to the under-representation of Irish experiences in South African studies. Although many South Africans, still carry distinctly Irish surnames, the historical and ethnic links of Ireland to the Southern Hemisphere are still in need of more detailed research.

What should be noted is that the experiences of the Irish diaspora in South Africa, although less studied by researchers, were significantly diverse by reason of a mixture of political and ethnic conflicts – which either extended from home or erupted locally. For instance, the intricacy of the Irish question profoundly troubled Irishmen overseas, who were divided in their attitudes: the fierce antagonism between Boers/Afrikaners and the British colonial government; the controversy of racial segregation between whites and blacks; the alliance between Boers and Irish nationalists against British rule and the mistrust between Calvinist Afrikaners and Catholic Irish Pro-Boers. These all lead to difficulties when examining the legacy of the Irish in Africa and defining their positions in South Africa as a former British colony. Although they had once contributed to "the fifth-largest immigrant population ... behind England, Scotland, the Russian empire and Germany" in the early twentieth century (McCracken, "Irish Identity," 9), academic attention paid to this minority all but disappeared when devastating events, such as the 1916 Easter Rising, the Irish Civil War, and the Boer War, drew the comprehensive attention of historians in both countries. The fact that the Irish were heavily involved in the most vociferous and "violent of the European pro-Boer movements"

Sabbatical," Donal P. McCracken's "The Irish Literary Movement, Irish Doggerel and the Boer War," and Deirdre McMahon's "Ireland, the Empire, and the Commonwealth."

[5]   In Victorian Ireland, the image of the "dark continent" appealed to many of the educated, skilled, and semi-skilled youth, unrestricted by marriage, who regarded the passage to South Africa as some kind of adventure (McCracken, "Irish Settlement," 146). This fascination was fulfilled by their being willingly enlisted in the British army and police forces. Their motivation for leaving home was thus very different from that of the famine refugees journeying to America. The colonial aspiration of cultivating an uncivilized land in "dark Africa" was acquired from the textbooks used at the above-mentioned State-run national schools in Ireland.

went unnoticed (McCracken, *Forgotten Protest*, 97), as did the manner in which the Boer War galvanized Irish nationalists at a time when the spirit of the Irish Parliamentary Party had sagged since the fall of Charles Stewart Parnell in 1889.

The two plays to be discussed in this chapter were produced at a time when the Northern Ireland Troubles had come to a somewhat peaceful end, after almost three decades of sectarian violence, resentment, and sacrifices. However, at the same time, racist attacks were emerging as a serious social issue that greatly concerned a government eager to present Ireland to the world as an emerging economic entity ready for the global market. This chapter will not only propose an examination of apartheid as a trampling of human civilization but also elaborate on how the South African experience can inspire the audiences of both Ireland and South Africa with a alternative perspective, or a possible paradigm for the resolution of racial segregation and tensions in the era of globalization.

Dolores Walshe's *In the Talking Dark*: Gendered Apartheid and Casting the Stones of Silence

The influence of the South African War (1899-1902) on Ireland became more pertinent when the British government started to look to the South African Convention of 1909 for a similar solution in the aftermath of the 1916 Easter Rising. The Convention created the Union of South Africa[6] a dominion within the Commonwealth, which seemed to some moderate Irish nationalists and pro-Boers to be a feasible key to peace between Ireland and Britain, although the Anglo-Irish Treaty of 1921 turned out to be an ill-fated imitation of the Convention that almost turned the Emerald Isle upside down in the subsequent Civil War (1922-1923).[7] The long-lasting consequence of the Treaty, ostensibly, was a partitioned Ireland, which not only incurred "unimaginable levels of violence" but was criticized by Edward W. Said as a "disastrously poor" type of solution to political disputes from which Ireland, Palestine, Cyprus, Syria, and the

---

[6] After the Second Boer War, Britain annexed the Orange Free State and the South African Republic (ZAR), which were independent Afrikaner republics before the War, renaming them as the Orange River Colony and the Transvaal. Expecting to draw all British colonies in southern Africa closer, the South African Convention of 1909 established the Union of South Africa, which included two other colonies: the Cape of Good Hope and Natal. For details, see "Boer" in the Britannica Online Encyclopedia.

[7] Details about Irish revolutionaries' activities in Southern Africa and their close tie with Afrikaner nationalists can be seen in Charles van Onselen's most recent published work: *Masked Raiders: Irish Banditry in Southern Africa 1880-1899*.

former Yugoslavia were not exempt ("Afterword," 185).[8] However, the common factor between the South African Convention and the Anglo-Irish Treaty was the ethnocentrism that bolstered radical nationalism and mimicked "the very structures of racism, ethnocentrism, and violence that Britannia perpetuated in order to subdue indigenous populations across the empire" (Schwarze 243). In other words, the South African Convention had led to a parliament that legalized the fifty years of apartheid and racial discrimination, whereas the Anglo-Irish Treaty gave birth to the Irish Free State that followed the administrative model of the British Empire.

Walshe's *In the Talking Dark* revisits the downfall of apartheid in South Africa in the late 1980s, in an attempt to critically mirror the ongoing sectarian violence in Northern Ireland, which was created by the Anglo-Irish Treaty of 1921. The after-effect of partitioning a nation is not only the sectarianism that arises between communities of different political and denominational persuasions but also the distrust engendered among individuals of different genders, classes and ethnicities – especially, from the late twentieth century onwards, after Ireland became a destination for asylum seekers and refugees. Specifically, the racial segregation of South Africa, as featured in this play, could be seen as metaphorical if the playwright intends to have Irish audiences rethink Irish stereotypes and prejudices against "the Other." The "Others" are not necessarily members of existing political or religious parties but those who are collectively silenced on the social margins.

Although *In the Talking Dark* does not appear to be a typical Irish drama with Ireland as its setting – and there is *only* a brief mention of an antimacassar made of "finest Irish lace" (246) – its Irishness is encapsulated in an intercultural framework that subtly mirrors the sectarianism in Walshe's homeland.[9] Set in an "affluent white suburb of Pretoria" during the fall of apartheid in South Africa (229), the play portrays the identity crisis of a die-hard Afrikaans family, the Schuurmans, when Mia, the mistress of the house, finds out to her distaste that she is the illegitimate daughter of her deceased mother and a black man. As Mia's

---

[8]   Instead, Said proposed a kind of bi-nationalism "in cases where rival communities overlap and must share a smallish territory" ("Afterword," 185). This political ideal is due to be tested, while the Middle East crisis is still at its peak.

[9]   *In the Talking Dark* is Walshe's second play and was premiered at the Royal Exchange Theatre in Manchester in 1989. Her debut play, *A Country in Our Heads* (1991), was performed at Andrew's Lane Theatre in Dublin. She has published a novel, *Where the Trees Weep* (1992), and a collection of short stories, *Moon Mad* (1993) with the Wolfhound Press. Her story, "Home Help," won second prize in the RTÉ Radio 1 Short Story Competition in Memory of Francis MacManus in 2009. In 1987, *In the Talking Dark* won the PEN Playwright Literary Prize. This play also won the staging prize in the 1989 *Mobil International* Playwriting *Competition*.

complexion is rather light, Paul Richardson, a white Londoner who was in love with her mother at the time, adopted the newborn girl in England, and the pair returned to South Africa as a married couple without revealing the secret to anyone. The truth about her origin is devastating to Mia, and is discovered when her biological father, Thulatu Mdala, breaks in to the house and reveals the secret, and demands that his daughter leave the household. What profoundly troubles Mia is that her upbringing in this white community, under apartheid for the past thirty years, is deeply ingrained with anti-black prejudice, and this resentment against the black community is unreservedly passed on to her stepson, Jan, whose biological mother has divorced Mia's husband, Piet. It is a family who not only feels exceedingly proud of being "true Afrikaners" – as illustrated by their brainwashing of Jan that "God [is] on our side" (232, 231) – but who also assume that the enslavement of the black community is a God-protected right: "by emancipating our slaves you have placed them on an equal footing with Christians. This is contrary to the laws of God, the natural distinctions of race and religion" (252). The teachers who are hired to teach in the Afrikaans community are even "handpicked" (253), so as to ensure the "correct" education of "Afrikanerized children" (254).

Even before Mia's self-recognition as a white, well-privileged woman collapses, her position in the Schuurman family is never secure, in that her father-in-law, Claus, an extreme racist, is not at all pleased that his son's second wife is not a "pure Afrikaner" but a woman with British blood, this despite the fact that she has grown up in a white community in South Africa. In order to be more accepted by the Schuurmans, Mia aspires to be a "great white swan" and often speaks in more racist terms than anyone else in the family (238), and refuses to face up squarely to Thulatu even once during his visit. All she cares about are the consequences of the neighbors by chance seeing her receiving a black visitor and subsequently gossiping about it. What she does not realize is that the more she makes herself "Afrikanerized," the more her "otherness" is confirmed. The fact she does not recognize, even before Thulatu reveals the secret, is that her prejudice against the blacks turns out to be the most bitter judgment against herself, while she by mistake applies the same condescension to "the kraal" whom her community demeans as "animals ... living in the squalor" and "worse than dirty linen" (256, 249). By exhibiting the socially constructed but mistaken identities that Mia is forced to demonstrate in public, it can be argued that Walshe aims to criticize Northern Irish politics as having become deeply immersed in the political correctness of a collective identity, rather than personal individuality. The society therefore becomes so sectarian that few people can escape from different ideological beliefs and sentiments in their divided community.

What is also noteworthy is that Mia's mental collapse results from her recognition that "[her] whole life's been a lie. A filthy, black lie," whereas she cannot immediately free herself from the fetters of prejudice against the blacks (272). This belated awakening costs her her life, not for merely questioning the apartheid system but for being, according to the apartheid nomenclature a "non-white" woman, who is subject to prejudice and who lives *within* a white, highly patriarchal community. Unable to fully accept her blackness, though it is implicit, Mia looks in a dictionary for the definition of "race," which denotes affirmatively that a white race "does not include any person who, although in appearance obviously a white person, is generally accepted as a coloured person" (276). The playwright's intention in having Mia plagued by this insular definition of "race," presumably, is to disclose its highly racist nature. It can be judged that the definition of "race" in the dictionary is made with prejudice in the first place and forbids people from seeing their own "colour" and only seeing that of "the Other." That the playwright has Mia "rub white cold cream on the lens of her [sunglasses] ... to re-examine her skin' is thus a symbolic challenge to the racialized definition of "race" (276). Feeling unable to identify who she really is by referring to the dictionary, Mia's world is completely shattered, and she cannot help taking constant showers to make herself "whiter," or dressing in black and staining her cheeks and sunglasses black. Her eccentric behavior is regarded as a symptom of mental disorder by a white, male doctor who suggests that she be sent to a sanitarium, because of the family disgrace she has brought on the Schuurmans.

Mia's difficulty in figuring out her race reflects the bigotry and violence of the apartheid system, under which a racially mixed person is an outcast from any community. Ironically, for Mia a sanitarium is a more suitable place than her home. It can be assumed that she, along with other mixed-race individuals, cannot be accepted in either white or black communities but must be demeaned as a "kaffir," "munt," "hotnot," "koelie," or "mongrel"; these being terms used derogatively to describe "non-white" people in this play.

Arguably, Mia's identity crisis in South Africa under apartheid can be likened to that experienced by those living in Northern Ireland (which is subject to the sovereignty of the United Kingdom), but local Irish republicans, for instance, members of the Provisional Irish Republican Army (IRA), were determined to create a United Ireland by forcing Northern Ireland out of the United Kingdom by the use of arms. Many cases have shown that some Northern Irish people, regardless of their religious persuasions, claim passports from both states, while some ardent unionists and nationalists behave in ways that are more British than the British, or more Irish than the Irish, depending on their political persuasion. The ambiguity of identities in Northern Ireland may have seemed to the playwright to be consonant, though not exactly, to that in South Africa under apartheid, where one's skin color defined who one was (not). In particular, that the degree of "purity" in one's origin defines whether one is (not) White/Black/Irish/British becomes "a matter of aggressively displayed credential" (Foster 596), a scale or spectrum to which one has to conform unmistakably. In Northern Ireland, the bigotry of identifying someone as either British or Irish, Unionist or Republican, Protestant or Catholic, has incurred sectarian conflicts, or, on a less serious level, the mild embarrassment of an Irish Jew when asked, "are you a Protestant Jew or a Roman Catholic Jew?" (qtd in Hezser 159).

In *In the Talking Dark*, the fact that Mia behaves eccentrically, but not insanely, due to her difficulties with her birth origin, serves as a good excuse for her father-in-law to cast her out from the family. (He had wished to do so due to Mia's distant Britishness.) What should also be pointed out is that the secret which her real father unmasks, though shattering, eventually liberates Mia from being "a well-dressed mannequin, a ventriloquist's dummy," and enables her to "see my new image... [which] goes with my new substance. The real me!" (290). The self-awakening is decisive, due to which she can relate the characteristics of her body with her black lineage: "I have black blood in me. Black as coal. Black as pitch. Black as hell.... Hard to believe ... apart from the eyes and the hair ... That woolly hair! ... That is the secret of my forked tongue" (292). Ostensibly, due to her infrequent contacts with the black community ever since her childhood, Mia has stereotypical ideas about the physical features of those considered "non-white." These stereotypes, which she later tries hard to, conform to suggest how the privileged, Caucasian minority in South Africa deceived themselves about the legitimacy of their ethnocentrism. For Mia, personally, what cannot be denied is that "my new substance" which she recognizes also results in a new language of her body in which her sexuality is awakened (291), unshackling the protagonist from the constraints of being a proper Afrikaans woman but not from being herself. She becomes the owner of her body, demanding sex at her will, no less explicitly than her husband who wants it "every night for ten years, not including lunchtimes" (289). She refuses to be an inferior object that always looks for "a sign that [my husband] loved me" in the marriage bed. (289). This new understanding of herself, more significantly, manifests itself through her intellectual well-being, in that she realizes how unpleasant she was as a "white" in this Afrikaans community: "Imagine what a difference that could have made to my ... wonderful childhood! I always loved music. D'you think I could have been a black and white minstrel in my youth?" (291). What she does not recognize is the tremendous pressure previously laid on her shoulders. Only when she realizes that she is by birth a racially-mixed person can she openly liberate herself from the unsympathetic social expectations placed on women. What Mia perceives after crossing the boundaries of skin color, however, is more than gender inequality in her Afrikaans community: she perceives the staggering fact that Afrikaners have enjoyed too much privilege without any return in terms of social justice, given that their numbers are far smaller than those of the black population of South Africa. The ethnocentrism of Afrikaners eventually results in their separation from the land, it deprives them of access to the wider world, and ensures that the cruelties they perform on one another and on the black, native Other are repeated.

It can thus be observed that the playwright's delineation of Mia's troubles over skin color can be read as her implicit criticism against any ideology that potentially splits a country into two, or several, parts based upon political, ethnic, or denominational aspirations, instead of recognizing and accommodating their differences. Mia's identity crisis is therefore not a personal but a social one that can challenge the "Population Registration Act" and the "Group Areas Act" of 1950 (Walshe, 297), as mentioned in the play, for denying her legitimate being and human rights.[10] The two Acts had not only proved "[Mia's] birth certificate falsified.... [and she] can't breathe without obtaining the right documents" (297), but crucified many of her mixed race for not being racially legitimate to have an equal status with Afrikaners. What is worse, in the play, is that the laws will force her stepson, a "pure" Afrikaner by birth, to be suspended from the Afrikaans school he attends and "[go] to one for coloureds" (297). More devastatingly, the whole family will, by law, be resettled in a black area, will lose the vote and "be a nothing" (297). The irony is that the institutionalized racism, as embodied by the two Acts, can be turned relentlessly against an Afrikaans community that is not as "pure" as it imagined itself to be.

In order to save the family, Mia, who has no social support due to her mixed blood, chooses to commit suicide. Her suicide becomes a solution to the troubles of this entire Afrikaans family, despite the fact that she dies with resentment against the racial segregation that sentences her to be a "carrier of an immoral disease fatal to humanity" (312). In particular, the decline of apartheid in the late 1980s does not rescue her in time but leaves her final protest to disturb the audiences of Ireland and South Africa, where sacrifices are still stirring in civilian's memories and many still experience living in states of partition.

---

10   The Population Registration Act and the Group Areas Act were both passed in 1950 in South Africa under apartheid. The former required every citizen to register in accordance with their racial characteristics, in order to determine his/her social benefits, political rights, educational rights, and so on. The latter assigned different racial groups to selected residential and business areas, so as to prevent so-called "non-whites" from mixing with whites living in well-developed areas.

In the afterword of the play, Walshe elaborates on how human lives are still conditioned inescapably by sectarian politics in many regions of the world, which may explain her intention in writing a play about South Africa and making innuendos about similar scenarios in her homeland. As she says,

> I believe the forced migrations of poor and hungry and disenfranchised people in a highly politicized world makes of every birth, every baby's first intake of breath, a political act in the eyes of our power-structured planet, instead of what it should be, a loving, wondrous act of creation in fruition. (326)

The partition of the Emerald Isle in the early twentieth century, although convenient, was not a well-thought-out solution to the Irish Question, and it has continually agonized people of different political shades in later decades. It is more than the land on a map that has been split, so too has the self-perception of the Irish, especially while they are mentally manipulated by political powers that sometimes cause them to fight against their own siblings. The play I will discuss next, *Soldiers of the Queen*, further dramatizes these identity crises and cultural conflicts over a span of four generations. An Irish soldier's nightmare of being haunted by the consequences of the Second Anglo-Boer War of 1900, and by contrast the pressing but not fully solved Northern Ireland Troubles, will be a major focus of discussion.

Damian Smyth's *Soldiers of the Queen*: Loyalty, Place, and Great Hatred at Home and Overseas

South Africa was a destination of choice for some Irish people during the mass emigration of the nineteenth century, with most of these emigrants, unlike the famine refugees journeying to America, being (semi-)skilled workers or sent abroad to occupy civil posts in the local British administration. Among these emigrants and civil service employees there was a relatively small number of Irish volunteers recruited by nationalists in support of the Boers, and established as Irish brigades in many regions of the colonies. What cannot be ignored is that, although the number of these pro-Boers was far smaller than that of those already serving in the British army, they had the potential to unsettle the colonial regime, influence public opinion and ignite riots back in their homeland.[11]

---

[11]   For example, in 1895 there were 400 Irishmen in an Irish Brigade led by John MacBride and John Black, whereas there were 28,000 Irishmen serving in the British army based in South Africa. Although the gap in numbers was wide, it reflects the political status quo in Ireland. The Irishmen among the British troops were not all anti-nationalists; some army deserters joined the Irish Brigade, which also included pro-Boer Irish miners on the Witwatersrand. *Soldiers of the Queen* is a play illustrating the subtle differences of political sentiments among the Irish in South Africa. Detailed records

The reason why the history of these Irish people in South Africa is ignored, apart from their small number and the fact that middle-class Irish immigrants intermixed with local communities more easily than deprived Irish Americans, is partially due to the dwindling influence of the British government after 1910, when South Africa gained its dominion status. The number of immigrants from Ireland was significantly reduced, "averaging 187 per annum between 1926 and 1939" (McCracken, "Irish Settlement," 149), although it had once reached 14,123 in a single year in the Cape Colony in 1891 (Akenson 135). What can be argued is that the divided politics of Ireland were brought to this foreign land by immigrants, despite South Africa being only a small corner of the Irish diaspora. That is to say, news about the Anglo-Boer Wars and other conflicts in South Africa, constantly attracted the serious attention of their families remaining in Ireland. The Pro-Boer Movement in South Africa and other countries inspired, to a significant extent, fervent Irish nationalists to think about ways of gaining their independence from the Empire through violence. In Sean O'Casey's memoir, *Pictures in the Hallway*, Boer leaders fascinated Irish nationalists who viewed the South African Convention of 1909 as a paradigm for leaving the "mother-ship":

> All fancy-goods shops and newsagents were filled with Boer symbols; streams of ribbons flashing the colours of England's enemies flowed through every street and sparkled in every second window. Every patriot carried in the lapel of his coat a button picture of Kruger, Steyn, Botha, Joubert, De Wet. (O'Casey 198)[12]

In contrast to *In the Talking Dark*, *Soldiers of the Queen* explores in some detail the Irish connection with the Boers in the late nineteenth century, this having been part of Smyth's familial experience, the effects of which still haunt not only his family but Ulster as a whole, the playwright's troubled home province.[13] The play unearths the difficulties

---

about Irish brigades in South Africa can be seen in D.P. McCracken's *The Irish Pro-Boers, 1877-1902*, and R. Ruda's "*The Irish Transvaal Brigades*."

[12] In 1899 Irish pro-Boer nationalists formed the Irish Transvaal Committee, the activities of which included fundraising for an Irish ambulance corps to be sent to the Transvaal to aid the Boers. Michael Davitt, an Irish labor leader at Westminster, also wrote a book entitled *The Boer Fight for Freedom* (1902). Details about the pro-Boer movement in Ireland can be seen in Donal P. McCracken's *Forgotten Protest: Ireland and the Anglo-Boer War* (2003), and Charles van Onselen's *Masked Raiders: Irish Banditry in Southern Africa, 1880-1899* (2010).

[13] According to Smyth, this play is based, fairly closely, on his own family history. The two major characters in this play, Henry Smyth and George Linton, were family members from nearly one hundred years ago. They served in India and South Africa respectively. Their nationalistic family backgrounds and the thorny political ideologies that defined "loyalty" and "disloyalty," identity and allegiance, Britishness and Irishness, during the Northern Irish Troubles, caused them to be nearly invisible for generations in Smyth's

and ambiguities of the experiences of the Irish soldiers in the British army who faced a depressing identity crisis, and the appalling history of the Pro-Boer Irish clashing with their countrymen in the British army and slaughtering one another. In particular, the main difficulty of being an Irish person in South Africa at that time was that they were both the colonized, within the administration of the British Empire, and the colonizer – albeit with powers given under supervision. It was almost impossible for the Irish to stand impartially between the two roles, whether denouncing both, creating an individual identity for themselves, or cutting the strong economic and political ties with England. It was also difficult for the Pro-Boer Irish to perceive the racist and patriarchal nature of Afrikaner nationalism, which later bolstered apartheid. Given the playwright's familial links with South Africa, and his observations on the lingering effects of the Northern Ireland Troubles, this play can thus be seen as a retrospective of the bleak reality of sectarian conflicts in both territories. Furthermore, it reflects on the cyclical nature of racial and political tragedies throughout human history.

What is peculiar about this play – set in 1900 and the 1970s to cover a span of four generations – is that it gives voice to ghosts who condemn, lament, and interrogate the ideologies to which they surrendered but which are still haunting them in the afterlife. The five protagonists all have "troubles" to fight for, concerning their given political identity or identities. George Linton, whose is presented in 1900 during the Second Anglo-Boer War, is a 25-year-old Irishman serving in the British army and tormented as an English hostage by a Boer sniper. His trouble is his difficulty in justifying to the Boer that he is neither a "Tommy" nor a "Paddy" (14), despite having enlisted in the British army.[14] Also, he is not able to demonstrate any support for the Boers unlike those Irish volunteers who have been "fighting for Boers, fighting for freedom" (14). In the eyes of the Boer sniper, because George Linton denies his "Britishness," he deserves as little respect as "the Kaffir" (14), both of whom are "the enemy

---

family. In order to trace the steps of these two family members more accurately, the playwright searched through the voluminous papers of the War Office and India Office in London for their records. I would like to express my heartfelt gratitude to Damian Smyth for providing first-hand information on his family's history.

[14] "Tommy" is slang for "British soldier," from Thomas Atkins, used as a sample name for filling in official army forms from 1815. In British English, "Paddy" is derogatory slang for an Irishman. In Ireland, it is short for Patrick and Pádraig (in Gaelic spelling). It was "black" slang by 1946 for any "white person." "Paddy wagon" was American slang around the 1930s, as many police officers were Irish. The different connotations of the same word may suggest the huge size of the Irish diaspora, many of whom eventually served in police and military forces in the New World and British colonies. Their work was mostly unskilled, unlike the marketable skills of other economic migrants to South Africa.

of my heart" (15). George Linton's conversation with the Boer sniper, with the constant howls of a tortured Zulu prisoner in the background, is actually an hallucination – the symptom of shell shock that lingers to his old age in the 1970s at home in Downpatrick, Northern Ireland. What causes his nightmare, however, is not just the identity issue which bothered him on the battlefield seven decades ago, but the guilt of being involved in wars by which his family have all been killed on different locations, leaving him as "the last of the Lintons," surrounded by ghosts "all over the place" and demanding justice (18).

The experience of Irish people, as demonstrated by George Linton in this play, may be largely off-record in the already limited documentation on the Irish diaspora in South Africa. He is an epitome of those Irish people who suffered and sacrificed in local anti-colonial struggles, regardless of their skin color. As George admits, the reason why many Irish people joined the British army is not because they identify politically with Great Britain but that they are simply "after money…. [as] it's called eating. It's called making a living. Ye can keep yer oul' oaths and yer blood lines and yer oul' fantastical rights to [Ireland]" (36). In other words, enlisting in the British forces provides a quick relief from hunger, although it is not very different from drinking poison to quench a thirst. It is a difficult but unavoidable choice for a destitute family like the Lintons, who are on the very lowest rung of the social hierarchy, as a result, the family gradually disintegrates with various members dying one after another on the front line.

Specifically, George Linton's father, Harry, was first sent to India as a British artilleryman but later resettled in South Africa to fight against the Boers and Irish Volunteers; he dies and remains unburied. A young man like Harry has no way of anticipating his death: "when I joined the [Hibernian] Rifles across the road [from my parents' house] that's where I'd be expected to stay" (38).[15] To fulfill his dream of being a real soldier and not to "[see] across the road is your own front door" (38), he re-enlisted in the British army, wishing he could thus "live [in India] for ever … with great girls altogether, up in the mountains, strong, wiry, great skin, polite even when you were huntin' their menfolk" (40). In the 1970s, George Linton's cousin, George Henry Smyth, follows in his uncle's and grandfather's footsteps in joining the Ulster Defence Regiment, a British

---

[15] The Hibernian Rifles was a small-scale Irish nationalist militia established in the early twentieth century. Its membership was exclusively Roman Catholic. It cooperated with the Irish Volunteers during the 1916 Easter Rising, and Patrick Pearse recognized its contribution in *Irish War News*. This publication was only issued once on 25 April 1916, featuring the Easter Rising of that year. For the full typescript of Pearse's article, see <http://www.his2rie.dk/fileadmin/user_upload/Kilder_Irland_Engelske/ EngelskKilde_9_01.doc>, for the image of this particular issue, see <http://trove.nla. gov.au/ndp/del/article/33605529>, both accessed on 11 Sept. 2011.

regiment, and also dies tragically by being blown to pieces by a bomb: "there was nothing of me in the coffin. They had to weigh it down with sandbags" (51). Ironically, his ghost has no clue about whose bomb it was that killed him. It could have been that of the IRA, or his own army; however, his life has so little value in these civil conflicts that a decent burial does not appear to be necessary.

What makes *Soldiers of the Queen* an unsettling drama is its portrayal of the naked truth which Irish and British historians, if clinging to a political preference, have yet not documented impartially, but which the playwright can potentially reveal to its full extent, especially through the illustrations of hidden voices that are often unattended by the mainstream media. The truth is that these soldiers all died feeling resentment and terror, inasmuch as the survival tip on the battlefield is that either "you plug him or he plugs you," regardless of whether "he's yer own blood and bone" (50). Although many of their comrades died "with half their faces blown away, the place looking like a butcher's shop" (49), these soldiers cannot escape from the fate of being manipulated in the interests of the British Empire, and collectively being called "[m]y brave Irish" in a speech given by Queen Victoria, while "we were still lying, untended, out on the hillside" in South Africa (52). The plight of those remaining helpless and hopeless on the social margins continues to be hidden as they only represent an "end product" of war (51). Among the facts that British right-wing politicians are not inclined to portray are national disgraces, such as the scene depicting the gang rape of Zulu women by British troopers in the play:

> An' troopers come and as they came on, there she was. They came and they pushed her rough and they took her. She lay there and one would go into her and go over and another one would come into her and go over and another, and every time, and somebody went, she laid with her arms open they would fish out a silver coin, Paddy, silver coin with the Queen's head and put it in her hand. (44)

Such sexual atrocities could be committed by anyone of the British troops, whether British or Irish. The brutality is made worse by the hypocrisy of the British colonial operation in South Africa, but it is not confined to them, as the racist Afrikaners continually devalue the black people. In *Soldiers of the Queen*, a Zulu man is continuously heard yelling, howling, or moaning in the background, along with the sounds of bombing. His unseen, offstage presence suggests the very marginal position of his people in the politics and economy of South Africa. That is, Zulus, as a local major ethnic group, had been intentionally wiped out or slaughtered by the European settlers – without any of their interests being catered to. As the play shows, they are physically abused offstage by the Boers as a threat to "Tommies," and can be killed at any time, if

British hostages act defensively against the Boers: "Black watch me too much I take the skin off their backs till they squeal worse …. They stop watchin" (24). The Zulus in this play, unlike those in *In the Talking Dark* (set in the late 1980s) who have more social support and attention from the international media, are treated by the Boers like disposable objects: "A nigger man's not a human man and nigger women's like cattle" (44). Being "cursed of the earth" (43), they can be lynched as often as the Boers wish and shot and killed on several separate occasions.

Nevertheless, none of the parties involved in the ethnic and colonial conflicts is the winner. The Boer in the play, for instance, suffers no less than George Linton because both his family members are killed during the Anglo-Boer wars, and he declares that he will kill all the British in revenge:

> You kills my sons. Now I gonna kill you, all of you, and when you killed I gonna find your mama and brother and everybody you love and kill them too, One by one…. You whole damned army. (26, *sic*)

This despite the fact that Linton makes it clear that "I didn't know your sons" (26).[16] The abuse and slaughter become cyclical due to the endless resentment, with the Union of South Africa established on the basis of racial segregation, and Northern Ireland and other political unities adopting a similarly problematic model.

Soldiers of the Queen presents the "troubles" of the five characters who talk to one another and the audience in the form of ghosts, rather than that of human beings. This creates a fresh perspective for seeing the troubles of the nation in conflict with those of individuals, in that the state always gains the upper hand in most aspects. This fresh perspective allows the audience to review elements that may not receive sufficient exposure in South Africa and Northern Ireland, which of both have long been overwhelmed by political turbulences.

The large number of soldiers who die in agony without official burials appear to be either ignored by historians or to exist only in the casualty figures in newspapers at the time or history textbooks. Their spirits linger on the battlefield without salvation, and await more tides of newcomers dying in savage ways, despite that "[t]here's so many [ghosts]. So many there's no room to move. No room to breathe" (54). Their blind sacrifices have meant that,

---

[16]   As it has been kindly pointed out by a reviewer that the dialogue here is an inaccurate mimicking of "Afrikaans English," it can be suggested that the play may initially have been aimed at an Irish audience with a focus on contemporary racial issues in Ireland, and most of the dialogues were therefore written in a type of colloquial English that was familiar to them. The play was premiered at Down Arts Centre, Downpatrick, Northern Ireland, on 2nd October 2002.

the whole world's haunted, … there's nat a spot that hasn't its own oul' horror hangin' over it, every bend in the road, every oul' ditch, the places ye'd never think like right in front yer own face, right in front of yer own face, under yer own shoes, in yer own hans. (56, *sic*)

What is ironic is that these spirits crowded together in an afterlife do not seem to care for their nationalities, ethnicities and skin colors, whereas their living family members and the communities to which they claim loyalty are still bitterly shackled by political zeal and racial discrimination.

In *Soldiers of the Queen*, although women's issues do not appear to be as dramatized as in *In the Talking Dark*, the suffering of black, Zulu women is alarming. The gang rape of a Zulu woman, as mentioned earlier, implies a similar predicament for all black women in a racist and patriarchal state under apartheid. Zulu women are always under the threat of being bullied, insulted, and raped by both Afrikaner and British soldiers, while their men are being tortured to death. The black women simply have no public and private voice in any existing forum, as is faithfully presented in Walshe's and Smyth's plays. However, white women are also constantly in all kinds of "troubles," as typified by the character mentioning those which her son delivered: "You brought trouble to your own door, for no reason, neither to make nor break bread" (Smyth 39). Living in fear of getting ominous news from the front line, all that these white women left behind can do is wait until the telegram arrives to tell them about the deaths of fathers, husbands, and sons, and they must bear the sorrow and other more difficult emotions.

The "troubles" or the deaths of family members, coming one after another, turn the women into bitter widows. The white women, in fact, share similar sentiments with the old Boer in *Soldiers of the Queen* as a result of losing their loved ones on the battlefield, however the heartbreaking experiences do not draw them closer nor make them more forgiving, but angry with each other. In the case of Bella, George Linton's mother, who is unable to accept the death of her son, she is determined to have revenge on all the Boers at the cost of destroying herself:

dar [Boers] get in the road an' the lot of ye can slabber all ye like, fer ye'll go through me first before ye get till any of mine an' ye'll nat get through me, I'll carry the head of the lot of ye, ye'll nat get through me. (Smyth 61)

The ethnic violence, which has been repeated throughout history, ironically, is regenerated by women in despair. What may strike the audience is that the old Boer, who has lost his sons and is grief-stricken, utters similar lines through which he declares his desire to erase all the British without sympathy:

I gonna take all of you and as many I can down into the mud. Down into death. One hundred, one thousand, five thousand, no matter, down into death for what you let be done to my boys. (Smyth 26)

In addition, what can be observed is that most of the characters in *Soldiers of the Queen* claim to be victims of violence and ethnic discrimination, while they are also abusers who cause harm to others and involve themselves in a vicious circle of hatred and conflict. That is, antagonism occurs between whites and blacks, or within the white Irish community where armed men of different political shades torture one another, regardless of whether they are at home, in South Africa, or in other British colonies. This vicious circle, however, causes further traumas within the black community, especially when formerly colonized people impose a similar racial discrimination on each other to the discrimination practiced by the previous administration. A number of South African writers have delineated how racial biases are still present in the public and private perceptions of blacks South Africans themselves, despite the onset of democracy. South African plays, for example Athol Fugard's *The Blood Knot* and Guy Butler's *Demea*, among others, represent a form of internal racism. Similarly, this kind of racism also brings pain not only to Smyth's Irish characters in South Africa but also to those still suffering from many kinds of visible and invisible division in contemporary Ireland.

What is also noteworthy is that the ending of *Soldiers of the Queen* is profoundly unsettling, in that the female protagonist promises to carry out more slaughter. In other words, the playwright does not create another female figure who fits into the stereotype of a woman grieving for nationalistic causes, as his predecessors have done.[17] Smyth does not recreate a heroic narrative for patriotic purposes, nor does he fabricate a happy ending in which all the parties are reconciled. Instead, he demonstrates the failures of heroic narratives by depicting the violence as cyclical. As a whole, this play re-examines the republican violence that has been passed down from one generation to another, including violence at the expense of civilians' lives. What is also implicitly reproduced from the Boers' experience is their mentality of abusing the Other or ignoring the Other's existence, and their ideology of creating an essentially white Eden on Earth. Metaphorically, what haunts the Irish is not merely the resentment of the ghosts of the Irish diaspora during the Boer War, but the ethno-centrism which produces violence and prejudice at both

---

[17]   Perhaps to the disappointment of Irish audiences, *Soldiers of the Queen* does not end heroically or nationalistically with a woman who, like the Poor Old Woman in W.B. Yeats's *Cathleen ni Houlihan*, requests a blood sacrifice to reclaim "four beautiful green fields" (250), asserting that "many a child will be born and there will be no father at the Christening" (255).

institutional and private levels, at a time when modern Ireland is being transformed into a multi-ethnic, cosmopolitan state.[18]

Conclusion: A South African Experience and (In)visible Apartheid in Northern Ireland

These two plays do not appear alike in terms of themes and backgrounds, and there is a twelve-year gap between the writing of the two plays. *In the Talking Dark*, written in 1989, focuses mainly on the awakening of a woman of mixed blood; *Soldiers of the Queen*, in 2001, highlights the haunting experience of Irish soldiers during the Anglo-Boer War, yet both plays end tragically and challenge the patriarchal nature of Irish nationhood. The common factor linking the two plays, is the ethno-political partition – based upon socially constructed and biological differences – that keeps South Africans from understanding and accommodating each other. Written by two contemporary Irish playwrights, these plays serve to provide the local Irish with a mirror to a similar scenario in South Africa, which is still experiencing the aftermath of apartheid. That is, what obstructs the achievement of peace in Ireland (and other countries) is not really the boundary that divides the nation, but the invisible apartheid that separates people and prevents them from accepting the truth regarding different political and religious commitments, as well as racial and sexual diversities. The apartheid, visible and invisible, prompts the sacrifice of the Irish to gain political insularity at the expense of the marginalized Other.

Writing about the peace process in Palestine, South Africa, and Northern Ireland, Tom Paulin, a cultural critic and founder of the Field Day Theatre Group, once remarked that only by putting the "'two traditions' as they're called (Protestant and Catholic) in some sort of communication, and to imagine a culture beyond partition" (11). To elaborate on his proposal, he quoted Robert McCartney's ideal of liberty from a unionist point of view: "a proper state constitution had to recognize and protect the rights of minorities" (11). Edward W. Said, in support of Palestinian self-determination, strongly denounced nativism that excludes cultural, racial, and political dissenters; he often referred to the Irish experience as a warning against social calamity as follows. In his view, peace can only

---

[18] Records and analyses of racial conflicts in contemporary Ireland can be seen in Ronit Lentin and Robbie McVeigh's *Racism and Anti-Racism in Ireland*, and Robbie McVeigh's "Racism and Sectarianism in Northern Ireland" in *Contemporary Ireland: A Sociological Map*. One of the most recent major attacks on ethnic minorities in Northern Ireland occurred when Romanian immigrants were hounded out of town by Belfast fascists in late July 2009. This has caused anxiety in the Polish and Lithuanian community which sensed the ire being directed against them.

be made when all parties admit to the existence of each other at present and in history:

> [T]o accept nativism is to accept the consequences of imperialism too willingly; to accept the very radical religious and political divisions imposed on Ireland, India, Lebanon and Palestine by imperialism itself. To leave the historical world for the metaphysics of essences like negritude, Irishness, Islam and Catholicism is, in a word, to abandon history. ("Yeats and Decolonization," 82)

What Said suggests is an open attitude regarding the facts about what happened and who has occupied the land in question throughout past history, instead of an insular and aggressive temperament with each side negating the Other. More specifically, nativist ideals, such as negritude, Irishness, and others of a similar kind, will lead to violence – at militant or conceptual levels – if they are over-emphasized. They can reproduce the intellectual violence inherited from the colonizer, incurring disquietude within local and/or neighboring communities. By affiliating the ignored experiences of the Irish diaspora in South Africa with those of the contemporary audience, these two Irish playwrights can be seen as unearthing the naked truth that derives from human ignorance. That is, apartheid in South Africa, sectarian violence in Northern Ireland, the Palestinian crisis arising from the expansion of Israeli settlement areas, and potential terrorist acts in other regions of the world, can all be seen as stemming from the ethno-centric mindset that usually "rehearse[s] positions from which there is no exit," making people constantly feel that they are "in grievous danger of being betrayed or have already been betrayed by governments" (Deane 15).

Having said this, we can boldly assert that the two Irish playwrights have proposed a dual or multiple recognition of ethnicities in a dramatic manner, especially for people who are in conflict over the control of a shared land. This situation corresponds to what Said advocates in terms of a "bi-national state," which "address[es] the difference between two collectives" and validates "a mechanism or structure that would allow [every party] to express their national identity" (*Power, Politics, and Culture,* 452). Walshe's focus on the neglected predicaments of racially-mixed women, alongside Smyth's delineation of resentful Irish ghosts in South Africa, exhibits an invisible apartheid based on skin color but which also involves deep-rooted gender and racial prejudice. Only when these cultural defects are realized by the general public can any peace process come to a successful conclusion.

This chapter does not intend to point towards an ultimate solution to the peace process in Northern Ireland, nor provide an elixir for countries already on the edge of war, as the historical, ethnic, and political conditions differ from country to country. The idea of transplanting the model of the Union of South Africa to Ireland has been proved to be a fiasco, and it can by no means ease the ongoing crises in Syria, Libya, Yemen, Burma, the *Korean Peninsula*, Tibet, or *the* unrest between Muslim Uighurs and Han Chinese *in* Xinjiang. These two Irish plays on South Africa, however, serve as a late-received mirror through which contemporary Irish artists have tried to inculcate a wider and deeper reflection on the Troubles. The two plays also testify that contemporary Irish playwrights, as opposed to their predecessors who tended to examine Irish issues by looking inwards rather than outwards, have started to situate relevant political occurrences in a global context, and have looked into the similar "troubles" or "crises" of other countries, so as to unearth the hidden facts, ignored by historians, ruling authorities and the mainstream media, in a more strategic way. South Africa, which has not yet become fully unshackled from the trauma of apartheid, and when seen alongside Northern Ireland with its painful memory of the Troubles, can thus act as a reference to those nations or areas where totalitarianism has been the cradle of unrest, social divides and injustice, but which await their timely mental and political liberation.

VI. Transnational Ireland on Stage: America to Middle East in Three Texts

Introduction: Between the Local and the Global on the Irish Stage

Historically, the comprehensive Anglicization of Ireland from the early nineteenth century, and the geopolitical location of Ireland in Europe, have laid the foundations for more Irish participation on the world stage. The rapid globalization process, however, has not fully removed the frustration buried deep in the Irish psyche about the country still being in partition, but it has encouraged many contemporary playwrights to express concerns regarding other areas that are just as troubled as the state of their country, despite the fact that the Northern Ireland issue is not yet fully resolved.

It is noteworthy that globalization, as the continuation of nineteenth- and twentieth-century imperialism in a new form, not only carries forward the exercise of colonial incursion but facilitates the oppressively homogenizing effects on the less advantaged Other. This is partly due to the rise of critical theory to "productively complicate the nationalist paradigm" by embarking on *trans*nationalism since the 1970s (Jay 1). One consequence of this was to prompt reevaluations of existing cultural productions, thus initiating cross-cultural and interethnic dialogues that had usually been absent in colonial and Eurocentric establishments, and prompting the public to envisage the Other across both real and imagined borders. Even more significantly, the meaning of a text starts to shift if it is studied in an international context, and this applies particularly to a text in which the characters venture into unexplored territories and impel "meaning [to] transform as it travels" (James 193). The transformation of meanings is further accelerated by intercultural encounters that are motivated by globalization that interconnects individuals and societies around the world. Our moral circle thus expands and is redrawn through such physical or imagined encounters with people of different ethnicities at distant locations. In the case of Ireland, how globalization benefits or frustrates the Emerald Isle has been a subject for inquiry in recent decades, alongside that of the rollercoaster ride of the Celtic Tiger.

It might be of interest to see how contemporary Irish playwrights, by creating *transnational* dramas that highlight border-crossing experiences, reassess more rarely regarded Irish experiences, past and present, in international scenarios. Their attempts at going beyond sectarian politics, partly to cultivate a transnational audience, may aim at challenging the Irish-centered convention that has existed since the movement toward Irish Independence and the Irish Revival. It is noteworthy that they contextualize Irish history not necessarily from insular viewpoints but in connection with other regional or ethnic experiences, thus initiating multicultural counteractions with predominant world powers.

The three texts to be explored here are Frank McGuinness's *Someone Who'll Watch Over Me* (1992), Sebastian Barry's *White Woman Street* (1992), and Colin Teevan's *How Many Miles to Basra?* (2006), which are set respectively in Beirut, the state of Ohio and Iraq. The questioning of narrow national models in these plays may open possibilities for creating meaning in a transnational context and reveal how prejudices and boundaries can be transmitted to distant locations and then become institutionalized.

Frank McGuinness's *Someone Who'll Watch Over Me* (1992): A Room without a View in Beirut

Born in 1953 in Buncrana, located in northern County Donegal, Republic of Ireland, and close to the border that divides the island, Frank McGuinness has admitted that in his youth the frequent border-crossing experiences from home to Derry had a significant impact on his writing, prompting him to be "a writer involved with politics" in an attempt "to cause a different type of bother" (Pine 29).[1]

Carrying these experiences into his adulthood, McGuinness developed a critical observational perspective concerning Irish relations with the outside world and those binary oppositions and ideologies that lead to political and religious sectarianism in Northern Ireland. Although some critics think that postcolonial studies, with their explicitly political nature of inquiry, have come under threat because of globalization, they are essentially two sides of the same coin and deserve "a dialectical relationship with each other, [as the] histories of the two are inseparable" (Jay 34). *Someone Who'll Watch Over Me*, set in a cell in Beirut where three hostages of different nationalities are chained to separate walls, offers a global and postcolonial space in which to examine the man-made

---

[1] For more detail, see Eamonn Jordan's "Frank McGuinness," *The Methuen Drama Guide to Contemporary Irish Playwrights*.

divides that trouble these characters from Ireland, England and America. As they have all been abducted randomly on the street simply for their skin color, the significance of their given identities, becoming void, challenges existing political philosophies.

Regarded as "his most accessible play" for American audiences, the play received international acclaim due to its "cultural references of brotherhood," as McGuinness mentioned in an interview (Hurtley 67).[2] Although this is not the first Irish play that has appealed to international audiences, it should be noted that its success is due to the presentation of transnational experiences that question sectarianism and suggest a humanitarian perspective on issues that are relevant in countries where the play is staged, despite the playwright once expressing the view that a political play cannot effectively change anything: "I don't think you can change people's attitudes and I don't think you should try" (Purcell 17). Nevertheless, what McGuinness was attempting was an experiment through which an international scenario can be presented that enables Ireland to be seen in a broader context. Although set in Lebanon, the play was written by an Irish playwright who has to cross the border to the Republic for study and work and has acquired mixed views as a result of being both an outsider and insider of Northern Ireland. This drama displays a similar stance in that it allows the audience to cross borders in order to understand the complicated relationships between the Middle East and Western superpowers. This play also illustrates how McGuinness, mainly based in Dublin, has expanded his attentions "well beyond the concerns of the local and the national," so as to produce an alternative view in which the public can see Ireland within an international framework and the wider world from an Irish perspective (Jordan 235).

The play may not demonstrate a ready-made solution to the Irish/ British political dilemma over Northern Ireland but it may, as Homi K. Bhabha claims, "emerge as the representation of a difference that is itself a process of disavowal" of current ideologies (*Location* 86). As Eurocentrism that has dominated western perceptions of the Orient that is disavowed, it is fair to say that it is not until these western hostages in the play are made powerless by their abductors that audiences can see how they are victimized by the Eurocentric myth *per se*. Take Edward, an Irishman and a hardline republican soldier who volunteers to join the UN's peace-keeping troops in Lebanon, for example. The reason that Edward would volunteer for peace-keeping duties in the Middle East is in

---

[2]   The play has won the London Standard Award, the Rooney Prise for Irish Literature, the London Fringe Award, the Harvey's Best Play Award, and the New York Drama Critics Circle Award. In addition, from its premiere to 1998 this play had been translated into twelve languages.

part to fulfill his desire for adventure: "[I was at] home wondering what it would be like to be here" (*Someone* 92)· His venture to the Middle East is not *a scouting* trip but is implicitly involved with European superiority over the troubled East, as far as the UN is concerned. The peace-keeping mission, protected by armed force, may fail to be accomplished but technically it is a defense of the failings of Eurocentrism. Interestingly, before Edward departs for the Middle East, he has sensed that at home in Europe he is trapped "in a bad hole" (*Someone* 92). As his home in Ireland has been a source of disappointment, his voluntary admission to the UN's peace-keeping troops is thus an intentional breakaway from home and an adventure that should bring him new excitements. Ironically, his adventure with the UN – an organization that operates beyond physical borders – is not as romantic as he had hoped but proves to be a fiasco, in that the European values he follows, perhaps unselectively, prompt him to be abducted and imprisoned in a windowless cell in which he has no idea of time, date, or year. Edward and his cellmates are faced not only with an endless predicament but the fact that they are the sacrificial victims of the Eurocentric illusion about ruling the East as a dominator and peace-keeper.[3] Ironically, the cell is as borderless as the UN, but the operation of the UN results in a prolonged war in which no one has "any sense of causality, development, fullness or even duration" (Bristol 197), as these hostages experience in their helpless state.

McGuinness's choices of characters give this play a confrontational air, since these hostages are, at least in the view of their abductors, political and cultural intrusions to the Islamic world. Adam, an American doctor, whose research topic is "the effects of war on innocent young minds," enacts American values in places where he is not welcome (*Someone* 94). The research that Adam conducts, which includes consideration of shell-shocked Lebanese soldiers, is not therefore simply a humanitarian task. Metaphorically, anywhere that American troops are stationed functions as an extended frontier within which American nationalism is celebrated and Adam's research is duly supported. Although Adam's presence in Lebanon may suggest the advent of modernization and globalism – albeit for the benefit of the West – the random abduction of the hostages signifies the unpredictability of the Middle East crisis. More specifically, for Lebanese civilians, taking three white men hostage is more than an expression of

---

[3]   McGuinness dedicated this 1992 play to Brian Keenan, who published *An Evil Cradling* (1991) to describe his four and a half years spent as a hostage, along with other captives from twelve nations, in Beirut from 1986 to 1990. However, McGuinness, perhaps to respect the privacy of the other hostages, has on other occasions claimed that this play has "nothing to do with Brian's life; there are parallels with what he suffered – but it isn't his story" (qtd in Mikami 95). For details, see Hiroko Mikami's, *Frank McGuinness and His Theatre of Paradox.*

animosity toward the military forces of the UN. That is, the UN, in which the US plays a pivotal role, affirms the necessity of keeping foreign peace-making troops in Lebanon, while its extended military presence may serve to enlarge the imagined territories, or areas under the domination of western superpowers. It is ironic that the peace-making mission – having been justified by the UN – prompts antagonisms between local Lebanese people and the outside world, or the West, but does not guarantee the interests of individuals. The windowless cell in which the three hostages are jailed and guarded by Lebanese warders therefore epitomizes those people who are most powerless and deprived in the international political power struggle. The frustration, helplessness and anger of Lebanese civilians therefore lead to random abductions from a Beirut street market.

The "three hostages" isolation from the outside world indicates that the clashes are not simply between two nations but are confrontations between modernity and tradition, imperialism and nativism, Christianity and Islam, or more generally the West and the East. Specifically, with the hope of being released, Adam recites passages aloud from the Koran so as to impress the soldiers that he has been properly converted. The Bible, alongside the Koran in the cell, is of little use to strengthen the faith of the three hostages but confuses them about whether they may be magi or actually sinners already abandoned by the Christian world. However, they gain comfort and help in relieving their anxiety by engaging in chitchat about sexual encounters, arguments about word choices in Irish and British English, and plots they make up for horror films, as well as undertaking minor physical exercise in the limited space. In other words, what has been assumed to be universally or globally feasible may be locally problematic, antagonistic or meaningless in the multi-cultural scenarios experienced by these hostages.

It is worthy of mention that, in one production of this play, in 1992, Adam, the American hostage, was played by Hugh Quarshie, a black actor born in Ghana.[4] The preference of the director, Robin Lefevre, for a black performer profoundly challenges the western perspective of the world, as it reminds the audience of ethnic biases against non-white communities in history. The intention of casting a black actor carries an irony in that American or European values have historically resulted in the dislocation of a huge number of non-white people from their place of origin, while

---

4   Analyses of McGuinness's *Someone Who'll Watch Over Me* have, since its first production, been abundant and in depth. However, discussion about employing a black actor to perform this American role is limited, albeit that "there is no mention of his colour in the published text play" (Jordan 168). The choice of a Ghanaian actor greatly complicates the transnational and cross-ethnic nature of the play and relates to two other plays to be discussed later in this article. See Eamonn Jordan's, *The Feast of Famine*.

Adam, being black, is seen as a scapegoat for the intrusion of the West in Lebanon. Although, metaphorically, the presence of a black actor in this production dramatizes the interethnic and transcultural elements in international politics, and involves an implicit call to examine racism in a West/East encounter, it also implies the vulnerability of border-crossing exchange, especially for dislocated non-white people, in that globalism still guarantees Eurocentric and American interests on the front line. This explains why Michael, an English lecturer, is the only one who is not released at the end of the play but left in a desolate state in the cell. He is thus an involuntary blood sacrifice in the confrontation between the UN and the guerilla forces in Lebanon – most likely for the strategic benefit of the former.

McGuinness's *Someone Who'll Watch Over Me* dramatizes a border-crossing experience by relocating Irish, American and English protagonists to a Middle Eastern scenario, which is symptomatic of the growing interest by Irish playwrights in visualizing their nation within a global context and in giving a voice to those who had hitherto been neglected during the social transformation of Ireland. In order to discuss further the enduring antagonisms of the global and the local in relation to the Irish experience in an international context, Sebastian Barry's *White Woman Street*, set in a small town in Ohio in the United States, will be explored in the next section.

Sebastian Barry's *White Woman Street* (1992): A Historical Revisiting of "1916" in Ohio

One feature of a number of contemporary dramas that concern the foreign experiences of Irish people is that their characters often wish to be away from Ireland or have recently returned home.[5] Only a limited,

---

[5]   Migration is a theme frequently visited by Irish playwrights with characters wishing to leave or recently returning. The settings may be across the Atlantic, within the British Isles, in Europe or the Southern Hemisphere. To name only a few: Brian Friel's *Philadelphia, Here I Come!* (1964), *The Loves of Cass McGuire* (1966), *Dancing at Lughnasa* (1990) and *Molly Sweeney* (1994), Martin McDonagh's *The Beauty Queen of Leenane* (1996) and *The Cripple of Inishmaan* (1996), Hugh Leonard's *Da* (1978), Tom Murphy's *Conversations on a Homecoming* (1985), Anne Devlin's *After Easter* (1994), Christina Reid's *The Belle of the Belfast City* (1989) and *My Name, Shall I Tell You My Name?* (1989), Jimmy Murphy's *The Kings of the Kilburn High Road* (2000), Sebastian Barry's *The Only True History of Lizzie Finn* (1995), and Jim O'Hanlon's *The Buddhist of Castlenock* (2002). Dolores Walshe's *In the Talking Dark* (1989), and Damian Smyth's *Soldiers of the Queen* (2002), both of which are set in South Africa under apartheid; Dermot Bolger's *In High Germany* (1990) and John Banville's *Conversation in the Mountains* (2008), set in Germany in the 1980s and 1960s respectively. Noticeably, there are also plays about non-Irish migrants in Ireland, for example Donal O'Kelly's *Farawayan* (1998), *Asylum! Asylum!* (1994) and Gavin Kostick's *The Ash Fire* (2002). However, I propose to focus on these three plays set

but not necessarily insignificant, number of Irish plays are primarily set overseas with an international cast, which diversifies the conventional Irish theatre – "by Irish authors, and plays relative to Ireland interpreted by *local* actors under a self-contained board of direction" (Hoare 566).[6] It can thus be argued that Barry's *White Woman Street*, looking at Ireland from an alternative historical viewpoint that is less keen to prove the universality of any perspective, illustrates an ignored Irish experience in a transnational context in America.[7]

A noteworthy fact about this play, set in 1916 in the wilds of Ohio, is its correlation with the Irish experience in that particular year, when the Easter Rising, which is lionized as a key signifier in republican discourse, took place. Although that event is only mentioned in passing through an Irish protagonist's description of home,[8] the playwright's choice of this significant year in Irish history creates a strong resonance among Irish audiences. Notably, by introducing a revisionist look at this crucial year in modern Irish history, the play touches on an often ignored but unsettling facet of the lives of Irish-Americans that had troubled their forefathers down the years, including those remaining in or emigrating from Ireland. In other words, in this play the Easter Rising rings its bell in a manner that is not obvious but is also not silent, in that the audience – watching a play set in Ohio in 1916 – returns to a historical year in which the Easter Rising took place and which has been consistently over-highlighted by Irish historians. This strategy allows the audience to observe, in a transnational context, how the Irish Famine and American Indian Wars had caused the Irish to be both victims and oppressors in the New World. This unpleasant facet of Irish life, however, was rarely featured by Barry's early predecessors who were more concerned about the Irish (cultural) nationalism that gave birth to the Irish Literary Theatre, later renamed the Abbey Theatre. The neglected experiences of the Irish diaspora in Ohio, as the play illustrates, can serve as a critique of the master-narrative of nationalistic dramaturgy and unearth those Irish-Americans who "do not fit with the way we want to imagine our history" (Grene 169).

---

in relatively unusual locations in Irish drama, in an attempt to explore those often marginalized Irish experiences overseas.

6   Emphasis mine.

7   Barry does not have many plays set outside Ireland. *White Woman Street* and *The Only True History of Lizzie Finn* (1995) are two clearly set overseas, while the latter – set at the turn of the twentieth century about a returned woman migrant's marriage with a descendent of the Big House in County Kerry – is partially set in Bristol. This play has a colonial subtext as regards the Boer War in South Africa.

8   The year is mentioned in the stage direction on p. 122 and Trooper and Clarke's conversation on p. 161.

On the other hand, it should also be noted that this 1992 historical drama illustrates, to some degree, an Ireland that is being transformed into a global state. This is done by presenting characters of several different nationalities – with only one character, out of six culturally displaced outlaws, being Irish. It can be assumed that, compared to the revisionist debates which have focused by and large on Irish *native* experiences, the geographical distance maintained in the play brings about a "direct challenge to the primacy of the nation-state in its present form," as well as an alternative perspective in (re-)writing Irish history (McGrew 63).

The alternative perspective resides firstly in the background choices of multi-national characters who all live on the margin of migrant society as gangsters who plan to rob trains that carry gold and their future. What draws them together, notably, is the force that edges them out from mainstream society. Trooper, in his fifties, came to America from Ireland in his youth, and was a laborer on canals and railroads. Without having the means to support himself, and being unable to go home, he has joined the gang in order to make his fortune. James Miranda is a black slave who, on seeing his peers killed and dumped in a ditch by their owner, has run away from a farm in Tennessee. Nathaniel Yeshov, a young man in his thirties from Brooklyn, and of Russian-Chinese parentage, constantly feels alienated for being unable to speak properly in either Russian or Chinese, and neither can he identify himself as an American: "It was prison the way I be in the head" (*White* 158). Clarke, in his seventies, is a native American Indian from Virginia who has experienced the mass slaughter of his people and watched women being raped by whites. He survived by becoming a pimp for colonial officers and speaking "damn good English ... [as] easy as white man" (*White* 155). Mo Mason, also in his seventies, is an Ohio Amish who has never returned to his puritanical community during the past fifty years but is still mentally trapped by its teaching, which is in conflict with his desire for whores. Blakely, an Englishman from Lincolnshire, is no less alienated than the other "poor robbermen without no homes" (*White* 130). Although they have been on the run together for five years and all have issues with each other, their common experience of having been in prison and wishing "to forget such places" prompts their comradeship and desire to stay in the gang (*White* 158), alongside their collective longing for being "a true man with gold ... Gold can turn a human creature any colour" (*White* 141).

The background of these six dislocated characters illuminates the creation of a "performative space" that potentially extends the realm of Irish historical revisionism by spotlighting the deprived Irish in the US and their little-documented experiences.[9] On the other hand, the fact that the play was premiered at the Bush Theatre in London, and the dramatization of the overseas Irish in relation to other ethnicities, imply the growing desire of Irish playwrights to boost the visibility of Ireland in the global network.[10] Despite the play focusing to a great extent on Trooper, the Irish wanderer, and his suspicious involvement in the mass slaughter of native Americans, his interactions with people of other ethnicities imply the double marginalization of those already silenced in a transnational context. That is, regardless of whether these six characters have arrived in America as low-skilled laborers or economic migrants – brought by the early stage of globalization – they are incapable of speaking with a public voice but have to survive individually on the lowest rung of society. Specifically, the tensions between the different ethnicities in the play and the killing of native Americans disclose the brutality inherent in the imperial rule of European settlers – usually unseen by the public or not featured in written histories – as it is always the winners rather than the defeated who get to write about themselves. Those who cannot be conveniently categorized as belonging to a recognizable nationality would be marked as inferior and consequently excluded from official documentation. Specifically, the six characters who deviate from their original courses in life would probably be written out of official history or, at most, be given only the merest mention in history monographs and textbooks. For this reason, as Ireland had not yet been recognized as a country in 1916, Trooper cannot help but fall through the cracks, which, along with his murder of a native American child prostitute, leads to him becoming an outcast in (Irish-) American society.

The emphasis on one's national identity is thus a matter of challenge, in that all the other five characters are in a similar quandary because of their ambiguous identities. For example, Nathaniel cannot identify himself as either Russian or Chinese because of his mixed origins, his incompetence in speaking his native languages, and being unfamiliar with either culture. As for James Miranda and Clarke, their skin color bars them from the political standing extended to white European settlers and their descendants, despite the fact that James, an escaped black slave, is

---

[9]   The performative space, or performativity, is a notion first created by Judith Butler, who describes it as a kind of "reiterative power of discourse to produce the phenomena that it regulates and constrains." Although Butler applied it mainly to gender issues, this notion has been used as an interdisciplinary term referring to the challenge to existing ideologies and traditions or the intention of constructing new ones. This play, by presenting a foreign scenario that coincides with the 1916 Easter Rising, may be performative in this sense. For more details on performativity, see Butler's *Bodies that Matter: On the Discursive Limits of Sex*, p. 2.

[10]   *White Woman Street* was premiered at the Bush Theatre in London on 23 April 1992 and toured to the Abbey Theatre for another run from 21 May of the same year.

also involuntarily relocated to America from a distant location. Clarke, the native American Indian, is on the cultural and political fringe in the "new world," even though no one in the play can be more *native* than him. Mo Mason's lust for women makes him religiously unfit in the eyes of the puritanical Amish community. Blakely, the only one who retains a recognizable identity as an Englishman, cannot return to his home in Grimsby, Lincolnshire, as it has been devastated by famine. Under these circumstances, the distinctions between their national or ethnic identities are gradually eroded until they are merely classed as robbers of gold trains – without any further critical explorations being needed.

Although *White Woman Street* is set in Ohio with multi-ethnic characters, the Irishness of the play rests on young Trooper's imagined encounter with an Irish prostitute whose presence is deemed to be unmentionable as a cure for the homesickness of Irish soldiers who are "sullied up by [Indian] wars" (*White* 149). Ironically, Trooper, traveling through "five hundred miles of wilderness" and not meeting the prostitute he has long desired (*White* 147), ends up raping an underage native American girl who slits her throat in his presence after submitting to him. Such a horrific experience should not be seen as an isolated case but as one of many undocumented incidents which happened during European colonial rule up to the mid-twentieth century. Satirically, what initially draws Trooper to White Woman Street, a red-light district, is the urge to ease his homesickness by visiting an Irish whore from Listowel: "a sight of home, a goddess of my own countrymen"(*White* 149), as she has been idolized as "a woman of a hundred stories, a hundred boasts, a kind of fire-hot legend of those days, such as had power over their talk and … was likely a goddess, and surely built that canal"(*White* 150). The playwright might well have intended to produce a counter image to Cathleen ni Houlihan, a mythical and over-politicized figure in Ireland, whereas this insalubrious image of an Irish whore in Ohio may potentially add problems to the nationalistic discourse. On the other hand, these culturally and geographically displaced characters, including the Irish and native Indian prostitutes whom the audience never see on stage, illustrate the darker side of American history that involves injustice, racism and infringements of human rights.

It can be contended that, by inventing characters who are constantly on the move as robbers and escaped slaves, the playwright may want audiences to see these individuals within the larger historical context of the American society becoming highly capitalistic after the Gold Rush. As the Gold Rush produced a westward flow of people to California for the first time in American history, the *nouveaux riches* were promptly created, and the resulting capital was redistributed with a mixed impact on class distinction, slavery, and interethnic exchange. Arguably, by presenting an image of how these migrants survive in an interethnic scenario, the play reroutes the moral direction of a national drama on the world stage. That these characters are of Chinese, Russian, native American, English and Irish origins implies an advent of intercultural exchange in the coming era.

Last but not least, the playwright's portrait of an Irish character overseas in 1916 unveils the parochial nature of the Irish nationalistic historiography in terms of its general dismissal of the experiences of Irish immigrants abroad. Notably, the play encourages the creation of an alternative perspective for the making of an *inter*national history of Ireland in which the Irish at home and overseas should both be considered in order to gain a more complete picture of the nation.

Colin Teevan's *How Many Miles to Basra?* (2006): From Patriots to Traitors?

Born in Dublin in 1968 and having worked for extended periods in Paris, Edinburgh, Newcastle, Leeds, New York, and for six years in Northern Ireland, Teevan is different from many fellow playwrights who have lived mostly in Ireland. Though based in London, his frequent border-crossing experiences have sharpened his sensitivity and led to shrewd observations about cultural clashes; only in London does he feel "least anxious about the issues of cultural difference" (Sexton 1). The mid-twentieth-century generation he was born into also experienced the Northern Ireland Troubles and their aftermath, witnessing how Ireland was transformed from an agricultural state into an economic power known as the Celtic Tiger.

Partly to examine how news can be manipulated, and partly to interrogate British policy in the Middle East under Tony Blair's administration, Teevan's *How Many Miles to Basra?* parallels the perspectives of different ethnicities and nationalities, in order to reflect on the imperial rule that once dominated Ireland and was now seen in another form in Iraq. First broadcast in July 2004 on BBC Radio 4 and later premiered at West Yorkshire Playhouse in Leeds in 2006, this anti-war play provides audiences with a critical distance from which to see the absurdities "in the white heat of the invasion of Iraq by Allied Forces," as the playwright stated.[11] What is of greater significance is that Teevan continues McGuinness's and Barry's attempt in contextualizing characters

---

[11] For details, see the interview with Colin Teevan on the website of the African-American Shakespeare Company, accessed 19 July 2012, par. 3. <http://www.african-americanshakes.org/AboutUs/AboutUs_Artists/AboutUs_Artists_ColinTeevan.html>.

of different ethnicities in a wider international context.[12] By questioning deeply the legitimacy of the British and American invasion of Iraq and their prolonged military occupation of the country, the play demonstrates how the two world powers had not only damaged the infrastructure of major cities, such as Baghdad and Basra, but also taken the lives of thousands of civilians as the country fell into anarchy.

Although the play challenges the rightfulness of the invasion under Tony Blair's leadership, it is Ursula, a woman journalist from Ireland, who initiates a series of journalistic assignments that would potentially embarrass the British government, despite her reporting being, to some extent, questionable due to her insufficient research, biases, assumptions and personal emotions. The problem of news-making in producing a favorable storyline is unfolded at the beginning of the play, when Ursula is seen at a news agency in London, complaining that the items she has submitted for a report have not been sorted in chronological order as she expected. Arguably, what the playwright would like to illustrate through Ursula is not just the work ethics of journalism but also the anti-terrorist ethos that is nurtured by the western media. The news agency that Ursula approaches, which is an embodiment of the western media, should be seen as partly responsible for popular images of the Middle East crisis. Its biased reporting prompts misleading impressions about the Iraqi government supporting al-Qaeda and harboring "weapons of mass destruction," despite there being no clear evidence of a connection or of such weapons being held. Incidentally, the play, which was premiered in 2006, reflected the playwright's highly critical views about the Blair government's justification for dispatching troops to Iraq. In the play, British soldiers" killing of a group of unarmed Bedouin civilians showcases this particularly unpleasant facet of the war.

Ursula's reports about the killing of civilians are certainly not welcome to the right-wing media, whereas such killings can be common but are often strategically covered up or by the authorities: Stewart, a low-ranked British officer in the play, has experienced them on the front line in different trouble spots. Specifically, in contradiction to Ursula's on-site observation, the cause of the deaths of the Bedouin civilians receives no

---

[12] Teevan is a well-traveled playwright, and these experiences may have contributed to a perspective, often seen in his dramas, in which the Irish, even a single character, should be examined through a broader framework alongside those of other ethnicities. Compared with McGuinness's and Barry's, Teevan's choices of setting are much more multinational. He not only adapted works by Euripides, Cervantes, Wu Cheng-en, Henrik Ibsen, Jaroslav Hašek, Edoado Erba, and Giuseppe Manfridi, but co-authored two plays with Hideki Noda, a Japanese playwright. He is one of the very few English-language playwrights devoted to topics on the Middle East Conflict. Other plays include *The Lion of Kabul* (2009) and *There Was A Man, There Was No Man* (2012).

mention in the British media, while the British military vehicle which is accidentally blown up by a British soldier is presented in the news as a result of terrorist action. It can thus be argued that the playwright intends to question the interdependence between the media and the British government. To achieve this, and partly to attract viewers/readers with visual or audible evidence and supporting matter, only those incidents which can be reconstructed by the media in a literal and lineal manner would be made public and they are often edited by people who have never been on the front line. Individual experiences, which Ursula thinks are more worthy of report, are often ignored or manipulated to suit political agendas, so as to solicit public support and to demonize the religious and cultural Other as potential terrorists.

A less discussed facet of the Iraq War, which this play explores, is how racism and sexism can be pillars of war. For instance, the soldiers' sexual fantasies about and assaults on Ursula, and their constant racist remarks about Iraqis, illustrate the excessive western chauvinism that exists in military operations. For soldiers, a female presence is deemed to be a potential interference with military action on the front line. Ursula is thus the detested Other to be removed, although her presence, as well as that of the ethnic, religious and cultural Others from the Islamic world, is necessary for the western superpowers to verify their (masculine) superiority and to confirm their domination over the less defensible. Specifically, the demonstration of masculinity exemplifies the continuation of colonial domination over the Other and the weaker sex – even metaphorically. That Ursula is often called "bitch" by the soldiers, and the fact that she appears in the sexual fantasies that lead to Freddie's attempt to rape her, are a metaphor for how imperial and patriarchal power still lingers in the twenty-first century. For these soldiers, Ursula is a much more convenient target for domination than the Iraqi guerillas. A further contradiction of the peacemaking mission of the Allied Forces is the verbal and physical abuse of civilians who are either carelessly killed like the Bedouin or are frequently dubbed "ragheads" (*How* 29). Unfortunately, how the violence is used is "classified information," as the (accidental) killing of Bedouin civilians in the play is immediately covered up, while the number of British casualties is soon made public through the media (*How* 29).

The play serves to illuminate agonizing truths about of the Iraq War, in that the portrayal of brutalities is to some extent faithful, given that the playwright had interviewed several war reporters and soldiers who confirmed that "accidental killings at roadblocks" and "payment of blood money" did happen (Sexton 1). Although highly critical of the military operations of the Allied Forces, Teevan does not seem to advance any perspective in describing the troubles in Iraq and their causes and effects, given that the reporting by western media about the Middle East was *not* always impartial and sometimes only reflected the interests of the winner, or the Bush's and Blair's administrations.

What is also noteworthy is a reference to Kabro a Generals, provided by Malek, an Iraqi taxi driver who is hired to take Ursula and the soldiers across the desert. As Malek explains, those enshrined in the temple as great generals by Alexander the Great are only "in his version of the truth" (*How* 71), while they are ultimately traitors in the eyes of the ancient Persians. Kabro a Generals thus represents "what was a sign of treachery to the East, [but] was a shrine to heroism in the West" (*How 71*). With this reference to the Persian version of a historical incident, the presence of Allied Forces in Iraq as "another western invasion" is comparable to that of the late Babylonian period, as Malek implies to his passengers (*How* 70). To Iraqis, the result of the extended war is not liberation but never-ending occupation that is regarded "more as arrogance" on the part of the West (*How 70*). There is therefore an implicit satire here, in that these soldiers who are undertaking an unauthorized mission are not only traitors to Britain but are similar to those Greeks who once showed the white flag to the Persian Empire but were later honored by Alexander the Great for political purposes.[13] It can be argued that the truth will only be fully appreciated when an interethnic or intercultural understanding of history is established. Ironically, as the reports written by Ursula are subject to re-editing by the news editors in London, exactly how the *coalition* forces of the UK and US in the Middle East operate would only be available to those who are deeply involved in the action on the front line

The Breakdown of Euro-Centrism in the Three Irish Plays

As was mentioned earlier, Eurocentrism has for centuries, both explicitly and implicitly, directed the making of the oriental Other, and it was only when postcolonial critics started to develop transnational perspectives that the insularism of nationalistic discourses could be examined and challenged. As for Ireland, its geopolitical and economic ties with Great Britain throughout history have provided a fixed point for critics from which to discuss the central-periphery model of (post)imperialism, and also provide a location for observing how transnationalism converts a nation-state into a global one.

---

[13]	According to Malek, the Greek generals found themselves surrounded by hostile tribes, so they decided to negotiate with the Persians. However, the Persians refused any negotiation but cut off their heads and displayed them in public. However, seventy years later when the Persian Empire fell to the Greeks, Alexander the Great set up Kabro a Generals to house their remains and to honor the generals who were thought to have been sacrificed for Greece.

The three plays discussed as a group exemplify a process that can be dated back to the native American conflicts, the Cold War, and the Iraq War, during which world power was reaffirmed through a series of military actions. Notably, the three plays demonstrate how the "zones of silence" which are exclusively created by "a [Eurocentric] diasporan axis of political, military and economic affiliations" have brought about the difficulties of lateral communications between and within oppressed countries (Fisher 14). The windowless cell in *Someone Who'll Watch Over Me*, the suicide of a native American girl in *White Woman Street*, and the miscommunication between British soldiers and Bedouin civilians in *How Many Miles to Basra?* all embody such communication failures as experienced by an individual or a group of mixed ethnicities in a transnational scenario.

One facet that these three plays have in common is that they were all premiered in the UK, rather than in Ireland. One reason might be because contemporary Irish playwrights hope to gain a wider audience outside the Emerald Isle with plays set in international contexts. They are also keen observers of the social and political transformation of British society and its problematic alliance with the US.

Both first staged in 1992, respectively at the Hampstead Theatre and the Bush Theatre, *Someone Who'll Watch Over Me* and *White Woman Street* reflect the changing attitudes of the public as regards British Dependent Territories and their colonial links to Britain,[14] particularly two years after Margaret Thatcher resigned from her post as Prime Minister.[15] Furthermore, although *Someone Who'll Watch Over Me* was adapted from the accounts of Brian Keenan, an Irish writer who attracted the attention of western media after being abducted in Beirut in 1985 and held captive for the next four and a half years, the play questions indirectly the British

---

[14]   The name "British Dependent Territory," introduced by the British Nationality Act 1981, was replaced by "British Overseas Territory," introduced by the British Overseas Territories Act 2002. The British territories overseas were still officially called "Dependent Territories" when the two plays were first staged.

[15]   Specifically, these two plays were staged after the first Gulf War (2 August 1990 – 28 February 1991) during John Major's premiership. Major's successful renewal of his term of office by winning the general election of 1992 was in part due to the success of the UN authorized coalition force to which the UK committed a major contingent, and in part to his replacement of Thatcher's unpopular Community Charge with a Council Tax. In spite of this fourth consecutive victory for the Conservative Party, it is probable that both playwrights would have wanted to draw the attention of the audience to the institutional deprivation of the disadvantaged in the British system. The English lecturer, Michael, who is the only person not released from the windowless cell in *Someone*, and Trooper, the Irishman wandering in the wilds of Ohio in *White Woman Street*, showcase the playwrights' concerns for these disregarded people.

alliance with the US during the Cold War, and reveals the extended consequences that afflicted civilians in the affected nations.

White Woman Street, by the same token, is a dramatic critique, from an Irish point of view, of the British imperial mindset embodied by the 1982 Falklands War, following which the Conservative Party received a resurgence of support in the next year's UK general election. The gap between the privileged and the powerless in an international scenario is further visualized in *How Many Miles to Basra?*, premiered in 2006 in London's Tricycle Theatre, which is a venue known for its left-wing stance. The position taken is that the Iraq War was prolonged by leaders who could have terminated it – seeing that no weapons of mass destruction were eventually found.

The three plays under discussion suggest not only the need to reassess Irish experiences in the present and the past, but more significantly they offer retrospective views of imperial violence and its impact on people of different ethnicities. By not endorsing any particular ideologies or cultures, the foci of these plays are on marginalized individuals and their struggles in a transnational setting, which notably counteracts the lingering effects of Euro-centric imperialism. Set *outside* Ireland, the three dramatic texts may correspond to what Steffen Mau implies by his proposal for a more interactive international community in which "the social life of each individual is less and less limited to the nation-state territory," the traditional borders of which are now constantly contested, de-naturalized and hybridized (23). As the three plays demonstrate, the more that confrontations are ignited by globalization, the greater the chance that transnational dialogues will be able to build a platform for all voices to be heard.

One of the shared characteristics of the three plays is the challenge by the playwrights to European cognition of the world since the Enlightenment and also insular Irish nationalism. In McGuinness's *Someone Who'll Watch Over Me*, the hostages' lives in Lebanon are entirely subject to people who revere the Islamic Koran, while audiences see Edward, the Irishman, and Michael, the English lecturer, argue over the correct use of certain English words. Their debate is meaningless, because what they believe to be appropriate usage is only ideological or simply customary. That is, when Edward insists that Michael should use "film" instead of "movie" to refer to a motion picture, it is the Irishman himself who holds on to a linguistic convention which makes him more English than his English cellmate. As a whole, what used to be regarded as major cultural values can be politically invalid or religiously void in the world of the Other. For Michael and Edward, their argument does nothing that contributes to their being released sooner from the prison of the Other, or their enemy.

Barry's *White Woman Street* also challenges the nationalistic histori-ography about the year of 1916 by setting it in a transnational scenario in that year, although 1916 is only mentioned in passing during the play.[16] Whereas fervent Irish nationalists were keen to posit a political identity that was different from the English one, and historians have documented and entered debates on the domestic turbulence, the ups-and-downs of Irish migrants are almost forgotten in the official records. For Trooper and other Irish migrants – whose love for Ireland is no less than that of any Irish nationalist – their bodily contact with an Irish whore, her smell and touch, is more important than the Easter Rising, in that her body prompts them to feel most physically in touch with Mother Ireland. Ironically, as Trooper has been physically and ethnically subjugated to the given social/ colonial hierarchy, his rape of the young Indian girl, or "that furrow" (*Someone* 163), has allowed him to receive a temporarily improved status as a white dominator, even though he is also a socially marginalized character in that settlers-dominated, migrant society.

The depiction of the conduct of the Allied Forces in Teevan's *How Many Miles to Basra?* can be seen as a strong critique of Tony Blair's administration and its anti-terrorist agenda. Although Ursula and the news agency in London both have their own biases about how British Intelligence "sex(ed) up the dossier on Saddam's weapon capabilities" (*How* 9), it is fair to assert that the extended occupation of Iraq allowed certain politicians to establish their interests through state machines and international networks. Ursula's strong concerns over how the news agency decodes her submitted items imply the possibility that the war may be misrepresented. Furthermore, how the war should be represented often mirrors fear of and imagining about the Other. Fear as such is not necessarily created by propaganda or within cooperatives like the news agency, but it can be a factor that prompts individuals" hostility to the Other, or whoever are regarded as potential terrorists. The indifference of the news agency in London to the three Iraqi deaths also emanates from such sentiments, leading to the killing not being worthy of inclusion in Ursula's report, as the victims belong to the fearful and deniable Other rather than being innocent Caucasians.

Irish dramas that have international appeal are not limited to the three discussed in this chapter, although they may reflect demands for reexamination of the Irish past seen from the broader perspective of contemporary Ireland. These three contemporary plays set in locations distant from Ireland demonstrate that borders are no longer prerequisites for defining one's identity, and that globalization often incurs a revisionist view of "historical breakpoint," as the "present premises and understanding

---

[16]   See note 8.

of history's dynamics must be treated as conceptual jails" (Rosenau 5). Through the compression of time and space, a transnational drama can present numerous, and sometimes contradictory, perspectives of those "jails" conditioned by major or minor players on the world stage. The quandaries that trap all the characters may thus portend the collapse of political and religious confinement that leads some regions or countries into war or leaves them in a constant state of conflict. In addition, the interactions of Irish protagonists with those of other ethnicities should not be taken only as a minor Irish experience, in that they showcase the demand for the reshuffling of political and economic powers so as to accommodate the Other more amicably. The three plays, perhaps a collective theatrical response to how justice should be firmly upheld in a transnational community, should be seen as opening a dialogue aimed at peace.

VII. Peace and Beyond in the Middle East: Colin Teevan's War Trilogy

Introduction: New Playwriting and Colin Teevan

Although globalization has heralded a new chapter of human life and been a key impetus for the furthering of international politics and economics, particularly during the last few decades of the twentieth century, it has not made, and perhaps never will make, much contribution to world peace. Sectarian conflicts and xenophobia still linger and are sometimes of greater intensity when the economic and military interests of superpowers clash. Competition between nations, whether regional or inter-continental, is often undertaken to achieve enhancement of international alliances, and/or to enable entrepreneurs to reach a wider market. This may demonstrate what Homi K. Bhabha predicted in his *Locations of Culture*, first published in 1994, about how the world would evolve irreversibly into a highly interconnected community, or global village, in that our existence cannot but be "marked by a tenebrous sense of survival, [...] for which there seems to be no proper name other than the current and controversial shiftinesss of the prefix 'post'" (333). What the world has experienced through, for instance, the September 11 attacks, the ensuing Iraq War, and the economic recession of 2008, may be seen as the symptoms of *post*-globalization which will be carried across boundaries, or between countries in the first and third worlds. The direct impacts and after-effects of these incidents have not bridged but widened the gap between the powerful and the powerless, and richer and poorer states, thus accentuating their differences.

Partly due to the advances of communication technologies, globalization implies that more natural, human and financial resources will be wasted or invested – sometimes from thousands of miles away. Wars and economic conflicts must be fought on battlefields that cross borders and for prolonged periods, if one superpower intends to dominate the distant, weaker Other and takes advantage of their sources.[1] The

---

[1] Debates on how the Other, as the politically and economically powerless, is forced to remain marginalized have been initiated by post-colonial critics and philosophers. Gayatri Chakravorty *Spivak,* drawing on Karl Marx's, Jacques *Derrida's, Gilles Deleuze's and* Michel *Foucault's theorizations on power struggles, argues in her "Can the Subaltern Speak"* that the Other is part of "Western intellectual production [...] [which is] in many ways complicit with Western international economic interest"

attempt to dominate the distant Other in the era of globalization has been a matter of concern in contemporary Irish theatre, which has evolved from an inward-looking forum into a venue that demonstrates how the country is being transformed by global forces. It is also noteworthy that many contemporary Irish playwrights, in part thanks to the status of English as an international language, and also in part to their strong interest in affairs outside Ireland, have learned to cater for more diverse audiences by dramatizing impending international issues.

Colin Teevan, born in Dublin in 1968, comes from this generation that has witnessed the rapid transformation of Ireland before and after the economic boom of the 1990s.[2] In common with many of his contemporaries who moved overseas for employment, he worked for extended periods in Paris, Edinburgh, Newcastle, Leeds and New York, and six years in Northern Ireland. These travel and work experiences are presumably what have prompted the playwright to consider multicultural subjects. His original works for theatre and radio and his adaptations of ancient tales and classical literature in modern contexts can be seen as examples of how the new generation of Irish artists is more engaged with non-Irish but important global matters than were many of their Irish predecessors.[3] Specifically, Teevan's concerns with ongoing humanitarian

---

(271). Concisely speaking, the UK's and US's foreign policies concerning the Middle East, which often lead to conflicts and international tension, are embodiments of problematic, "subjugated knowledge" against the Other in traditional European humanism (Spivak 281).

[2]   Born in 1968, Teevan experienced the impact of the Northern Ireland Troubles and their prolonged aftermath. Differently from many established Irish playwrights whose plays are often set against this domestic upheaval, Teevan, having traveled widely, shares with non-Irish playwrights an acute observation of wars in many parts of the world, both historical and current. His contemporaries include Edward Bond, David Hare, Mark Ravenhill, Robin Soans, Ron Hutchinson, Lee Blessing, David Greig, Amit Gupta and Nick Stafford. A long list of contemporary dramatists who have used experiences of war to inspire plays can be seen in two anthologies: *The Great Games: Afghanistan* and *The Bomb: A Partial History*.

[3]   To name a few: Frank McGuinness, Brian Friel, Dermot Bolger, Donal O'Kelly, Conor McPherson, Jimmy Murphy, John Banville, Jim O'Hanlon, Dolores Walshe, among others, have all set works outside Ireland and/or in an international context where characters, not necessarily all Irish, struggle to survive. Another reason why a greater number of contemporary Irish writers are concerned about international affairs is that Ireland has long been an emigrant nursery. Compared to people of other European countries, Irish people have relatively closer links to family members residing overseas. According to the Office of National Statistics of Ireland and a survey conducted by *The Irish Times* in December 2012 about dual citizenship, "the number of residents who held a passport that was not a UK passport was nearly 4.8 million. Of these 2.3 million were EU passports (other than UK) and 2.4 million were other foreign passports." The large number of passport holders who have dual citizenship suggests how the Irish, particularly those overseas, regard their historical and familial ties with Ireland.

crises have taken his *The Lion of Kabul* (2009) to Washington DC "for a private performance attended by Pentagon staff, policymakers and the military."[4] In order to explore the significance of his works in depth, this paper will focus on three of his political plays that present the causes and effects of current international conflicts in the Middle East, and demonstrate the controversial roles of NATO, the UN, and British and American operations alongside their scandalous conduct and interactions with local Muslims and detainees.[5] Set respectively in Iraq, Afghanistan and Iran, the war trilogy to be discussed comprises *How Many Miles to Basra?* (2004), *The Lion of Kabul* (2009) and *There Was A Man, There Was No Man* (2011).

How Many Miles to Basra? (2004): A Mission to Reveal Hidden Facts in Iraq

The traditional Irish theatre has been known for its highly political nature, in that many playwrights since the turn of the twentieth century have been keen to demonstrate their observations on social inequality and have initiated cultural movements and public debates that have changed how the Irish see themselves and their problems. This is despite the fact that not all their plays have presented an optimistic view of Ireland but rather one that expresses disappointment.[6]

Teevan, having being part of this theatrical force that has offered resistance and rethinking about Irish social problems, has directed the attention of audiences overseas, by challenging those foreign powers that claim to be world peacekeepers but ultimately are adding fuel to the fire. On being asked about his intention to write political dramas, he remarked that "Safe theatre is boring […] Theatre should always explore doing

---

See Mark Hennessy, "Irish-born population in England and Wales falls sharply in last decade."

4   "Dramatic Insights for Pentagon," *The Times Higher Education Supplement*, 27 January 2011, p. 14.

5   With his background knowledge of the classics, Teevan has been devoted to adapting classical works in modern and cross-cultural settings. Apart from the war dramas under discussion in this paper, he has adapted works by Euripides, Cervantes, Wu Cheng-en, Henrik Ibsen, Jaroslav Hašek, Edoado Erba and Giuseppe Manfridi, and has co-authored two plays with Hideki Noda, a Japanese playwright. Few Irish playwrights have been as prolific as Teevan in employing such a wide range of cultural and literary materials.

6   Apart from the writers listed above, Teevan's predecessors and contemporaries who have written works dealing with the transformation of Irish life include: Tom Murphy, Sebastian Barry, Brendan Behan, Martin McDonald, Marie Jones, Christina Reid, Anne Devlin, etc.

the wrong thing and therefore challenge our preconceptions about what the right thing is" (*Dewhurst* 248). Although his plays do not offer any solutions for combating terrorism or weapons of mass destruction, they might, in the playwright's own words, "have a massive impact in raising awareness[...] [by] paradigmatic depiction of injustice rather than their topical sociological interest" (*Dewhurst* 248).

As a theatrical response to the Iraq War and its controversies over the intentions of Tony Blair's and George W. Bush's administrations in attacking Iraq, Teevan's *How Many Miles to Basra?*, first broadcast in July 2004 on BBC Radio 4 and later premiered at West Yorkshire Playhouse in Leeds in 2006, is a play loosely based on a canonical Greek adventure tale, *The Anabasis* by Xenophon. The play begins with Ursula's frustration when presenting, at a news agency in London, her first-hand experiences in Iraq with soldiers and local civilians. Through this Irish woman journalist, the play challenges the convention of reporting which often distorts war news for either propagandism or sensational headlines.

However, the truth that Ursula insists on is made more problematic by involving personal biases, in that her mission to the front line in Iraq was aimed, as she admits, to revenge her deceased brother who was killed by the Royal Ulster Constabulary in Northern Ireland with the truth subsequently being covered up by the authorities concerned. Partly to embarrass the Blair government about the sexed-up dossier concerning Iraq's weapons of mass destruction, and partly to investigate the war crimes of the Coalition Forces, her reporting has the preconceived idea that "the army is always [...] the baddy," and she aims "to make [her] stories suit [the] agenda" (*How* 54-5). It can thus be judged that *How Many Miles to Basra?* aims to be politically inflammatory so as to interrogate the reliability of information from the government and the credibility of Blair's "New Labour" administration.

Recognizably, what Teevan intended to create may not have been so much a politically correct character but more likely a call for justice for victims silenced by the British and American military presence in Iraq. Whether justice can be restored may not save those characters in danger, but the play allows audiences to digest what is unveiled about the Iraq War.

This play can also be regarded as a modern adaptation of Xenophon's *The Anabasis*, which detailed Cyrus the Younger's failed expedition to the north of Babylon with a large army of Greek mercenaries in 401 BC, in an attempt to wrest the throne of the Persian Empire from his brother, Artaxerxes II. In *How Many to Basra?*, the Coalition Forces resemble the Greek mercenaries, many of whom did not wholeheartedly swear fidelity to Cyrus but had their own agenda about how to benefit themselves in the army.

As the play unfolds with an accident in which a number of innocent Bedouins are gunned down at a vehicle checkpoint by over-stressed British soldiers, the audience gradually sees the problems of military operations on the front line. Not only the language barrier between English-speaking soldiers and Iraqi civilians but also the lack of proper supervision and discipline contribute little to peacekeeping but result in more accidental killings, as researched by the playwright in advance of writing the play.[7] The neglect of the soldiers' mental health when they are stationed alone in the desert can lead to misconduct, including verbal and physical abuse of detainees and even their own colleagues, especially women, who are also serving in Iraq. Journalistically portraying these inappropriate military operations, the play draws an effective picture of the malfunctioning of the UK/US-led Coalition Forces in Iraq.

The incidents in the play begin with an accidental killing at a vehicle checkpoint in Southern Iraq, although the cause of the accident should, to a great extent, be attributed to the overstress and low morale of the depressed soldiers. Not only they are ill-equipped – without proper desert boots and other necessary items – but they feel that they have been forgotten by their own country. As Freddie complains to Ursula in a recorded interview, "look at it: this country. What the fuck are we doing here? It's not like they're grateful or anything. It's not like the people at home even want us here in the first place. So who the fuck are we fighting this for?" (*How* 10).

The mental stress and the extremely arid conditions make the soldiers impatient at following the standard operational procedures before firing at suspects, and this situation prompts Stewart, the officer in charge, to go on an unauthorized mission to deliver a ransom to Kabro A Generals on behalf of a deceased Bedouin whose wife and child are being held hostage there: "Saving his wife and son's life is the least we can do" (*How* 26). Apart from the issue of whether Stewart's self-appointed mission is a humanitarian act, Teevan also shows facets of the ill-starred military operation in Iraq including the soldiers' racism towards local civilians by constantly addressing them openly as "raghead," "bastard," and "you animal." This circumstance leads to Ursula almost being raped by Freddie,

---

[7]   Teevan told David Sexton, an interviewer from *The Sunday Telegraph,* that he had talked to four or five "embedded" journalists before writing this play, and confirmed that "[there] have been accidental killings at roadblocks in Iraq, and there is evidence for the payment of blood money." He wished to interview more soldiers in the Ministry of Defence, but was denied this, "probably because of his accent, he thought." See David Sexton's "Interest in Conflict Radio."

who outspokenly excuses his physical attack as her rightful punishment for the death of a fellow soldier during their journey deep into Iraq.

All these incidents demonstrate an embarrassing fact about the quality of these soldiers, in that the play reveals that none of them has joined the army for patriotic reasons but either to pay off credit card debts like Geordie, or to run away from a loveless marriage, in Stewart's case, or simply through having been fooled by a job center which does not warn new recruits that "all your actions have consequences for [the death of] someone," but only impresses them with a picture in which are seen "tanks rolling through woodlands and guys patrolling through trees" (*How* 62).

The setting of Kabro A Generals, the temple in which Alexander the Great placed the remains of Greek generals who were beheaded by the Persians, implies that political authorities in the past and the present all create "[their] version of the truth" to attract and convince followers (*How* 71). As Malek, an Iraqi who drives these soldiers around in the play, explains, Alexander the Great had claimed that those remains were of "early martyrs in the civilization of the barbarians" in Cyrus the Younger's failed expedition, so as to cover up the treachery of these generals – who had actually waved the white flag to the Persians but whose surrender was refused and they were all killed. The temple that houses their remains is therefore also a reminder not only of the historical hiatus between two warring bodies but of the unending attempt to assimilate the political and religious Other. It is even more alarming, as Ursula finds out during this unauthorized mission, that this historic temple is where the "Allies … dumped more bodies" (*How* 88). If this is factual, "[the] discrepancies [Ursula] wish[es] to expose [will] strip the men of the dignity the official version affords them" (*How* 88).

It could be argued that the playwright's intention in alluding to Xenophon's *The Anabasis* is to stress the unreliability of truth when issued by a political party. Dramaturgically, although Teevan chooses naturalism to approach each individual's troubles and the international crises, the reference to *The Anabasis* suggests, on the one hand, how history can be politically interpreted in favor of an authority or as disfavor of the opposition. On the other hand, what the Iraqi driver condemns through this story is how the Other has to bear mistreatment in an ethical sense when western superpowers adopt an attitude of conscious superiority during wartime or through peace-keeping missions. As the play does not appear to suggest a definite perspective on the Iraq War, audiences do not have to take Teevan's critique of the Coalition Force for granted, despite the fact that Ursula – with her preconceived agenda – is eager to testify to her own version of the truth. What should be noted, however, is the significance of

Teevan's naturalistic approach to contemporary international crises – with metaphors employed in his plays to be explored in the next few sections.

The Lion of Kabul (2009): Two Cultures, One Fallacy in War-torn Afghanistan

If Xenophon's *The Anabasis* illuminates the historical discrepancies between the Persians and the Greeks and different interpretations of treachery: "what was a sign of treachery to the East, was a shrine to heroism in the West" (*How* 71), what underlies the discrepancy, however, are the clashes between different cultural and religious persuasions, many of which still linger to the present day. It should also be acknowledged that, although globalization technologically shortens the geographical distance between West and East, it does not necessarily lead to effective communication and is often for the cause of international crises involving different political alliances. The war in Afghanistan (2001 to the present), the background against which *The Lion of Kabul* is set, redraws, alongside many other conflicts in the Middle East, the archetype which *The Anabasis* portrays, despite all the parties claiming their legitimacy against terrorism either by calling for Jihad or liberating the religious Other.

Set during the war in Afghanistan, Teevan's *The Lion of Kabul* features how Rabia, a woman UN representative of Pakistani/Indian origin who was born and educated in Britain, investigates the disappearance of two Afghan citizens who are working for the UN.[8] Through a meeting with a mullah who sympathizes with the Taliban, Rabia learns, before she arrives to rescue them, that the two UN workers have been devoured by a lion at Kabul Zoo.

It soon becomes clear just how savage the Taliban is; however, although the US troops do not kill or abuse any lesser number of Afghan locals, the fact is that Rabia and the Taliban/Islamic extremists have become blinded by their own interpretations of justice. That is, Rabia's upbringing in Britain prompts her to feel superior to the Afghans. Her arrogance is portrayed explicitly at the beginning of the play when she promises Ismael, another Afghan working for the UN, that "someday I'll take you, Ismael, I'll show you the world outside" (*Kabul* 154). She also acts as Ismael's mentor, giving imperious instructions about the way to think like

---

[8]   Commissioned by Nicolas Kent and premiered on 18 April 2009, at Tricycle Theatre in London, *The Lion of Kabul* is one of twelve plays in *The Great Game* sequence about Afghanistan and was directed by Indhu Rubasingham. Tricycle is known as Britain's foremost political theatre and often produces plays that concern the status of minorities and their cultures, including Black, Irish, Jewish, Asian and South African experiences. *The Great Game* covers Afghan history from 1842 to the present.

a Westerner: "You've gone into Afghan mode. You're not looking at me. You must sense the enemy at hand" (*Kabul* 155).

Despite most reviews focusing on the portrayal of the horrors of Taliban rule in the play, acclaiming the play as "a highly watchable slice of blood-soaked life under the Taliban" (Mark par. 11), it can be argued that Rabia never learns that her patronizing attitude is an unfortunate symptom of Western culture when dealing with the Other. It is ironic that she does not seem to realize that there has been discrimination imposed on her own ethnic origin, whereas she fails to question the Western values that she has acquired and demands that her Afghan coworker thinks like a Westerner. It should be pointed out that, although she appears to be a well-educated, articulate and independent career woman, the mullah's disdain for her is a collective reproach on the Western forces for having consistently ignored the cultural differences between the Islamic and Western worlds, and the inappropriateness of justifying their *own* cultural codes as universal.

It can thus be understood that, for the Taliban, a quicker way of restoring the dignity of Islam would be through defeating the West and evoking anti-Western sentiments among Afghans as a backlash against the extended military intervention of the UN. As the mullah makes clear to Rabia (and thus to the audience), the Taliban should not be held liable for the current thorny troubles of Afghanistan and other Islamic countries that enjoy more amiable relations with the West, but they are a consequence of the Cold War: "when the Russians left, the world forgot Afghanistan [...] Warlords of Mujahideen [...] killed anyone who got in their way [...] Each one, if you couldn't pay what they demand, you were raped, or robbed or killed" (*Kabul* 163). Simply put, the spiritual leader of the Taliban, Mullah Mohammed Omar, the new Amir ul-Momineen,[9] "led us from these dark times" and restored the social order (*Kabul* 163). In the view of the Taliban, the West, or the coalition of the US and NATO, should be blamed for those unsolved crises in the Middle East.

What the mullah would like to remind Rabia, the UN representative, is that Muslim countries are not necessarily the troublemakers but the Western superpowers should pay the price for having taken advantage of the Islamic world. That is, although there seemed to have been many diplomatic talks and negotiations, understanding of Islamic culture had not been effectively deepened but more domestic or tribal contradictions were created. This is partially why the Taliban and Muslim fundamentalists would, often in extreme ways, resist the values imposed by the West and wreak havoc against them. It can be seen as a satirical comment in the

---

[9]   *Amir ul-Momineen* means a Commander of the Faithful or Leader of the Faithful in English. It is a legitimate title for leaders in Muslim countries or communities of Muslims.

play that Rabia, "wearing a scarf loosely over her head" (*Kabul* 153), never doubts those Western values but acts on them faithfully. Rabia not only cannot convince the mullah about the human rights issues she brings up but also fails to even slightly bridge the gap between the UN and the Islamic world thanks to her ethnic origin. In other words, the more desperate she is to convince the mullah, the more problems she evokes.

It is also ironic that the mullah can speak fluent English with Rabia, since he was trained in Mumbai. It can thus be judged that the English language does not necessarily help assimilate the Other with its cultural codes but only functions as a medium to testify to the differences between each other. Nevertheless, both Rabia and the mullah are ignorant of the fact that they have been closely trapped by the ideologies of their communities and are only able to see half of the truth. In other words, they are no different from the half-blind, senile lion trying to restore its past glory at Kabul Zoo.[10] Nevertheless, the handicapped lion as a key image in this play about the controversy surrounding the British presence in Afghanistan can be seen as profoundly ironic in that the lion was also employed to personify the qualities of Britishness, particular during the expansion of the British Empire in the nineteenth century.[11] What Rabia witnesses and finds fearful can be regarded as a reflection of Britain being fractured and unable to defend itself, rather than as an enemy that is about to show the white flag.

All the characters are apparently frustrated because of their incompatible cultural peculiarities, while they do not know how *not* to answer violence with violence, nor know how to break the vicious circle rooted long in the past like a historical nightmare. Rabia's anger and helplessness imply the failure of (Western) individualism and its inapplicability to other cultures. On the other hand, the mullah's insistence on justifying the status of the Taliban and its use of terror in Afghanistan reveals his lack of confidence in other Muslims and their ability to make sensible judgments. All these factors lead to disrespect between Islamic states and Western countries,

---

[10] Known as "a symbol of survival against the odds," according to a BBC report, Marjan the one-eyed lion died of old age in 2003. Born in captivity, he was a gift from a zoo in Cologne, Germany, in 1978 and witnessed the turbulent history of Afghanistan. While many animals were stoned to death by the Taliban and suffered hunger and ill health, Marjan miraculously survived the ordeal. For more details, see "Lion of Kabul Roars His Last" on the BBC website.

[11] The use of the lion as a national symbol may be traced back to the eleventh century, when Henry I (c. 1068-1135), also known as Henry the Lion or "The Lion of Justice," adapted the Anglo-Saxon legal system effectively in the royal administration. Several English monarchs, for instance Richard I, Henry I and Henry II, had used lions on their arms. The adoption of lion in association of the British Empire as a national symbol for strength, courage, dignity, and pride became more consistently used in the nineteenth century.

causing repeated failures in assimilating the religious and political Other and communicating with it. By showing the cultural impasses that trap these characters, the playwright may have intended to suggest that what each party needs is a deeper understanding of their *own* cultural fallacies, rather than eagerly promoting a common spoken language, before peace emerges.

There Was A Man, There Was No Man (2011): Espionage and Gender in Palestine

The political tension and military conflict between two antagonistic states as presented in Xenophon's *The Anabasis* have had lingering repercussions in the Middle East from 401 BC to the present day in different forms. Notably, the twentieth century has witnessed turmoil involving Western superpowers and Islamic communities, especially around the time that Israel was established with the support of the UN in 1948, and, since then, the consequent Israeli-Palestinian and Arab-Israeli conflicts. Although some countries, through the coordination of the UN/US/UK, have signed peace treaties with Israel, some still see Israel as an adversary to be removed from the Palestinian region. It should be noted that Irish nationalists have mixed sympathy for Israelis and Palestinians, inasmuch as some perceive the Irish nationalistic experience as being parallel to the Zionist retrieval of the Promised Land; while some offer consolation for the Palestinians who were forced to leave their homeland, despite British and UN interventions in the Gaza Strip and West Bank.[12] The sentimental link to the Israeli-Palestinian conflict in the Irish consciousness may suggest why the playwright would choose to write about the nuclear arms issue in the Palestinian area and the impending humanitarian issues.

Also premiered at Tricycle Theatre as part of the series *The Bomb: A Partial History*, and directed by Nicolas Kent,[13] *There Was A Man, There*

---

[12]   For many Palestinians, the Israeli-Palestinian conflict arose from the intervention of Britain and the UN since 1946 and the Israeli government's aggression in occupying lands that were not outlined in the Balfour Declaration in 1917, which forced local Palestinians to move out of their homeland. Some Irish nationalists thus condemned Britain, the US and UN for their tacit support for Israel's (wrong-)doings. Support from some Irish nationalists – mainly Catholic – for Zionism is drawn from a similar experience of occupation and their struggle for self-determination against the British.

[13]   Born in 1945, Nicolas Kent grew up during the Cold War, the Cuban missile crisis and the early years of the Campaign for Nuclear Disarmament. He had served for 28 years as artistic director at Tricycle Theatre by 2012, and is known for his theatrical inquiries, based on documentary evidence, into many dark undercurrents of societal injustice. Apart from this project, *The Bomb: A Partial History*, which includes ten plays about the history of the nuclear bomb, his dramas about Stephen Lawrence, the Hutton inquiry, and Guantánamo were thoughtfully written.

Was No Man presents an episode of espionage activity between Israel and Iran. The play dramatizes how an Israeli woman spy, Amira, tries to hack the nuclear arms program of Iran through the use of a USB stick. However, the espionage gets more complicated due to a love affair between Amira and a married Iranian nuclear arms scientist. The scientist, called a professor in the play, is murdered by a group of Iranian agents after he is found meeting Amira at a conference in Jordan and later in his hotel room. The intrigue grows with the revelation that Amira and her younger brother Meir were formerly Iranian citizens who have sought shelter in Israel for having joined the anti-Khomeini movement. Torn between romance, morality, loyalty, familial ethics, and the risk of being murdered, Amira and the wife of the Iranian professor both suffer a "liberal conscience […] in a twist" (*There* 140), and have to make a choice between protecting their loved ones, making a confession about the secrets on the USB drive, or submitting to the authorities which threaten to kill them.

While covering the agendas of Israel and Iran in developing nuclear weapons for unlawful purposes, this play also explores an extreme condition in which patriotism for and loyalty to either country remains a top consideration in one's work, rather than merely personal and familial preferences. Despite the fact that Amira and Meir have both taken an oath to support Israel, their sibling relationship is, however, subject to Muslim patriarchy according to which Amira's political and private life and espionage work have to be under Meir's surveillance. Specifically, although Meir is junior to Amira by age, he has rights that allow him to question Amira in respect of her everyday life: "Everything is politics, sister, even no-politics is politics. Sitting in your chalet in the Alps with your Mercedes in the drive and your banker husband and your two blond children and your fridge full of Swiss chocolate, that's politics" (*There* 143).

The point to be addressed here is that even though Amira has been given the USB drive by the Israeli agency – containing a hack program – to be forwarded to the Iranian nuclear arms scientist, she is under strict supervision and is not fully trusted, not only because of her formal Iranian citizenship but also because she is female. Suspected of having had a sexual/love encounter with the scientist in his hotel room, she is accused by her younger brother (and other Israeli agents) of being a counterspy for Iran, in spite of the fact that her conscience tells her that the Iranian professor is eventually "in the opposition, a Green, a reformer" (*There* 144). Although she may not be able to explain clearly her relationship with him, the fact that she is charged by the Israeli agents, and consequently the Iranian scientist is murdered, suggest the complete ignoring? of human values in an over-politicized society where people suspect rather than have faith in each other (*There* 133). None of the characters can defend him/

herself but are used as chess pieces or spokespeople for the state. That is, even though Amira has realized that the Iranian has no intention of killing people with a nuclear bomb, she cannot stop the state from murdering the scientist out of suspicion of his loyalty: "[The professor] opened up their whole system to you and then you sacrificed him. Just another piece in a game. But a man, not a piece, has died here" (*There* 148).

The manipulation of women in a highly patriarchal society is also exemplified through the way in which the Iranian scientist's wife, Gully, is treated. She is abducted by the Sep⬛h and interrogated by her own elder brother, Mahmoud, after her husband is murdered by Iranian agents. Notably, as male siblings are entitled to dominate their female siblings in a traditional Muslim community, Gully has no choice but to listen to the recording which Mahmoud plays of her husband's voice during his extramarital sex with another woman, although the authenticity of the recording can be questioned. She is then forced to admit to the press that her husband has been murdered by Israeli assassins and is persuaded that she should then work for Iran as a counterspy in the opposition party, if she would like "you and your children [...] [to] continue to live in the comfort and security you presently enjoy" (*There* 154).

Having illustrated the prejudice against Gully and Amira and portrayed their dilemmas, the play suggests that the failure of Amira's espionage does not necessarily reside in whether Iran's nuclear arms project has been undermined by counterspies, but is due to the distrust of females and what they report. It is also ironic that both Gully's and Amira's brothers – as victimizers of their sisters – are never aware of their own contradictions in their arguments. That is, Meir does not trust his own elder sister as his close family member but tries to convince her that whatever he does is in her interest: "you and I aren't that different. We are still the two kids looking for a home" (*There* 148). As for Mahmoud, he is embarrassed by Gully's incisive question: "You conspire with your enemy to keep your own people in fear?" (*There* 155). The remarks from their female siblings illuminate that not only is national security often achieved at the expense of gender equality and ethics, but also show that the conflict over nuclear arms between Iran and Israel in the Middle East region does not promise peace but more wrestling with superpowers, even those far away.

Conclusion: A New Tower of Babel

Briefly referred in *How Many Miles to Basra?*, and featuring the failed expedition of Cyrus the Younger and his Greek mercenaries deep into Persia, alongside Alexander the Great's intention of enshrining the beheaded generals as heroes, *The Anabasis* not only provides an archetype that runs through Teevan's war trilogy, but also exemplifies how the Other is demonized, (mis-)interpreted, and (mis-)treated. What should be noted is that, in spite of the playwright being Irish, all three of these plays were commissioned, developed and premiered in the UK and were largely focused on the political relationship between Britain and the Middle East. More interestingly, London's Tricycle Theatre, where *The Lion of Kabul* and *There Was A Man, There Was No Man* were produced, has been a renowned venue for staging realistic plays severely critical of political issues in Britain and which alert the public to issues concerning social injustice, particularly in relation to the working class.[14]

One may thus have doubts about Teevan's political leanings in his writing, and place his works in the British rather than Irish canon. Nonetheless, such labeling and the intention of sustaining political divides have seemed to Teevan to be ideological and irrelevant: "[w]hen an Irish Playwright from either North or South writes a play about, for want of a better term, 'the human condition' he is an Irish writer, but when he writes about the Northern Troubles, he's bloody Northern Irish" (Teevan, "The Boards and The Border" 60). It can therefore be assumed that what concerns him is the attempt to create the Other, or the marginalizing of those with critical opinions in political and non-political scenarios, which should be more consciously inspected. Although the conflicts presented in this war trilogy continue, explicitly or implicitly, from the historical rivalry between major religious and political persuasions in the Middle East, whether they be Judaism and Islam, modern democracy and feudalism, individualism and dictatorship, or other ideological divides, the gaps are seemingly not bridged but often result in more threats from weapons that can cause mass destruction.

This archetype about creating a hero and justifying a preferred interpretation is manifest in the way in which war news is produced in *How Many Miles to Basra?*. However, only through Ursula does the audience get to know these soldiers in a personal way and is able to witness those untold or twisted stories in the war news, even though Ursula also fails to present Stewart, the commanding officer, through a tragic heroic narrative intended to impress the news agency in London. More specifically, the truth that Ursula covers up about Stewart, but which is understood by the audience, is that his insistence on fulfilling the last wish of a Bedouin is to make expiation for his having killed an Irish girl by accident when stationed in Northern Ireland. He is also a husband who constantly betrays his wife when serving overseas. Therefore, Ursula's aspiration of sanctifying Stewart as a national hero in a documentary she hopes to make cannot be justified due to her personal feelings. Needless to say, the

---

[14]   *How Many Miles to Basra?*, as mentioned earlier, was first broadcast on BBC Radio 4 in 2004 and later staged at West Yorkshire Playhouse in Leeds in 2006.

news broadcast via the radio from London about British soldiers being attacked in Iraq contradicts the facts that the audience have just witnessed on stage and appears to be farcical and ironic in the play.

The Lion of Kabul also presents a version of how a political incident can be interpreted differently when incompatible agendas are involved, and challenges the assumption that the acquisition of the English language may assimilate the Other and bridge the gap between different cultures. That is, although both the UN representative and the Islamic mullah can communicate in fluent English, their divergence of opinion has little to do with the language *per se* but the essentially different ethical values held by the West and the Islamic community in general. The historical traumas arising from relevant conflicts also prevent recognition of the failure of their faiths and moral idealism.

With greater irony, in *There Was A Man, There Was No Man*, the espionage and counter-intelligence activities of Iran and Israel intensify the competition over nuclear arms and keep neighboring countries under the threat that such weapons could be deployed. The threat, being open-ended, thus becomes "a paradox [...] contain[ing] a deeper truth beyond the simple logic of language" (*There* 144), thus profoundly worsening the regional tension with unexpected terrors. Consequently, few individuals can be spared from the manipulation of the state but become part of it, thus defining their relationships with others, including family members. All they can do is to survive with the fear lingering in the history and live with the lies, which leads to Gully criticizing her brother by saying that he "fear[s] internal opposition more than [he] fear[s] [his] enemies" (*There* 155).

As well as demonstrating Teevan's particular concerns for the Middle East crisis and its enormous impact on civilians, these plays, when considered in a wider context, can be seen as sharing the humanitarian appeal of many of Teevan's other plays and adaptations. Examples of the latter include *Iph...* (1999), adapted from the Iphigenia of Euripides, and *Svejk* (1999), which was inspired by Jaroslav Hašek's novel *The Good Soldier Svejk*.

Iph... highlights a woman's plight when the state expects her to sacrifice herself for the common good. This corresponds to the moral struggles underscored not only in *There Was A Man, There Was No Man* but also as a common experience in a patriarchal society where women's rights over their bodies are usually ignored. Iphigenia states: "our lives should not be lived for just ourselves alone" (*Iph* 70). On the other hand, *Svejk*, set against the backdrop of World War I, focuses on the "dehumanizing nature of war and the brutality of life lived in a state of fear," as a reminder to audiences of "a seismic event not unlike 9/11," as stated by Teevan in an interview (Dewhurst 248). These plays can be studied alongside Teevan's Middle East trilogy as being thematically linked but there is also room for further research by seeing them as cultivating a non-western viewpoint of terrorism and the violence it incurs, be it cognitive, mental or physical.

Teevan's engagement with issues in relation to war, human rights and terrorism, and his theatrical focus on conflicts in an international context, reveal his intention in calling for public attention to be directed towards imminent and existing crises in our global village. His works not only show how younger Irish playwrights are accommodating themselves to global issues by making use of cross-cultural materials, but they are also demonstrating how localities are affected, for good or ill, by both local and global forces. A study of Teevan's dramas can therefore spark a new perspective and show how audiences can be brought to face a new political framework that accommodates diverse identities and allegiances as well as their ancestral heritage. Most importantly, such a study could enable a more effective dialogue to be initiated that could lead to a more peaceful world.

VIII. Voices from Two Theatrical Others: Labor Issues in the Theatres of Ireland and Taiwan

Introduction

At first appearance, the working classes of Ireland and Taiwan do not appear to have much in common, living on opposite sides of the world and speaking unrelated languages. Further, the two countries have never established standard diplomatic relations or had much cultural exchange. The leaders of their labor unions do not engage in reciprocal visits, nor do they support each other on relevant issues. Nevertheless, the working classes of the two countries have affected each other at a distance, long before the term "globalization" arose as the focal point of attention toward the end of the twentieth century and transformed social, economic, and cultural situations worldwide. Specifically, Ireland has borne the unpleasant consequences of Taiwan, and other Asian countries, dumping their low-priced and machine-made products on other countries since the 1960s. The consequences, interestingly, are illustrated in Frank McGuinness's 1982 play, *The Factory Girls*, which portrays Irish women workers' failure to maintain their production of hand-made shirts after machinery has taken the place of human labor: "do you know what a flooded market means? Shirts selling for half nothing from Korea and Taiwan" (34).[1] This mention of Taiwan, though brief, suggests that Taiwan should not be excused for its role in causing rising unemployment in Ireland in the mid-twentieth century, although Ireland may also have benefited from transforming its economy from reliance on labor-intensive farming to high technology. Ireland's (pre-crash) title of "Celtic Tiger" and Taiwan's title of "Asian Little Dragon" was at the expense of socially marginalized workers. What is worth noticing is how, due to their under-representation in the public domain, lack of education, and the domination of transnational enterprises, workers in the two countries have been largely disadvantaged and their interests are often ignored. Only a small number of playwrights, particularly those with a working-class background, have attempted to mark the vicissitudes of their lives with certain social agendas. This chapter will explore the similarities, differences and contradictions in the theatrical representations of workers and the social and political concerns

---

[1]   The distant but influential interactions between Irish and Taiwanese workers are discussed later in this article, including an analysis of female aspirations in McGuinness's *The Factory Girls*.

common to both countries. Interest will be focused most particularly on how contemporary Taiwanese playwrights create new dramaturges to illustrate new representations of exploited laborers and empower their once-suppressed voices. A post-colonial approach will thus be adopted to examine the deprivation that has persisted into this century's era of globalization.

Ireland and Taiwan are often treated as comparable subjects, in that geographically they are both small island countries on the fringe of a continent and liable to isolation. Economically, they do not possess substantial natural resources; politically, there is a history of tense relationships with their neighbor: Great Britain is Ireland's former colonizer, while China is an emerging world power which takes Taiwan for granted as part of its territory. The working classes, as the silent but essential foundation of the industrial development of both countries, are objects easily neglected and unnoticed. However, Irish and Taiwanese playwrights, some with blue-collar backgrounds and sensibilities toward the deprived, have dramatized their nations' dilemmas and concerns as a way that calls attention to social inequalities, unsettling national male-dominated social hierarchies. Moreover, many Taiwanese and Irish women laborers are still subjugated by ideologies which can hardly be resisted, Confucian or Catholic. Without other role models available, many women workers continue to be silent, submissive, and self-restrained in the context of male-centered families.

Despite liberation from colonialism, the working class may remain "re-colonized" or continuously subjugated by political antagonisms, literary censorships (against leftism), denominational vendettas, local corporations and transnational enterprises dominate, and working-class subjectivity remains vague and divided. Oppression may also come from within workers' social circles or unions. The dramas which this chapter will discuss illuminate, to differing degrees, the working class sub-culture and the prejudices which force the working classes into the social margins. In this way, they attempt to provide a voice for the deprived and to construct a recognizable identity with particular social agendas.

In the post-colonial perspective, theatres are perceived not only as places of entertainment, but also as centers for the exposition of different self-reflexive responses to national formation. Playwrights do not always endorse "the pedagogical" discourse of nationalism, socialism, or religious ideologies, but, as proposed by Bhabha ("Dissemination" 293-322), instead maneuver the power of "the performative" to critically examine political and cultural intricacies. In Bhabha's view, "the performative," which applies repetitious, recursive strategies in nation formation, conflicts with "the continuist, accumulative temporality of the pedagogical," in that the former always "intervenes in the sovereignty of the nation's self-generation by casting a shadow between the people as "image" and its signification as a differentiating sign of Self, distinct from the Other of the Outside" ("Dissemination" 146-147). Acting as meta-novelists, some playwrights challenge conventional dramaturgies by presenting the fictional and the real in more ambiguous ways, questioning authority, omniscient authorship, and historical chronology. This chapter considers how dramatists jeopardize the pedagogical given, noting how socially marginalized characters interact with the politically and economically advantaged, and how dramatists produce recursive strategies. Issues of social hierarchy, gender, and politics are considered, as well as how some working-class dramas create a "third space of enunciation," or a "contradictory and ambivalent space," for the isolated and unprivileged (Bhabha, "Dissemination" 35, 37).[2] This chapter will attempt to reconstruct the "third space of enunciation" of the working class particularly through the experimental tent theatre of Chung Chiao in Taiwan.

The chapter focuses on several plays that address class issues with a distinctly political, but not necessarily socialist, agenda: Fred Ryan's *The Laying of the Foundations* (1902); Sean O'Casey's *Juno and the Paycock* (1924); Brendan Behan's *The Big House* (1957); *Castrated Rooster* (1943), by Wen-huan Zhang and Tuan-qiu Lin; and *The Wall* (1946), by Guo-xian Jian and Fei-wo Song.[3] The current chapter will also consider the Uhan Shii Theater Group and the Assignment Theater Company, founded respectively by Ya-ling Peng and Chiao Chung, with the agenda of addressing the exploitation of laborers in the age of industrialization and globalization.[4]

---

[2]   The "third space of enunciation" is phrased by Bhabha as a mode of articulation, referring to a hybrid identity emerging from a contradictory and ambivalent space. This "space" "m[ight] open the way to conceptualizing an international culture, based... on the inscription and articulation of culture's hybridity" (Bhabha, *Location* 38). It aims to blur and test the boundaries and limitations of existing identities and culture.

[3]   Jain was a novelist and playwright whose work was banned, and he disappeared during the 2-28 Massacre in Taiwan. Song was a cultural activist and radio broadcaster

[4]   Other plays which also deserve mention in this context include A. Patrick Wilson's *The Slough* (1914); Oliver St John Gogarty's *The Blight* (1917); Daniel Corkery's *The Labour Leader* (1919); James Plunkett's *The Risen People* (1958); John Arden and Margaretta D'Arcy's *The Ballygombeen Bequest* (1972); and Jimmy Murphy's *Brothers of the Brush* (2001). The first three were premiered at the Abbey Theatre. *The Slough* was regarded as the first play at the Abbey Theatre that specifically addressed Irish urban poverty and was written nine months after the Great Lockout of 1914, "indict[ing] the political and economic structure of the city for its urban conditions and to arouse his Dublin audience's sympathy by exposing the plight of Dublin's starving poor" (Burch 66). The effectiveness of these dramas lay in the fact that the working-class struggle was brought to the Abbey's predominantly middle-class audiences. *The*

The "New Theatre" movement (1923-1936) was initiated by a group of Japanese-educated Taiwanese elites, some with leftist leanings. They aimed to create new plays with Taiwanese scenarios, using more refined styles. The pioneers were the Star Drama Society, founded by Wei-xian Zhang in 1924, and the Ding-xin Society, and they garnered a great deal of critical acclaim. The Pacific War brought this dramatic movement to a halt after 1943.[5] Most of the "New Theatre" scripts are no longer extant, and are traceable only sparingly through secondary sources such as memoirs and newspapers.[6] Martial law from 1949 to 1983 further cut off Taiwanese intellectuals from the theatrical legacy of their "New Theatre" predecessors. Consequently, there are only a few plays which challenge sensitive labor issues. Zhang's *Castrated Rooster*, which was commissioned by the Hou-sheng Drama Society, was performed in 1943 and was probably the final play of the movement. It was banned by the Japanese for having characters refer to Taiwanese folklore. Nevertheless, Zhang's original short story is widely recognized as a masterpiece, and it is one of the very few "New Theatre" stories which still returns to the stage from time to time, most recently in a 2009 adaption by the Tainaner Ensemble at the National Theater in Taipei.[7] Jian's and Song's plays provide

---

     Wall, by Jian Guo-xian, portrayed the huge social gap between rich and poor, was produced before the 2-28 Massacre.

[5]   The details of the "New Theatre" movement can be seen in Chiu Kuen-liang's *Old and New Dramas and his Taiwan Theatre and Cultural Development: Memories and Civil Perspectives*; *New Theatre Research "Castrated Rooster": The Comparison of Presentational Activities Between 1940's and 1990's* by Mo-chun Jiang, details all recorded performances by 1997.

[6]   For possible reasons for this loss, and for the history of theatrical productions, see, for example, *A History of Cinema and Drama in Taiwan*, by Su-shang Lu, and also *Taiwan's New Theatre Movement Under Japanese Rule*, by Yang Du. In 1991, Chiu Kuen-liang expended Lu's and Yang's studies to cover "new dramas" after 1936 in *Old and New Dramas: A Study of Taiwan's Dramas under Japanese Rule (1895-1945)*. These publications, however, are mostly sociological and historical, and do not consider textual sources which would help to reconstruct the neglected experiences of laborers. In contrast to other forms of literary endeavor, research into theatre during the Japanese ruling period is very limited.

     When writing up this article, the author attempted to approach the families of a few playwrights for scripts; for instance, that of Qian-yun Chen, the renowned organizer of Xun-feng Theatre Group active from the 1930s to 1940s. According to his family, the scripts of his theatre might have been either destroyed out of fear during the "White Terror," or simply lost during several home moves. It is likely that the unavailability of scripts is due largely to political considerations of the period. Public awareness of the historical significance of those playscripts came too late. Chen himself no longer gives interviews. A record of Chen's contributions is provided in Chiu Kuen-liang's *Floating Stage: The Development of Taiwanese Professional Theatre* (227).

[7]   Zhang's original short story was first published as a short story in Japanese and has had a number of translations. The original script for the 1943 premiere has been lost; the

an in-depth understanding of the social contexts of the following period, during which the Kuomintang (KMT) government retreated to Taiwan, while the contemporary Taiwanese theatres of Peng and of Chung show how the critical agenda of the "New Theatre" has been restored through groundbreaking dramaturgies.

In the case of Ireland, although early scripts are still likely to be available, the public suspicion of playwrights' political motives and denominational leanings would often dismay those who wanted to dramatize the truths they perceived. Riots following the premieres of W.B. Yeats's *Cathleen ni Houlihan* and J.M. Synge's *The Playboy of the Western World* are notable examples from the early twentieth century, even though these playwrights contributed to the revival of Irish culture and identity by highlighting working class experience in rural and urban areas.

The Irish and Taiwanese dramas analyzed below, though not quite inter-textualized in terms of their plots and characters, will place them into a critical and international perspective. In other words, the intertextuality, if discernable, lies in the social, or sometimes socialistic, concerns that playwrights hold for the lower stratums of the working class.

The Long Wall/War between the Classes

Irish and Taiwanese playwrights in the early twentieth century approached colonial bureaucracy and social corruption in a similarly Ibsenian style. Their shared approach testified not only to the effectiveness of modern dramaturgy in dissecting social issues, but also to their intention of making the theatre "perfomative," in contrast to "the pedagogy" of capitalistic and other prevalent mechanisms. One example is Fred Ryan's *The Laying of the Foundations*, which was staged by the Irish National Drama Company in 1902, and which dealt with the conditions of tenement dwellers. Ryan exposed how jerry-builders and landlords would make fortunes by evicting tenants and using the land for other purposes. In this play, the tenements are demolished to make way for an abattoir, thus showing how the underclass and poultry are alike strangled for the benefit of the rich. The evicted tenants and their families become homeless or, if lucky, find temporary shelter in an asylum. No working-class characters ever appear on stage, but their living conditions ("unfit for beasts") and impoverishment are constantly brought to the audience's attention through a socialist protagonist, Michael, who is also the son of a member of a building syndicate. The father and his contractors care only about

version used in this article was translated by Ming-tai Chen and collected in *Complete Works: Zhang Wen-huan*, vol. 2, published in 2002. According to Jiang, at least five amateur and professional theatre groups have worked on productions of *Castrated Rooster* in Taiwan since 1990.

maximizing profit through using "the worst class of yellow brick and... the cheapest stuff" for a new asylum (Ryan 30). The "rights of labor' are for the most part absurd to the builders, who support Irish patriotism only when it can maintain their profit: "[patriotism] doesn't run to two shillings a week for an Irish workman. Patriotism, to the capitalist, is for use only at election time" (Ryan 28, 32). The class distinctions appear to be almost inviolable, while Michael, the young inheritor of the syndicate and a city architect in charge of public security, is firmly opposed to his father's the contractors' the municipal jobbery. His stance as a socialist is typified by his refusal of a bribe and insistence on justice as the basis for building a new Ireland:

> We are building a new city and we must build square and sure. In the city of the future, there must be none of the rottenness which you and your class made in the city of old; in the new city you will have no place... The city whose foundations are laid in Liberty and Truth... The city of the future demands it. It can be nothing else but war. (Ryan 36-37)

Ryan's play is socialist propaganda rather than a work of art, directing the audience to see current Irish troubles as a struggle between capitalists and proletarians, or between exploiters and the exploited, in contrast to a nationalist perspective. This socialist, or leftist, influence also gave intellectuals in Taiwan a theoretical basis for how the oppressed could be liberated from their downtrodden condition. Some of the Taiwanese elite involved in the anti-Japanese movement in China greeted the "New Theatre" with expectations that the movement would solidify ethnic identity and therefore strengthen cultural and nationalistic awareness; this was similar to how Irish Revivalism was received in Ireland, and it has been noted that many Taiwanese anti-imperialist advocates regarded Irish independence as a paradigm for Taiwanese cultural separation from Japan (Yang 50).[8]

Mid-twentieth century Taiwan, especially after the Japanese defeat, was marked by social corruption, inequality, price fluctuations, and political agitation, and there were the same kind of class exploitation as found in Ireland. Politically, most of the native Taiwanese elite were excluded from key government positions, and many were executed without trial during the 2-28 Massacre for suspected socialist leanings or for making anti-KMT criticisms. Disillusionment with the nationalistic

---

[8]   According to Yang, the example of Ireland was introduced by Qi-chao Liang, during his visit to Taiwan in 1911. This was at a time when the Japanese colonial government was trying hard to erase Taiwanese culture and identity. Xian-tang Lin, who hosted Liang at his estate in Tainan was one of these. However, it seems likely that Liang meant "independence" in the context of minimizing Japanese influences, rather than politically separation of Taiwan from China (Yang 50; Cai 285).

KMT government led some playwrights to turn to Marxism to explore the social functions of literature. Their devotion to the exploited – who suffered hierarchal suppression – was in expectation of building up a new nation, not necessarily independent from mainland China, which would ensure proper social development. Guo-xian Jian, Fei-wo Song,[9] He-ruo Lu, and Ming-gu Lan, among others, endowed their dramas with socialist concerns about the suppressed Other, or the proletariat, whose own voices were censored by the KMT government, and promoted a new Taiwanese literature.

Like Ryan, Jian was deeply concerned about the divisions that created an underclass, and *The Wall* has similar concerns to those of *The Laying of the Foundations*. Jain portrays two families, from very different social classes. These are the families of Jin-li Chen, an affluent and snobbish landlord and business magnate, and of Beggar Hsu, who rents a small and squalid next-door room from Chen. The stage is divided by a high wall, on either side of which Hsu and Chen lead strikingly different lives. The play begins with Chen repetitively calculating his income, identifying him as a miser at a time when a large number of families are just above the starvation line. As a landlord, he is delighted that his house is "awash with money;" he feels that "business is no different from playing a cheap trick;" and he experiences gastric distress from overeating (Jian 159).[10] By contrast, Hsu, his tenant, is ill and impoverished, barely able to afford the rent and making his son earn a living as a peddler. Class distinctions are shown even more clearly when Hsu's hungry son is forced to steal food from Chen's livestock, which are well-fed on human leftovers. Having been caught stealing, Hsu's family is evicted. Ironically, the eviction is carried out by a monk who is over-friendly with Chen and avaricious of secular wealth. Hsu, in despair, after poisoning his son and blind mother, commits suicide by banging his head against a wall. The play ends tragically with his cry of desperation:

> 'The wall, the wall! On the other side of you is rice hoarded as high as the house, with all the luxuries that only a paradise deserves, while you are only a hungry ghost on this side of the wall, scarce with food. I am so doomed in this hell that I cannot but end my life now... Oh, the wall is so thick and high that my little fists and thin arms cannot break it. Oh, the wall, the wall! Why cannot this wall be shattered? Oh, the wall, the wall!' (Jian 176)

The play, which realistically portrays the bitterness of the proletariat and contrasts it with the nouveau riche and the working class, enjoyed

---

[9]   Song Fei-wo was the pseudonym of Xian-zhang Song, and was used from the age of seventeen to express his anarchist ideals. In Song's own words, "Fei-wo" means "not I for myself" (cited in Lan, *Song Fei-wo* 65).

[10]   Translation mine.

huge success and positive reviews. A reviewer from *Xin-Sheng Daily* commented that, "*The Wall*, in order to present a contrast and dramatize the complex facets of society, is most critical of the unreasonable social hierarchy, and urges the necessity of social reform. This play, which has become popular through word of mouth, is worthy of recommendation" (1946, cited in Lan, *The Writers* 47). Another reviewer, Lin Qian-da, from *People's Directives*, elaborated on how a realistic play such as *The Wall* could promote the solidarity of the underclass, and speak to the needs of reformists:

> Arts enrich human spirituality, and human beings cannot be parted from community life and social reality. Thus, a drama that is both artistic and pragmatic must show social contradictions between the dominator and the dominated, and the struggle between the exploiters and the exploited. Only this kind of play can incur the empathy of the audience and maintain its modernity. (1946, cited in Lan, *The Writers* 51)

However, *The Wall* was banned after four runs as "unsuitable for the public" (1946, cited in Lan, *Song Fei-wo* 120) and for provoking class conflict. [11]

Ryan's *The Laying of the Foundation* and Jian's *The Wall* share similar sympathies for those in the lowest social stratum, and provide a new perspective from which social injustice can be revealed to the audience. The stage, in this way, helps formulate a socialist discourse and possible solutions to relevant social complaints. In Ryan's drama, Michael, the savior or hero, is celebrated for his courageous stand against corrupt builders, with a call for "class war." Intellectuals noted that *The Wall*'s banning "makes clearer the intention of the authorities concerned, for they expect citizens not to reveal the truth... If the government supposes that social satire is illegal, and is unwilling to overturn the ban, we could not feel more helpless" (1946, cited in Lan, *The Writers* 56).

The following year, Jian was arrested as part of the 2-28 Massacre, and he was sentenced to death in 1954. Lu He-ruo and Lan Ming-gu also perished during this period of "White Terror," while Song Fei-wo was exiled to China. [12] The KMT regime further suffocated theatrical development in Taiwan over the next four decades, until the late 1980s. Only dramas morally unproblematic and securely in line with the prevailing patriotism could be produced.

---

[11] Jian was arrested during the 2-28 Massacre in 1947 and sentenced to death in 1954.

[12] Song returned to Taiwan in 1987 and left again in 1989. Reportedly, he died in a car accident in Quan-zhou in 1992.

The "New Theatre" on Radio

The playwrights of the "New Theatre" movement also wrote radio dramas and worked as broadcasters, thus highlighting the close relationship between radio entertainment programs and political argument. [13] Song Fei-wo stated that "through the wireless I simply wanted to indirectly bring the anti-Japanese campaign into effect" (cited in Lan, "Looking for the Flagman" 27), and in an interview with Lan Bo-zhou (*Song Fei-wo* 87), he recalled that "my scripts were often based upon Jian Guo-xian's drafts in Japanese... and I was the first one who criticized the government and its policies through drama." The mobility of underground broadcasting, and of radios, allowed broadcasters to evade censorship and brought drama to those unable to attend the theatre. Radio dramas therefore reached their anticipated performative effects against the rulers and deserve serious study. [14]

Jian's *The Wall* was among the plays broadcast, and Song also produced a series of plays entitled *Tour of the God of the Land around Taiwan*, which continued to be broadcast even after the defeat of Japan. These plays told the story of how Tu-di-gong (the God of the Land), a respected household deity, dealt with the social corruption prevailing in almost every corner of the island. Tu-di-gong and his wife, both in human form, are greatly displeased with the corruption of officials and the desperation of the people. As expected (by the audience), the deity became a man of justice, fearless of revenge from social superiors. The plays' popularity derived from the truth they manifested. Although no script is extant, Song is known to have structured his plays in a lively manner, "calibrated with twists and humor" so as to "allow the social problem to be dissected more precisely" (Lan, *The Writers* 66). Song's

---

[13] The first radio station in Taiwan was set up on 16 June 1925, to Nipponize Taiwanese people and to celebrate the thirty-year anniversary of Japanese rule in Taiwan. Broadcasting lasted for ten days, and resumed on 1 November 1928. Despite its Nipponizing purpose, the station began to air radio dramas in Taiwanese from October 1942. Although there are few records as to why the Japanese government started to air programs in the Taiwanese dialect, Lu (1961, cited in Chen 39) notes that many programs during this period were war-time propaganda, and it seems likely that the government wanted to counteract underground stations which they could not censor but which were popularizing anti-Japanese sentiment.

[14] Research into radio dramas as a source of entertainment during the Japanese period has been hindered by the attitude of the KMT rulers after Japan's defeat. The KMT had a Chinese-centered historiography, and Japan's contribution to Taiwan went unrecognized. Documents were not preserved, and Japanese publications were banned, in the words of governor Yi Chen, in order "to quickly eradicate the slave mentality of Taiwanese people and to construct a revolutionary mindset" (cited in Huang 103-4). The ban effectively forbid Taiwanese elites and creative writers from using Japanese, their most familiar language, to communicate with the public.

mastery of the Japanese and Taiwanese languages also contributed to the popularity of his plays, which not only reflect the everyday situation of the underclass, but significantly deepen listeners' understanding of social problems and of their government. Jian and Song's collaboration continued until the outbreak of the 2-28 Massacre in 1947.

Similar to Song, Brendan Behan was also a prolific writer for both theatre and radio. One Behan radio drama, *The Big House*,[15] revolves around an Anglo-Irish landowner who resides in a big house, and his tenants, who can only entertain themselves in a pub ironically named "The Big House." The lives of all the characters are lived in or around "big houses," while the rigid social class structure drastically differentiates them in terms of life quality. Mr Baldcock, the landlord, has strong prejudices against the Irish: "If an ass is born in a stable, does that make it a horse?" (Behan, *The Big House* 362). In his eyes, nationalists such as Eamonn De Valera, who are jeopardizing the given superiority of the Anglo-Irish aristocracy, are rebels to be condemned. As landlords become afraid of the growing Irish unrest and grow desperate to return to England, rent collection and evictions are entrusted to local police and to land agents, represented in this play by Mr Chuckles. Agents form a new class between landowners and tenants, and take all manner of advantage behind the landlords' backs. Their lands are sequestered by agents who, politically, always fall between two stools like "a tea leaf," should there be a fortune to make (*The Big House* 374), and they justify their illicitly-taken advantages with observations such as "old Baldcock got the land off Cromwell's soldiers by using his load... the same as I'm using mine" (*The Big House* 374). The greater suffering remains that of the proletariat, who own almost nothing but are subject to all the classes above them. Mr Chuckles is presented as deserving little sympathy from the audience.

Behan, Song, and Jian, among other Irish and Taiwanese playwrights, have contributed significantly to working-class historiography, challenging the official line that is usually imposed by the social elite and/or which favors the advantaged. Nevertheless, their shared sympathy for deprived laborers does not bar them from depicting their wickedness, but rather illuminates how oppression passes down unrelentingly from one social rung to another. In *The Wall*, the monk who works for the rich landlord as a messenger to Beggar Hsu, and those who refuse to give Hsu spare change, are depicted metaphorically as the murderers of his family.

---

[15] Behan's *The Big House* was first commissioned as a radio drama in 1957, and staged at the Pike Theatre Club on 6 May 1958. It can be said that the radio served as a more economical channel for playwrights as the budget for performances was limited, and possibly had more far-reaching effects on the working-class audience nationwide, as they were unlikely to be able to afford to buy theatre tickets.

Likewise, Behan, whose father had been a house-painter, stated about community that: "I think that the Irish that I know and the Irish who I like, who are ordinary blokes, taxi-drivers, house-painters, bookies' runners – I don't say honest workers... some of them are extremely dishonest workers – but they're the people I care about" (Behan, "Meet the Quare Fella" 145). The Irish and Taiwanese playwrights under discussion seem always to present their homelands in a bitter way, although another remark by Behan can also apply to his Taiwanese comparators: "the world is divided into two classes: invalids and nurses. I'm a nurse... I'm a nurse in the sense that in my plays and in my books I try to show the world to a certain extent what's the matter with it, why everybody is not happy" (Behan, "Meet the Quare Fella" 142-143). Consequently, their characters are less the products of authorial imagination as drawn from real people with whom the playwrights once talked, drank, and celebrated life. However, they also form part of national memory, to be re-awakened, re-justified, re-built, and possibly refuted, but not easily erased.

The Silence and Defiance of Women Laborers

The experiences of lower-class women also feature in Irish and Taiwanese drama; two examples are Sean O'Casey's *Juno and the Paycock* (1924) and *Castrated Rooster* (1943), from a short story by Wen-huan Zhang and adapted for the stage by Tuan-qiu Lin.

Castrated Rooster, as discussed above, is one of the most significant works performed during Japanese rule as part of Taiwan's "New Theatre" movement. The play depicts the rise and fall of two traditional families in the 1920s, when a town is about to be urbanized. As a plan to acquire some valuable land, Yu-li, the daughter of a Chinese pharmacist, is forced to marry the only son of a local shipping magnate, A-yong. The marriage is arranged for Yu-li's father to obtain the "golden area" near a planned train station in the neighborhood of the shipping company, and for A-yong's father to procure the pharmacy as Yu-li's dowry.

As a woman laborer in a patriarchal society, Yu-li, although possessing much passion and intelligence, has no freedom to acquaint herself with other suitors, nor is she able to protest against the arranged marriage. The marriage becomes a deadly shackle, for she is expected to be a decent woman, unconditionally faithful to A-yong so as not to disgrace her family. Unfairer still are the circumstances which soon follow; A-yong's father dies very soon after Yu-li's wedding, A-yong becomes ill with malaria and is unable to work, and the government's urban planners decide not to build a railway in the anticipated "golden area" after all. Facing huge debts and lacking options but unwilling to sell her soul, Yu-li becomes a pig famer at home while also working part-time in the city, and has to endure jeers and derision levelled at her by her community.

Urban planning is a game of involving various interested parties and the government; its decisions do not necessarily benefit the working classes, but rather further disillusions them with government. Unable to resist all these subjugating forces, Yu-li can only suppress herself, comforting her husband as a proper wife: "I am pleased that you don't want to give up. You see how tearful I am now..." (Zhang 133). Lin's stage adaptation simplified Zhang's story to make Yu-li less passionate and sexual, but his adaptation consolidates the sense of patriarchal morality and fits into the general expectation of an ideal wife, whose hardships are all for others but not for herself.[16] Regardless of Lin's intention, *Castrated Rooster* shows how women laborers in a land-based farming community are constantly under exploitation and emotionally oppressed. Her tears are thus signs of all the unpleasant feelings and experiences in this arranged marriage. She is no more than an object, under double deprivation of traditional patriarchy and Japanese rule. Both Yu-li and A-yong are the embodiments of the "castrated rooster," which is not only physically incomplete but dysfunctional, and they both have to bear the capitalistic, colonial, and patriarchal violence that casts them from the social center to the margin.

Yu-li's story exemplifies how Taiwanese women were/are subject to the patriarchal teachings of Confucianism, whether loyal assistant or sole breadwinner. Likewise, their counterparts in Ireland were/are also under the double influence of Catholicism and Victorian culture, often restricted to the domestic arena as "the angel in the house." Specifically, most women in Taiwan have to fulfill patriarchal obligations, behaving in accordance with the "three rules and four virtues of obedience", as Confucian teachings prescribe. Self-esteem is bound up with devotion to sustaining the dignity of their fathers, husbands, male siblings, and relatives. The same expectation is also applicable to Catholic Irishwomen, who should by all means honor their husbands: "if [women] want to find out about something, ask their husbands at home. It is a disgraceful thing for a woman to speak in church" (1 Corinthians 14: 35). Unmarried women should be as "consecrated virgins," and restrict themselves from any intimacy with men. This highly conservative ethos in Taiwan and Ireland thus prevented female workers from being prominent in labor movements, and usually from leadership positions. Only in recent years

---

[16]   As noted in footnote 7, the original script has been lost. However, the stage version referred to in this article is believed to be closest to that of the premiere, although the ending is different from that of the original short story. In this stage version, Yu-li is consistently faithful to her husband in her arranged marriage, while in the short story she has a love affair with an artist, with whom she later commits suicide. Yu-li's striving for freedom is remarkable, and so are the curses against her.

in Taiwan have female activists outspoken on issues of employee rights, domestic violence, female sexuality, and the rights of sex workers received some degree of respect and media attention.

In O'Casey's *Juno and the Paycock*, Juno, the mother, is the only working member of her Catholic family, in contrast to her drunkard husband, Jack Boyle, who continually evades work by feigning illness. Her son, Johnny, has lost an arm in the Irish Civil War and is thus unable to work. Mary, her daughter, joins the lock-out, as the trade union expects. The family is economically deprived by the forces around them and is almost below the starvation line. Worse, a lawyer who falls in love with Mary and makes her pregnant later brings a false message that a distant deceased relative has left them a large amount of money as a bequest. Expecting, but not having received, the money, the Boyles purchase a few luxuries on a mortgage. The whole course of events turns out to be a disaster for the family, as the lawyer disappears after taking advantage of Mary, and the Boyles fail to pay back the loan and are evicted by the landlord. Jack spends the last of their money in a pub; Johnny is killed by the IRA for being unwilling to join its campaign after losing his arm. Mary is disowned by her father and has to find shelter, with her mother, in a relative's house. This play, overshadowed by the Civil War, criticizes the war's inhuman consequences and how those in power take advantage of the underclass and drive them further into destitution.

The play has received mixed reviews. According to Raymond Williams, "O'Casey fails to dramatically engage with the "feelings of the fighters" or with the "need and the oppression" which drove them to take up arms... [the play became] the sound... of a long confusion and disintegration" (Williams 151). By contrast, Christopher Murray judged *Juno and the Paycock* to be a social drama in which the traumatic birth of the nation is "most passionately, most powerfully and most memorably dramatized," with "a greater range of vivid and original characters, male and female" (88). The mixed reviews of the play suggest that what concerns the playwright is not the social privileges enjoyed by the well-to-do, but the tyranny that is imposed on the oppressed.

O'Casey grew up in a working-class Protestant family, and was at one time secretary to Jim Larkin, a socialist leader during the 1913 Dublin Lockout. He skilfully draws the attention of the audience to the problematic natures of Irish patriotism and the labor movement, through the eyes of ignored female working-class characters and across denominational divisions. In other words, what prompts Juno to find work is not just her husband's joblessness or idleness, but also the long-term political unrest that has resulted in a widespread economic depression. She can only take a few odd jobs on an irregular basis; as for the "workers' principle," for

UNIVERSITY OF WINCHESTER
LIBRARY

which Mary is an enthusiastic, she may not have realized that its anti-capitalistic agenda also involved an anti-colonial element, as most of the economic advantage from work went to the Anglo-Irish ascendancy and British investors. It is probable that she does not even think about the fact that the trade union, whose members are largely Catholic, does not consider gender equality. Her position in the union is doubly marginalized, so that its patriarchal nature remains secure. Her out-of-wedlock pregnancy further implies her failure in this power struggle, given that the runaway lawyer not only takes her virginity and leaves her holding the baby, but also shatters the family and leads to its dispossession. Johnny's lost arm, meanwhile, makes him a damaged man with no job prospects. Ironically, the union, which has been incapable of helping those who are physically well but hungry due to joblessness, cannot secure Johnny's working rights. That he is murdered by the IRA is thus no less different from being starved to death, as he has no chance either way. The Boyles, inarguably, are under the tight control of capitalism and can survive only with extreme difficulty.

Many of O'Casey's works were banned in Ireland, including *Within the Gates*, *I Knock at the Door*, *Pictures in the Hallway*, and *Windfalls*.[17] Comparing *Juno and the Paycock* with the Taiwanese dramas of Jian, Song, and Zhang discussed above, it can be seen that their plays were banned or led to controversy most probably because of their supposed Marxist standpoint in favor of the dispossessed. Further, the working-class characters whom these playwrights portray are either ill or disabled in some way; they are thus like the "castrated rooster" which is to some extent dysfunctional, but they still manage to live on with some little dignity.

The role of working-class women as breadwinners, or as the central pillars of a family during a national crisis, means that their voices need to be taken into account in social and political analysis. The following section will therefore examine how contemporary Taiwanese and Irish playwrights delineate the ignored experiences of women of the underclass, in order to build up a working-class "her-story," within a still male-led historiography.

Social Minorities and Transnational exploitation

As discussed above, theatres can be political or "performative" spaces where dramatists express criticisms or suggest areas for reform. Theatres

---

17   Clerical antagonism against works by James Joyce, Samuel Beckett, and O'Casey prompted O'Casey to forbid all professional productions of his plays in Ireland until 1964.

can provide the audience with an escape to the unreal, or a chance of self-recognition through the stories being enacted on stage. Contemporary Irish and Taiwanese dramatists engaging with this approach pay particular attention to minorities in different corners of society, whether defined by ethnicity, geography, or economical situation.

We Are Here,[18] was written and produced in 2000 by Peng Ya-ling, director of the Uhan Shii Theatre Group.[19] The play is particularly concerned with the almost *triply* marginalized women of the Hakka Diaspora. What is peculiar about this play is that it aims, as the dramatist specifies in the prologue, to unearth "the ignored experiences of this Diaspora around the world, while their familial ethics, musical conventions, language, culture and traditional industry, of which they used to be proud, are being buried consciously and unconsciously," (Peng 237). The drama consists of four episodes, and features the lives of working-class Hakka women of differing ages and the hardships which they bear but which are largely ignored outside their community. The four episodes, though performed by different characters and consisting of disparate stories, are connected by the oldest actress carrying a blue cloth shoulder pack throughout the play. The working-class women of the Hakka Diaspora are shown to be subjected to male domination throughout their lives: as infants, they can be "exchanged" for daughters of other Hakka families as future "daughters-in-law."[20] They are mostly deprived of personal choice, or even of an identity, long before they can be aware of having one. The price for choosing their own husband is heavy, as shown by the protagonist Jiao-mei in the fourth episode. She is disowned by her family for marrying a mainlander, rather than a Hakka.[21] She is warned by her own mother that she will be "chopped into pieces of pig food," and

---

[18]   The play is available to watch online: <http://catalog.digitalarchives.tw/dacs5/System/Exhibition/Detail.jsp?OID=2510203>.

[19]   The Uhan Shii Theatre Group was established by Peng in March 1995. The actors and actresses are mostly seniors, aged sixty-five years old or older. Their repertoire consists of plays based on the real experiences of the theatre members, who come from different ethnic groups in Taiwan; these include Minnan, Hakka, and mainland-born. The aim of the group is to introduce theatrical performance to both seniors and young people, attempting to bridge the generational gap and to present the overlooked historiography of the socially marginalized. The group has toured with the Age Exchange Theatre Trust in Europe and the USA, and been well received.

[20]   This is probably done in order to maintain the purity of the Hakka Diaspora, which is constantly on the move. Also, as soon as they are able, future daughters-in-law can provide labor for a working-class or farming family.

[21]   "Mainlander" here refers to immigrants from China who are unable to speak Hakka. Their immigration to Taiwan began in the seventeenth century, and huge numbers arrived with the KMT from 1949. Mainlanders claimed most of the political and economic advantages, and tense relationships ensued with local ethnic communities.

warned: "do not ever come back home" (Peng 274). Nevertheless, those of her siblings who marry Hakka men are not necessarily guaranteed a good life, but can usually expect to be "blamed, abused, without respect, spending their whole life with endless complaints" (Peng 255). They can never be financially independent but must rely on the meagre incomes of their working-class husbands. The lack of money is a common cause of family dispute, and Hakka women are often forced to take odd jobs. Never receiving adequate attention within the patriarchal Hakka community, they often keep a blue cloth pack with them to take wherever they are exiled, and they have to come to terms with all manner of hardships.

The Hakka women in the separate episodes of the play do not know each other, although the audience can see that they share similar circumstances in that their happiness is determined by capitalism. Their individuality is usually undeveloped, and integrated within the male-led community, and they are triply marginalized by a multitude of political, economic, and cultural forces. As the Hakka community will never be a political majority in Taiwan, unlike the communities of mainlanders and Minnans, there is little political, economic, or social support they can claim. Lacking social assistance, many even choose to conceal their minority identity outside their own community. Women in the Hakka community are thus disadvantaged and always remain lookers-on from the social margins. It is ironic, but also a factor evoking sympathy, that often only when these working-class Hakka women have retired, or after their children have started their own families, that can they start to reconstruct their own individualities. Peng's Uhan Shii Theatre Group therefore provides these senior amateur Hakka men and women with a chance to demonstrate themselves as artists.

While *We Are Here* provides a voice for largely-neglected working-class women on the social margin in Taiwan, Frank McGuinness's *The Factory Girls* might be its Irish counterpart. *The Factory Girls* realistically exemplifies how Irish female workers are subjugated by local patriarchal forces, and, distantly but influentially, by Taiwan's extensive export trade. Superficially, the Irish and Taiwanese working classes have never shared any reciprocal relationships, but Irish workers have been affected by Taiwan's cheap labor and low-priced exports; this is documented in *The Factory Girls*, as quoted at the beginning of this chapter. The low-paid Hakka women workers of Taiwan, along with other ethnic groups, have caused female factory workers in Ireland to lose their jobs. Underpaid and aware of the threat of being laid off, the women workers in *The Factory Girls* go on strike by locking themselves inside a factory, disregarding the condemnations of the parish priests and pressure from their own community. Although Taiwan is mentioned only in passing, it can be argued that McGuinness intended to show how workers, exploited by a socially privileged class, can clash across borders. The winners will never be the exploited but the entrepreneurs, who not only dominate their human resources but enjoy all the social and economic advantages that industry brings.

What makes *The Factory Girls* special among working-class dramas is not only that it revolves around issues concerning the working conditions of a small factory in Donegal, "a jiggeldy-piggeldy bit at the top of the country" remote from Dublin, but that the factory is presented as an epitome of the power conflict between the classes during the early stages of globalization (*Factory* 23). That is, a global market can be of little benefit to those who are always on the lowest social run, and they continue to be exploited. In McGuinness's observation, Irish entrepreneurs facing massive imports from abroad and possible bankruptcy are rarely concerned with the welfare of employees, but always on maintaining their pecuniary advantage: "A unit of production that I need to see go out this factory quicker and in greater numbers if against all the odds I'm to make this hole of a place survive" (*Factory* 37). To increase the factory's output of hand-made shirts and in the face of machine-made imports, the owner sacks older employees, cuts salaries, and, worst of all, disallows the workers from taking breaks. These female workers are therefore turned into cheap "slaves" competing against machinery, and describe themselves as such (*Factory* 33).

Ironically, the workers' union takes a condescending attitude toward these female laborers, who can get support from nowhere else and so resort to rioting. The union disapproves, and indeed helps the factory owner to turn down their petition, resulting in more tension between the oppressors and the female working class. The male representative from the union, Bonner, boldly condemns senior workers who do not accept "voluntary redundancy" as "very foolish" (*Factory* 35). Lacking community support but under tremendous pressure, these women workers are greatly isolated, or even demonized for not behaving with proper respect toward God.

McGuinness, by depicting a rather small-scale Irish riot in a remote shirt factory which is close to being closed down due to imports from Taiwan, demonstrates that the exploitation of the working class is transnational. In both *The Factory Girls* and *We Are Here* inadequately educated female workers are deprived of career choices but devote themselves to working primarily for their families. *We are Here*, as noted above, shows how Hakka girls would be exchanged with other families to provide labor from a very young age. There is no independent female role model for them to aspire to in their community. In *The Factory Girls*, women have to support themselves by either "tak[ing] the boat [to emigrate] or getting married" (*Factory* 45). Those who are unable to get married and cannot afford a passage abroad have to find a factory job, as the Irish economy was so depressed at the time. They ask: "where will [Irish men] get the work to support us?" (*Factory* 45). Compared with the frequently-abused and underrepresented Hakka women, the Irish female workers, though not physically injured in *The Factory Girls*, suffer a similar mental suffocation. However, whether or not they choose to riot against the given power structure, their action will hardly change the fact that they are born to be "martyrs" on the social fringe, lacking choices. If working conditions remain unimproved and there is continuing and relentless deprivation of workers, "martyr" looks set to remain a current term in the context of globalization. A transnational corporation will probably be more desperate to find cheap labor from across national boundaries, but this will leave class conflicts unresolved and lead to prolonged suffering.

Although the reference to Taiwan in *The Factory Girls* implies that Taiwan gained the upper hand in the 1980s through cheap exports, its success actually resulted in even worse conditions for Taiwanese workers during the following two decades. The enormous impact of transnational enterprises on the disadvantaged working class, although not fully developed in *The Factory Girls* and *We Are Here*, resonates in the productions of the Assignment Theater Company, founded in 1996 by Chiao Chung. Unlike the dramas discussed above, most of Chung's plays are in the style of magic realism, and are often produced in an open-air tent with an explicit concern for the most deprived of the working class in the age of globalization. The "assignments" to which his tent theatre is committed, according to the playwright, include "to accommodate those completely broken souls in the dominion of imperialism and capitalism; the tent is thus a performative arena in which these souls can be conjured up through imaginative power struggle," and so counteract the conventional, capitalistic manner of performance (Chung, *Magic Tent Theatre* ix). Specifically, most of Chung's characters have been injured or poisoned during the process of manufacture, or are characters on the social margin whose lives have been directly or indirectly subject to the actions of gigantic native and foreign corporations.

One example is *The Platform of Memory*. A-gen is a victim of dioxin pollution to which he has long been exposed in a hardware factory; Little Red and Shen Hui suffer from radiation poisoning emitted by a nuclear power station. In *The Hotel at Sea* (2001), a group of nameless, illegally-hired Chinese fishermen work night after night in fishing vessels that offer little comfort. *The Darkness of Tide* (2004) deals with a larger number of people at the very bottom of the society, and their much-ignored voices; for instance, foreign brides living with domestic violence, illegal immigrants who are drowned; a dying veteran who has given most of his life to fighting in the civil war but received little in return; homeless and aboriginal people who are desperate for social recognition. These socially under-represented characters and the open-air venues substantiate a distinctive collective discourse and aesthetic, providing "an alternative to the highly stylized and commercialized mainstream theatres" (Chung, *Homesickness* 188).

By illustrating the misery of the socially marginalized, Chung's dramas challenge not only imperialistic capitalism but also social bureaucracy and stereotypes of the blue-collared. In this way, he reveals the distressing facts of gender inequality and the unequal distribution of social welfare. The playwright's magic realism allows the traditionally less attended working class to freely express their experiences and dreams in a convention that is more creative than is the case with naturalistic dramas. On the other hand, the visualization of neglected communities serves as a healing practice through which mentally scarred individuals may vent their resentments and rebuild their identities, although the harm caused is unlikely to be lessened so long as the tide of globalization keeps coming in. In terms of theatrics, Chung's magic realism is a significant breakthrough in the dramatization of social and humanitarian issues. That is, his plays create a platform on which the socially suppressed can visualize their dreams, unconstrained by traditional realism. Chung's series of tent dramas thus portrays exactly working conditions endured under the cloak of economic success. Notably, his theatre does not have a regular audience like other commercial theatre companies, but his non-mainstream, tent theatre allows him to conduct many theatrical experiments in characterization, theme, and setting. His theatre is, in the post-colonial sense, more "performative" and conceptually radical, and in practice unerringly resists the transnational exploitation which subjugates lower-skilled laborers during the process of globalization. [22]

Conclusion

The story of Taiwanese dramas on labor issues as discussed in this chapter contains a hiatus between the 1940s and the 2000s. This is because of unrelenting censorship between 1949 and 1987 which left Taiwanese theatres and other media with few innovative dramas to produce, and which prescribed either patriotic and anti-communist or apolitical works.

---

[22] Another notable play is *The Story of Nei-Wan* (1994), written and directed by Juan-juan Chiu, founder of the Corn Field Theatre. This retrospective play documents the deprived life of miners during the period in which Taiwan was in a transition from farming to industrialization. Miners transferred to cement plants, which offered the most benefits but took little responsibility for deaths or injuries. These miners contributed to the globalization of Taiwan's industries, but their lack of education and voice have meant that their contribution has not been well documented.

Critical plays on sensitive labor issues and social corruption like Jian's *The Wall* are scarce, as they tended to irritate the KMT. Most media "consciously or unconsciously served themselves as a tool of propaganda for the ruling regime, and promoted the expected loyalism to the KMT/state" (Chen 76); KMT censorship resulted in self-censorship.

Irish artists also had to deal with "The Censorship of Publications Bill," passed in 1928 and only gradually relaxed in the late 1970s. This censorship was not against alleged communist influences, as was the case in Taiwan, but rather had a moralistic mission of forbidding obscenity and information about abortion. This official censorship brought about a "spiritual emptiness" which disabled Irish artists from producing new dramas as remarkable as those of their predecessors (Merriman 148). Once censored, playwrights in Ireland and Taiwan could only look inwards for insular and safe topics, rather than trying experimental theatrics. However, it in turn gave impulse to the playwrights of the next generation to produce works which either express critical views or are experimental. Taiwanese plays by Peng and Chung, for instance, are celebrated for their unconventional innovation and theatrical significance. It is worth noting that Chung and Peng, like their predecessors, Jian, Song, and Lu, and a contemporary critic, Lan, are all of Hakka origin. This does not mean that there are few playwrights of other ethnic origin prominent in Taiwan, but Hakka playwrights, being an ethnic minority, seem to know how to create plausible works from their usually harsh and exploitative everyday experiences. Ireland's Fabulous Beast Dance Theatre, established in 1997, can be viewed as a counterpart of Chung's experimental theatre, with a new dramaturgy that "fuses the visual immediacy of dance with the narrative strength of theatre" (Fabulous Beast 2010). One key difference between Chung's theatre and Fabulous Beast is that the latter has made a successful transition from local experimental group to globally-renowned commercial project, while their productions are no less artistic and creative.

Having examined different styles in representing labor issues on Irish and Taiwanese stages, it can be seen that playwrights in both countries have endeavored to give voice to the politically and economically marginalized. They take either a journalistic approach to the working class, or audaciously try a mixture of experimental dramaturgies: from naturalism to magic realism, framed stage to open air, professional playwriting to amateur story-telling, and narrative drama to dance theatre. Ireland and Taiwan, culturally and politically, have both experienced a de-colonial process; many nativists and intellectuals have strived to raise public awareness of lost tradition by reviving local languages or ethnic identities. Working-class dramas should thus be given more recognition within discussion of nation formation in Taiwan. Significantly, although

Jian, Song, and Zhang always delineated the social problems of their times through an idealized, socialist lens, their plays were mostly produced in Taiwanese, a language most familiar to their less educated native audience, rather than in Japanese, a foreign tongue which can easily reveal a self-endorsing elitism.

The Irish playwrights discussed in this chapter, from Fred Ryan to Frank McGuinness, do not appear to have considered language issues, and their work is in English rather than Gaelic. Although the public prevalence of English in Ireland is due partly to a failure of cultural nationalism in the early twentieth century, the use of English for theatrical performances does not bar Irish playwrights from critiquing local or transnational enterprises which subjugate personal life or the State. It has been suspected that globalization, once so celebrated in Ireland, has not ensured the stability of the Celtic Tiger, but has rather triggered an increasing number of redundant, low-skilled (migrant) workers. Irish laborers, both local and migrant, are still heavily exploited in the global market. In both locations, workers have become similarly aware of the imperative need for counteracting the exploitation of cheap labor. Theatrical performances may not bring immediate relief to the unemployed or the exploited, but the collaboration of playwrights across national borders, in different forms, can help create a securer space of enunciation, as Bhabha suggests, in which laborers can identify with each other and their pending challenges. They may be able to forge an alliance, rather than, as McGuiness prophesies in *The Factory Girls*, remaining as foes or competitors in a global sweat factory. The working classes of Ireland and Taiwan, co-acting more cohesively and amplifying their voices in this age of globalization, might more effectively resist (in)visible powers wishing to exploit them. The power they accumulate will only be louder through words on stage, and it will set an inspiring example for those still suffering in the Third World.

IX. Samuel Beckett in Taiwan:
Cross-cultural Innovations and Significance

2006 has been notable in world theatre as the centennial of the birth of Nobel Prize-winning writer, Samuel Beckett, with a series of festivals, conferences, book launches, and theatrical performances around the world. These celebrations almost coincidently characterized Beckett as one of the most distinguished Irish playwrights, although his Irishness is so vague that favorable critics, such as Vivian Mercier, Sighle Kennedy, Sinead Mooney, and Eoin O'Brien, could not persuade all reviewers with their book-length expositions.[1]

It could be argued that the centennial festivities, to some degree, reinitiated the unsolved debate in that Beckett's dramas could still be performed around the globe in places without the slightest trace of Irish influence and still be well-received in different regional, cultural and linguistic contexts. This debate, however, has lingered on since the 1950s and reinforced the cross-cultural nature of Beckett's theatre, typifying the fact that the compilers of the MLA bibliography had trouble indexing his work as French, English, and/or Irish up until the early 1980s.[2]

---

[1] A number of critics have been engaged in the debate from the 1950s up to date. Vivien Mercier was the most prominent figure who demonstrated Beckett's Irishness in a number of articles and monographs, arguing that Beckett was fully aware of the aims of the Irish Literary Revival and was well-learned in the Gaelic cultural heritage, sharing the satirical tradition with Oscar Wilde, W.B. Yeats and James Joyce. Sighle Kennedy figured out the implicit Irish elements in Beckett's novels; Eoin O'Brien elaborated how Beckett's plays, for instance *All That Fall*, *Happy Days*, *Krapp's Last Tape* and *Waiting for Godot*, might be set in the background of post-war Dublin. Sinead Mooney, furthermore, linked J.M. Synge, Sean O'Casey and Beckett to a tragic literary tradition celebrating "ritualistic sacrifice, heroism in defeat, nobility" (478). However, Martin Esslin, an expert in the Theatre of the Absurd, demonstrated that the playwright's deep existential anguish "clearly originates in levels of his personality far deeper than its social surface" (1). John P. Harrington, in line with Esslin, rejected Irish revisionists' claims to the political nature of Beckett's drama for not "consequently construct[ing] a positive [and] evident alternative" to the Irish Troubles (190-191). The details of the debate can be found in: Kathleen McGrory and John Unterecker (eds) *Yeats, Joyce, and Beckett: New Light on Three Modern Irish Writers*; Eoin O'Brien's, "Beckett Centenary," *The Irish Times* 16 June 2006: 8; Sinead Mooney's, rev. of *Tragedy and Irish Literature: Synge, O'Casey, Beckett*, by Ronan McDonald, pp. 477-8; Martin Esslin's, *The Theatre of the Absurd*; John P. Harrington's, *The Irish Beckett*.

[2] The entry for Beckett was first located in the "French Literature" section of the MLA bibliography in 1955. From 1959 through the 1960s, his *œuvre*, located in the French section, was cross-referenced in the "British Literature" section. Only after 1981

Nevertheless, the cross-references to Beckett's identity, or identities, do not eloquently define him as a national icon out of any political correctness, but rather reveal the ambiguities that he presents, through his absurdist theatre and choice of subject matter, across national borders. However, some critics have not taken into account another fact, namely that Beckett voluntarily departed from Ireland – the "land of my unsuccessful abortion" – for France, because "the little operation [in France] is cheap, safe, legal and popular" (qtd in Nixon 43). His departure from Ireland was partially due to the effects of the stringent Irish censorship which banned three of his early novels. His disappointment about Ireland was more explicit in his displeasure about *Waiting for Godot* being labelled as an Irish play: "some Irishisms in the translation liable to mislead" (qtd in Nixon 44).[3] It can thus be appropriate to judge that the universalism of his drama was born out of his disfavor of a narrow Irish label, while he was more interested in depicting poetically the failures of existing political and cultural mechanisms and creating his own absurdist aesthetics.

To illustrate how Beckett's cross-cultural legacy has contributed to world theatre, this chapter will exemplify the contemporary theatre of Taiwan, which has gradually taken its form since the 1960s amidst the movement of modernization. Japanese theatres, like those in Taiwan, and some local critics had also approached Beckett's drama to "find possibilities in revolutionalizing or revitalizing their theatre" (Tanaka 47). Being more than a cultural bridge between Western Europe and the Far East, the avant-gardism of Beckettian theatre became an arena where young Asian directors challenged both the traditional dramaturgy and social norms, calling for a theatrical alternative, with native devices, to a political impasse. More specifically, the productions of his plays in an Asian theatre – with barely any connection to European conditions – were often endowed with an unconventional cultural agenda and led to divisions among cultural activists, in that "the theatrical 'space' and 'physiology' of Beckett do not fit those of [the traditional Japanese theatre]" (Tanaka 47). This chapter, following Tanaka's illustration of Beckett's legacy in Japan, will address how his theatre has been endowed with non-European significance and has contributed to the experimental theatre of Taiwan, giving rise to a theatre of cultural hybridity under

---

did the MLA omit these cross-references and position him in the Irish and French "Literature Bibliographies."

3   The above two statements of Beckett are taken from his correspondence with George Reavey, 8 March 1938, and with A.J. Leventhal, 26 Jan. 1956. Details can be found in Mark Nixon's , "'A Brief Glow in the Dark': Samuel Beckett's Presence in Modern Irish Poetry," *The Yearbook of English Studies* 35.1 (2005): 43-57. The three banned publications are *More Pricks than Kicks* (banned on 23 Oct. 1934), *Watt* (22 Oct. 1954), and *Molly* (23 Jan. 1956). Details can be found in Nixon's article. (*op. cit.*).

the influence of globalization, or cultural imperialism. To expound more carefully how Beckettian theatre can appeal to an Asian audience, this chapter will explore if the cultural and political antagonism of the Emerald Isle has counterparts in Taiwan. This comparison may help to elaborate the transcultural nature of his drama and its influence on world literature, opening up new polemics in regard to his universalism and implicit Irishness, and more accurately picturing his attitude towards the conventions of European theatre.

Beckett's dramas have been the most frequently presented and adapted within the experimental theatre of Taiwan since the 1960s. Most of his major plays have been introduced to the local audience. To name a few: *Waiting for Godot, Endgame, Come and Go, Footfalls, Play, What Where, Act without Words I, Act without Words II, Krapp's Last Tape,* and *Ohio Impromptu,* among which *Waiting for Godot* has often been presented in Mandarin by a number of theatre groups, and *Endgame* was once performed in the Minnan vernacular in 2004 (by the Tainaner Theatre) in response to the call of the de-Chinese movement.[4] They were, however, staged at different historical turning points for Taiwan, during the process of rapid modernization, mirroring the impact of "exteriorisation, distance, removal, and alienation" in many developing countries (Roof 147).

Moreover, the preference of young directors for Beckett's absurdist drama reflects their discontent about media censorship. That is, it was not until 1987 that martial law was lifted in Taiwan after thirty-eight years, during which time the media were subject to censorship as the nationalist government set up an official literary policy that predominantly promoted patriotic literature against the spread of socialism, as well as preserving the Chinese/Beijing culture as opposed to the fervent Cultural Revolution in Mainland China. A comparison can be made with the time when Beckett left for France in 1928. The Irish Free State had not been less insular but barricading itself into being a Catholic Gaelic society with nationalists having the upper hand, and operating a censorship no less severe than that during the period of British government, so as to "contain or limit possible Irish identities into a single abstraction" (Leverich 102). Beckett, James Joyce, George Bernard Shaw and forty-one other writers were all banned between 1924 and 1929.[5] It might therefore be observed that both

---

[4]   Apart from the nine aboriginal languages, the three major languages in Taiwan are Mandarin, Minnan and Hakka, of which Mandarin is the official language and Minnan is spoken by approximately 75% of the population. *Waiting for Godot* was first produced in 1965 by the Theatre Quarterly Association. This performance – to be reviewed later – was a failure if judged in terms of audience attendance but it made a relevant impact on young fellow artists.

[5]   It is well known that the media censorship sought, on the one hand, to ban publications that carried information on contraception and those alleged to be indecent. On the other

Taiwan and Ireland cultivated a very cloistered ethos which prompted a number of intellectuals to seek to challenge these social restrictions in the arts. Aware of such cultural predicaments, artists such as Beckett and some of his contemporaries thus chose to write in exile and introduce new theatrical styles to set against the existing conventions. Their predicaments and approaches were also recognized by young directors in Taiwan in the 1960s.[6]

One common feature shared by Beckett and the young Taiwanese directors was their strong discontent with the intense cultural movements of their times. Particularly, Beckett was known to be versed in Gaelic literature, mythic art and oral tradition (he was trusted by Joyce with making the French translation of *Finnegans Wake*) whereas he was ultimately opposed to the aims of the Celtic Revival.[7] In his 1934 essay, "Recent Irish Poetry," he was critical of the Celtic Revival that led to some Irish intellectuals becoming antiquarians without a sense of "self-perception," which other European modernists would have acquired:

> Thus contemporary Irish poets may be divided into antiquarians and others, the former in the majority, the latter kindly noticed by Mr. W.B. Yeats as "the fish that lie gasping on the shore", suggesting that they might at least learn to expire with an air. (71)[8]

---

hand, it also aimed to maintain the stability of the new nation founded on Catholic principles. Between 1924 and 1929, forty-four writers and seventy-seven books were banned. The censorship was not eased until the 1970s. For further details, see Michael Adam's, *Censorship: The Irish Experience*, p. 215, and Julia Carlson, ed., *Banned in Ireland: Censorship & The Irish Writer*.

[6]   The development of Taiwanese literature should be attributed to a few literary magazines, amongst which *Theatre Quarterly* and *Europe* in particular introduced news of European literary developments to Taiwan. They were known for acquainting local readers with the philosophy, literature, art, history, films, paintings and cultures of Western Europe. *Europe* was founded by the Overseas Chinese Students Association in France in 1965; some of their issues featured French dramatists and artists, such as Eugène Ionesco, Albert Camus, Jean Genet, Paul Claudel, Jean Cocteau, Henri de Montherlant, Jean Giraudoux, Jean Anouilh and Romain Rolland, as well as Pablo Picasso (Spain), and Samuel Beckett (Ireland). Due to insufficient funding, this magazine was unfortunately closed down in 1968 after nine issues in total. Although the circulation of the two magazines was mostly limited to those with higher education, their influences were known to be far-reaching. Two other literary magazines which are worthy of notice are *Literary Magazine* (1956-1960) and *Modern Literature* (1960-1984).

[7]   Research on Beckett's Irishness, and his extensive knowledge of Gaelic tradition and myth, has been abundant. John Fletcher's bibliographic studies on Beckett show that the playwright's knowledge of Celtic culture was by no means tangential. Laura Barge also compiled a list of articles in regard to Irish influences on Beckett's drama. See Laura Barge's, "Out of Ireland: Revisionist Strategies in Beckett's Drama," p. 204.

[8]   This essay was first published pseudonymously under the name Andrew Belis. In this article, Beckett was critical of those Revivalists for "delivering with the altitudinous complacency of the Victorian Gael the Ossianic goods," advocating the sense of

Interestingly, the young editors/founders of *Theatre Quarterly* in Taiwan, which first produced Beckett's play *Waiting for Godot* and translated *Krapp's Last Tape* in its fifth issue, was critical of the effects of reviving a conservative Chinese tradition in Taiwan and the welcoming of rapid industrialization on western standards, which, they claimed, would incur ineffectually romantic sentiments and intellectual cultural impotence. In "A Note before Performance" of *Waiting for Godot*, Daren Liu, one of the organizers, wrote as follows:

> The entire membership of Theatre Quarterly Association has deeply sensed that the current movement of modernization is tossing us around the issue of whether we should despise romanticism; of whether we could rebuild a pure modern China by both fixing the tradition and adopting the western one. We become so weak, nearsighted and head-in-the-clouds. We are uncritical, irrational, and unable to scrutinize the reality and react to it. The breadth of our mind is abortive; our creation is malnourished, and no more than an expression of anaemia and sexual impotence. We are all impotent, and our efforts only bring forth a city of impotence; what we lack is more than some bull-headedness. (266)

Observing the social contexts in which Beckett wrote *Waiting for Godot* and Taiwan's Theatre Quarterly Association produced it, we might contend that this play, on the one hand, mirrors the senses of helplessness, nihilism, speechlessness and despair that troubled young Taiwanese critics struggling for artistic creation on their own, under the media censorship as well as the tremendous burden of restoring an ancient tradition reinforced by the nationalist government in retreat from mainland China.[9] On the other hand, the choice for performance of this particular "anti-play" was a challenge to the established standards of the arts, including films and stage plays. That is, the formula of Taiwanese and imported Hong Kong films in the 1960s had been, according to Ying-Zhen Chen, "too rough to lead to any remarkable aesthetics. Moreover, Hollywood films – which had dominated the taste of the Taiwanese audience – could not be more superficial in any serious standard" (5).[10] Their dissatisfaction and frustration, therefore, "allowed the space for the introduction of intellectual trends and aesthetics from western Europe" (Y.Z. Chen 5).

"self-perception" of European modernism (71). See Samuel Beckett's, "Recent Irish Poetry," *Disjecta*, pp. 70-71.

9   The Chinese Nationalist Party (Kuomintang, or KMT), led by Chiang Kai-shek, retreated from mainland China after being defeated by the Communist Party of China in 1949. The nationalist government declared martial law for nearly five decades and turned Taiwan into a one-party authoritarian state until the 1990s. The official media policy was to maintain a tight grip, which hindered the speaking of Taiwanese vernaculars and suppressed nativist awareness.

10   Chen was one of the editors for *Theatre Quarterly*.

Chen's comments are true to a relevant degree, as the director, Gang-jian Qiu, writing in his own notes for direction in 1966, stated that, in terms of language, "no Beijing accent should be allowed on stage but that of local Taiwanese Mandarin" (279-280). It seemed to him that the Beijing accent had "paralyzed the appreciation of the audience for a long time" (Y.Q. Chen 277). It could be assumed that the abandoning of that Beijing accent, significantly, was to free dramatic practice from the so-called "standard" accent widely used in nationalist-government-funded television channels and broadcasting media.

It could be claimed that Beckett's influence on world theatre, taking that of Taiwan as an example, was the idea of the "anti-play." Half of the Taiwanese audience could not appreciate it, and left the theatre after the first act (which action was criticized by a local critic as "unmannered"), which suggests that the aesthetic taste of those invited "sophisticated few" had been pushed to its limits and would be subject to challenge (Yao 272).[11] The effects of the challenge lasted for the next few decades and laid the foundation for more experimental theatre in Taiwan. Interestingly, the organization which assisted the Theatre Quarterly Association in producing this play was the Tien Educational Center in Taipei, a Catholic organization founded in 1963 by American and European clergymen of the Society of Jesus.[12] Unlike Catholic clergy in Europe, who are often regarded as conservative, these foreign missionaries in Taiwan often provided dissenters with a protective umbrella and introduced the latest western artistic developments that could unsettle existing literary styles and values. Their contribution, if judged by the size of the audience for *Waiting for Godot*, would not have been thought to be very large at the time; however, they created a channel of cultural exchange between the West and the Far East. The introduction of Beckett's "anti-play" thus promoted a relevant reexamination of traditional Chinese dramaturgy and cultural aesthetics.

What should also be worthy of attention is the reason why Beckett's modernist drama would be of minor interest to the Taiwanese audience,

---

[11]   The audience was "by invitation only." That is why Yao would describe them as the "sophisticated few" (272). This restriction was probably because all performances, under the censorship, had to be inspected by the authorities beforehand, whereas the Theatre Quarterly Association had failed to notify them, or had refused to do so. Nevertheless, the "invitation letter" was printed in its magazine and could be retrieved by interested members of the public.

[12]   In 1976, the Tien Educational Center established the Tien Experimental Theatre Group, which was the first such fringe group in Taiwan. The clergymen also compiled Spanish, Latin, and French-Chinese dictionaries, and organized creative writing classes and social services for aboriginal Taiwanese. Some of them taught at both public and private universities, such as Fr. Frederic J. Foley S.J..

whereas *Waiting for Godot* had been performed in Paris and other major cities on more than four hundred occasions by this time. Their lack of appreciation was partially because there was no western dramaturgy that Beckett's "anti-play" could counteract in Taiwan. A supporter of the Theatre Quarterly Association was Fr. Frederic J. Foley, S.J. of the Tien Educational Center, with a doctorate in English literature from Harvard University, who consequently commented that, "as [the] audience in Taipei [was] far from familiar with western dramaturgy, a rather traditional play would more possibly ensure success" (273). Foley's comments might be tenable, while it could be argued that the audience's disinterest in Beckett probably resulted from the strong influence of non-European public agencies that operated in Taiwan. The United States Information Service (USIS) was the most dominant among them over many activities of cultural exchange, systematically introducing, translating, and propagandizing American/ western culture, providing scholarships for prospective students, and sponsoring research.[13] Noticeably, as Taiwan and the US had shared a close partnership during the Cold War since the 1950s, Taiwan was "a strategic military base against socialism, a new cultural colony [of the US], and a capitalistic society on the fringe of international politics" (Y.Z. Chen 5). The cultural exchange, to be precise, operated more in a one-way direction than mutually with the US, which westernized young people to an American standard but did not yet allow them to be intellectually critical. As a result, the rapid westernization up to the 1960s was roughly at an industrial level. The cultural values of the West, which Beckett's "anti-play" questioned, were still far from sufficiently rooted to allow for reactive impacts in a postcolonial framework.

It could further be said that, although the first production of *Waiting for Godot* in Taiwan did not make a great impression in face of the westernization apparent at the time, it attests to the consciousness that local intellectuals had of the literary modernism and theatrical experimentalism that were gradually being brought into the island, whereas the emergence of the two artistic trends had come about almost fifty years previously in Western Europe.[14]

---

[13] Fr. Frederic J. Foley, and Fr. Jack Deeney, S.J., who assisted the Theatre Quarterly Association in producing *Waiting for Godot*, are of U.S. nationality. They worked for the Society of Today's America, sponsored by the U.S. Embassy, publishing a series of pamphlets on American writers.

[14] According to a survey by Ou-fan Lee, not until the 1930s was Modernism introduced to China. It was the young editors of *Modern Literature* magazine who, in the 1960s, successfully drew the attention of the public to modernist novels written by Chinese writers (122). The Theatre Quarterly Association was closed down in 1968 due to lack of funding, and the young editors involved split up because of their incompatible interests – some turned to socialism. Nevertheless, this laid the intellectual foundation

The legacy of Beckett, interestingly, found its new life twenty-three years after that first performance in Taiwan in 1965.[15] In 1988, Stan Sheng-chuan Lai, a promising director with a doctorate in drama from the University of California, Berkeley, led a group of student actors from the National College of Arts to perform six plays of Beckett, including *Come and Go, Footfalls, Play, What Where, Act without Words II*, and *Ohio Impromptu*. What is noteworthy is that Taiwan's experimental theatre had become more flourishing and mature due to ambitious young directors, such as Lai, receiving higher degrees overseas. Lai's production of Beckett's six plays, unlike that of his predecessors from the Theatre Quarterly Association, was extraordinary by not being performed on a traditional stage, which separates actors and the audience, but in a traditional Chinese rectangular courtyard, or "Si-hey-yuan"[16] That is, the audience was to see the six plays in adjacent rooms within this Chinese courtyard. The application of environmental theatre as such seemed to Lai "a better approach to present the mental quandary of Beckett's characters and bring the audience a fresh viewing experience" ("Footfalls" 9). It can be pointed out that Lai's production is a recreation of Beckett's drama by not only re-conditioning it with a Chinese ambience but also applying an unconventional theatrical mode, namely environmental theatre, in which the audience could become greatly immersed during the performance.

According to Lai, his choice of the six plays to be performed in an environmental theatre setting was made because their characters shared a common quality of being regretful spirits who asked "who am I?" ("Beckett" 5). A bare traditional rectangular courtyard could, in his opinion, highlight these characters' failed explorations of life, their frustrations and broken memories; most importantly, the audience could understand better the torments that haunt them as episodes in the real world ("Beckett" 5). His production of Beckett's drama in a Chinese setting, on the one hand, might technically link the Taiwanese audience to a classic modernist one. On the other hand, the combination of Chinese architecture, the environmental theatre and Beckett's nihilistic drama

---

for the literary debates of the 1970s: "The Debate on Modern Poetry" and "The Debate on Regional Literature." These debates gave more shape to Chinese modernist writing.

[15]   The performance of *Waiting for Godot* in 1965 can be seen as only the first step for experimental theatre in Taiwan. It is well known that not until 1976 did Taiwanese experimental/fringe theatre become more mature. What changed Taiwan's theatrical scenario was, however, the first showcase of "Experimental Drama" at the National Taiwan Arts Education Center in 1980. "The New Match of He-Zhu," adapted from a well-known drama from the Beijing opera and produced by the Lan-Ling Theatre Group, was regarded by local critics as the most groundbreaking production (Ji 12).

[16]   "Si-hey-yuan" is a compound with traditional Chinese houses of greybricks and tiles built around a courtyard. In the old days it was a big compound of houses for wealthy families.

might have thus created a "third space of enunciation," as Homi K. Bhabha describes a hybrid identity emerging from a contradictory and ambivalent space. Specifically, it formulated a mode of articulation, and "m[ight] open the way to conceptualizing an *inter*national culture, based … on the inscription and articulation of culture's hybridity," calling into question the established identities and culture by blurring and testing their boundaries and limitations (Bhabha 38).

One of the significant features of this "third space of enunciation" is, given a postcolonial provenance, its "productive capacities" (Bhabha 38). Although Taiwan was never a European but a Japanese colony in the twentieth century, its rapid modernization has allowed for "cross-cultural exchange" in a single direction, if seen as a consequence of American cultural imperialism, and this "usually implies negating and neglecting the imbalance and inequality of the power relations it references" (Ashcroft 119).[17] Lai's production of Beckett, however, counteracted such an unbalanced exchange. That is, Lai and his contemporaries' theatrical elites, particularly those graduating from western institutes in the 1980s, chose not to be entirely subject to Beckett's dramaturgy but, more creatively, not necessarily more maturely, to utilize the signifiers of native culture. The application of environmental theatre to Beckett's plays in a Taiwanese context, as a result, engenders a spatial politics which includes, rather than excludes, new possibilities of performance, "initiat[ing] new signs of identity, and innovative sites of collaboration and contestation" (Bhabha 1). In an interview, Lai expressed his excitement about this East and West "collaboration amidst conflicts" ("Classical" 9). Lai's theatrical experiment, expectedly, set an inspiring example for his fellow young directors, leading to a number of more original productions later on.

It could hardly be denied that *Waiting for Godot* was a drama that most of the aspiring Taiwanese directors would have liked to tackle in their careers and thus to engender cross-cultural interpretations that Beckett, presumably, could not easily have predicted during his lifetime. Lai's example was followed in 1996 by Ai-ling Lu, a director receiving professional training in directing in France.[18] Her interpretation, as she claimed, was close to the original work by translating Beckett's play directly from its French edition; the pauses and silences were not omitted but only some long-winded dialogues, in order to more effectively attract the attention of an Asian audience and ensure their better understanding of the play. Most importantly, Lu introduced native theatrical elements

---

[17]   Taiwan was an on-and-off Dutch and Spanish colony from the mid-seventeenth century. Japan ruled Taiwan as a colony between 1895 and 1945.

[18]   Lu received her doctorate from the Drama department of the Université de la Sorbonne Nouvelle in 1995.

that made the play more entertaining than Lai's version. Specifically, techniques of both Chinese and western theatre were employed for the performance, such as those of Beijing ballet, Taiwanese folk opera, and Chinese cross talk (or Xiang-sheng). These innovations strategically unsettled the categories of the performances and physically created new cross-cultural dynamics to be performed on stage, as compared to Lai's application of environmental theatre. The newly added Asian elements, on these grounds, vivify what critics have characterized as the "in-betweenness" of postcolonial theatre, which allows different cultures to be transferable:

> [The postcolonial theatre is] celebrated and privileged as a kind of superior cultural intelligence owing to the advantage of in-betweenness, the straddling of two cultures and the consequent ability to negotiate the difference. (Hoogvelt 158)

Having exemplified two Taiwanese directors' interpretations of Beckett's drama, we could assume that, apart from their syntheses of western and Asian theatrical components, they were greatly concerned with the audience's accessibility to this absurdist classic. They did more than follow the stage directions given by Beckett himself but applied various cultural elements with which the local audience was familiar. Nonetheless, not all young directors were interested in producing a half-Beckettian, half-Chinese play, in effect a Chinese version of, for example, *Waiting for Godot.* Ching-mei Chu, director of an expressionist production of this play in 1997, discarded all those popular Asian elements that had been employed earlier, concentrating instead on the original, anguished nature of the play.[19] She intended to acquaint the audience with the play itself without giving it an Asian mask, except that the actors were Taiwanese and performed in Mandarin. To express the various emotions of characters, while also assuring the audience's empathy with them, Chu replaced the one and only setting – a tree – with a stepladder, which she assigned as an "ironic symbol for Didi and Gogo's endless waiting for God, rather than a ladder of hope."[20] The little boy "who carried a pair of black broken wings was to symbolize the broken hope."[21] Most importantly, Didi and Gogo were dressed up as identical "clock dolls"

---

[19] Chu belongs more or less to the same generation as Sheng-chuan Lai and Ai-ling Lu. They all went abroad for professional theatrical studies. Chu earned her Ph.D. in directing from Bowling Green State University in the USA.

[20] The quote is taken from Chu's note written before the performance and shown at the beginning of the video recording of this production. Thanks are due to Dr. Chu for her kindness in lending me the video. In *Waiting for Godot,* "Didi" and "Gogo"is short for the names of the two protagonists: Vladimir and Estragon.

[21] See the note above.

with pale makeup, through which Chu proposed to demonstrate "their distorted mentality, and the loneliness and anxiety for life of twentieth century people."[22] Precisely, their distorted mentality is shown through not only their colorless makeup but also their almost indistinguishable costume. In particular, Didi was cross-dressed, being played by an actress. By using the concept of mixed gender, it could be argued that Didi's and Gogo's individualities were erased in a highly industrialized society in which machinery is dominant.[23] The cross-dressing, which significantly turned the gender of the characters to ambivalence, attested to the mechanical standardization that demoralizes individual creativity. It can thus be observed that the expressionist dramaturgy that the director adopted in presenting the inner turmoil of the characters through their faces, makeup, body language and costumes made this play less abstract to the audience, as the characters' anger, helplessness and fear were more concretized than in previous productions.

What is noteworthy about Chu's production is that the director devised a prologue of black comedy, or farce, in which the four main protagonists become members of a circus instructed only by order and without distinct personalities. This device, apart from being relatively entertaining, might have prepared the audience for the jarring nature of *Waiting for Godot*, in which mental distortion, exaggeration, primitivism and fantasy were to be animated. It could thus be suggested that Chu's expressionist interpretation was revolutionary, not necessarily only among Taiwanese directors' productions, as she effaced the gender difference and creatively applied a number of theatrical devices so as to challenge the stage directions given in the script. It could also be maintained that Chu's production, with no recognizable Asian elements, could be appreciated without cultural constraints, as she managed to turn human inner workings "inside out" through a new stage setting.

In regard to gender, Chu's approach might be thought to be less provocative than that of Lai's new production of *Waiting for Godot* at Taiwan's National Theatre in 2001. It was Lai's second production of the

---

[22] See the note above.

[23] The replacement of the tree with other objects has been done in several other productions in various countries. Chu might have shared the view of Joël Jouanneau, a French director, who substituted Beckett's original setting: "A country road. A Tree," with a modern, disused factory. In Jouanneau's production there was no tree but an upright, huge and old electric transformer with electric wires around the stage. This modification aroused much debate, but he argued that, after studying Beckett's works in depth, the playwright must have allowed freedom in the setting and costumes as he was opposed to any authority, including an authoritative interpretation. For details, see Lu Ai-ling, "Where is Godot? When Will he Come? – A Few French Productions of *Waiting for Godot*," *Performing Arts Review*, pp. 37-38.

play, as he had directed it for his degree presentation in 1982.[24] Lai did not simply duplicate his first production, performed nearly two decades' previously, but made a few experiments. One of these was to employ two *young* actresses as Didi and Gogo, with no cross-dressing involved. This change is still an issue for debate, as Beckett himself had eventually taken legal action to ban a Dutch theatre group, Haarlem Toneelschuur, from producing *Waiting for Godot* with four actresses; "he did so because the characters he had created for this play were men, and men are different from women" (Abbott 718). Beckett's insistence on the gender of the performers is even more distinct in his own words: "[w]omen don't have prostates" (qtd in Ben-Zvi x).[25] It is therefore fair to assume that any attempt to change the gender of roles could incur an over-interpretation or an unjustifiable one. In particular, this play, though debatable, is known to have an anti-Christian nature. Lai's employment of two actresses as Didi and Gogo could thus be regarded as more than a gesture of counteracting the patriarchy of Christianity but a revelation of problems that face both women and men in the twenty-first century.

Three unconventional aspects of Lai's production are worthy of notice: the gender of the roles, the stage setting, and the Chinese translation of the title – *Waiting for Godot*. As to the choice of performers, Lai's employment of young actresses – in their early thirties – created a fundamentally different interpretation from those that highlighted the heaviness and gloominess of the original play. More specifically, instead of presenting Didi and Gogo as old, restless and tiresome, the two young actresses were playful with tender and delicate voices. That they were able to run around on stage and discuss the whereabouts of Godot with laughs seemed more entertaining, while the script itself was not much modified but simply dramatized in a different tone. The effect, expectedly, allows this tragi-comedy to be more comic than tragic, and leaves room for the audience to contemplate the would-be endless waiting for Godot of two young woman protagonists.

The consequences of changing the gender of the roles could be more effectively understood when seen alongside the change of setting. In this production, the stage was rebuilt – in bright orange – across the audience seats from the back to the front of the theatre. This design was not, however, contradictory to Beckett's stage direction, which only indicates "a country road." It could be argued that this visualization of "a country

---

[24]   Lai's first production of *Waiting for Godot*, which was for his doctoral degree in Drama, was applauded by the critics as "definitive," according to reports (Chi 6).

[25]   This is from Linda Ben-Zvi's interview with Beckett, Paris, December 1987. According to her, Beckett was "too precise a writer," believing that "women do not experience the suffering of being the play depicts" (x).

road" might be significantly closer to its symbolic meaning as "the road of life" on which life is transient.[26] The audience could therefore be provided with a rather omniscient viewpoint from both sides of the "road," silently observing Didi's and Gogo's quandaries and seeing themselves from different angles in that the opposite audience was their "mirror," as Lai noted.[27] This effect cannot be achieved with a traditional "framed stage." More interestingly, what was under the "road," or an overpass across the audience seats, was an icon of Taiwan with a blue light, symbolic of the ocean. With this stage setting, it could be suggested that the director intended to contextualize the play in a local scenario in which Taiwan is constantly troubled by its ambivalent national status due to the unresolved issue of political independence. People have been confused, agitated and disillusioned by politicians' promises, and perplexed about their own positions and individual identities amidst endless political disputes. If Lai's production reflects the local sectarian politics of Taiwan, it might be suggested that the nihilism in most of Beckett's dramas, among which *Waiting for Godot* is the classic, has its roots in Irish national questions and shows his concerns over the human condition in the cold-war era. More note-worthily, the translation of the title of *Waiting for Godot* was "Waiting for Dog-head" in Mandarin; the English title, however, remained the same. This change not only effectively dissociated the play from a Christian reading that presumes Godot would be God, but also cynically implied that it could be d-o-g that was being awaited, rather than g-o-d. A local critic, Ching-hsi Perng, thus remarked that the change of the title "[was] not necessarily blasphemous but because the director realized in depth and with pain the degradation of human nature, the hopelessness of salvation [...] Whether this play could penetrate the minds of a great number of superficial audience in Taiwan, and bring them real shocks, is not a trial for only Beckett and Lai."[28] The revised title might more accurately reflect the cynicism of human life that Beckett has produced in *Waiting for Godot*.

---

[26] A description of the stage can be found in Mo-lin Wang, Rev. of *Waiting for Godot*, dir. Lai Sheng-Chuan, *Min-Sheng Daily*, 25 Oct. 2001: A12.

[27] The expected effect of this rebuilt stage can be found on the website of the Performing Workshop, founded by Lai. See "Waiting for Godot," Performing Workshop, 1 July 2014, <http://www.pwshop.com/portfolio-cht/zht-theater/%E7%AD%89%E5%BE% 85%E7%8B%97%E9%A0%AD%EF%BC%882001%EF%BC%89/>.

[28] Ching-hsi Perng's, Rev. of *Waiting for Godot*, Performing Workshop, dir. Lai Sheng-Chuan, 1 July 2014, <http://www.pwshop.com/portfolio-cht/zht-theater/%E7%AD%8 9%E5%BE%85%E7%8B%97%E9%A0%AD%EF%BC%882001%EF%BC%89/>.

Arguably, if Lai's production was a trial for the audience, the trial was effective because the western/traditional dramaturgy of *Waiting for Godot* was discarded, and a new interpretation was introduced for an Asian audience. It could be maintained that a new understanding of the script was generated, and demonstrated what Umberto Eco stated about infinite interpretations: "a text can foresee a model reader entitled to try infinite conjectures," so as to incur multiple and contradictory interpretations (64). The "infinite conjectures" lie in the intention that the author holds while writing, but those who actively participate in the reading process, including the reader, critics, directors and performers, may tackle the limit of the playwright's intention. In other words, "[t]he question then becomes not whether intention is the best criterion by which to measure a given interpretation but rather what definition of intention one ought to use" (Quillen 44). Eco's argument for the flexibility of interpretation according to the reader's preference, which allows the keen reader to construct meaning, might thus endorse Lai's and his fellow directors' new dramaturgies. Their interpretations with Asian elements, though unconventional, are not necessarily incorrect or over-interpretations, in that they have explored and redefined the limits of the script by positioning it in a cross-cultural condition.

It could be stated that the directors – mentioned above – agreed with a common aim of the experimental theatre: "there is nothing [we] cannot try," as Ai-ling Lu elucidated in her production of *Waiting for Godot* in 1996 (qtd in Xie, D25). The productions which followed hers, by Chu and Lai, to varying degrees, were meant to acquaint the Asian audience with either an expressionist dramaturgy or local geographic elements. Nevertheless, their theatrical training in the West merely allowed them to interpret *Waiting for Godot* seemingly within the given limits of the western theatre. That is, those local elements still functioned only as better symbols, icons or silent decorations. The acting itself clearly followed the convention of the western stage play.[29] The traditional Chinese theatre was still dominated by the Chinese opera – with singing, music, dancing and martial arts. Apparently, there existed, and still exists, an immense gap between the western and eastern theatres, inasmuch as their separate and much consolidated traditions circumscribed most of the artists from being revolutionary in forms and contents; the long traditions in which they were immersed have probably hindered them from seeing the limits which determined their theatrical creativities. *Waiting for Godot*, as an anti-play,

---

[29] Not until the turn of the twentieth century did the western style play make inroads in China. The introduction of the western style play, or hau-ju, was in 1919, during the May Fourth Movement, advocated by noted intellectuals, such as Du-Xiu Chen and Shih Hu. The "hau-ju" was popular and promising in the 1930s, but soon declined due to years of civil wars involving the KMT and the Communist party.

was therefore meant to challenge the existing dramaturgy, particularly the theatre of realism, which had for a long time prevailed on the taste of audiences and critics.

In Taiwan, however, *Waiting for Godot* served as a platform on which the Chinese/Beijing opera performers who never received western theatre training could confront their own weighty tradition, which originated in the late seventh century. The most ambitious movement was initiated in 1986 by Hsing-kuo Wu, a rigorously trained Beijing opera actor and founder of the Contemporary Legend Theatre, which sought to rejuvenate the traditional theatre by giving it a fresh lease of life and thus to attract a new young audience to replace the loss of older audience members. The theatrical controversy he instigated was alarming, in that he attempted to produce the classic repertoire of the western theatre in the style of the Beijing opera, a step which went much further and was more groundbreaking than the actions of his fellow directors who had been trained in the West.[30] More specifically, Wu introduced the working of the western theatre to that of the Chinese one, seeking "a change of style, a new spirit, new thinking, and new attitudes that reflect contemporary society."[31] Based upon this, *Waiting for Godot*, a well-known play for the local audience, featuring the uncertainty, predicament, and despair of modern life, was employed to extend the boundaries of both eastern and western theatres.

---

[30] Since 1986 the Contemporary Legend Theatre has adapted a series of plays by Shakespeare, including *Macbeth* (renamed as *The Kingdom of Desire*), *Hamlet* (*War and Eternity*), *King Lear*, and *The Tempest*. Euripides's *Medea* and Aeschylus's *Oresteia* are also in their repertoire. This theatre group has performed its repertoire, on invitation, at major festivals around the world.

[31] This quote is taken from the introductory note in its program for the performance of *Twenty Years of Legend: Oriental Shakespeare*, Contemporary Legend Theatre, Taipei Cultural Centre, Taipei, 10-15 Oct. 2006.

Photograph by Te-mao Tsai. Waiting for Godot, *by Contemporary Legend Theatre, 2005, Taiwan.*

The revolutionary adaptation of this play in the style of the Beijing opera should be partially attributed to Beckett's stage directions, which Wu followed exactly – without instrumental music, whereas music is an essential of the Chinese theatre. His adaptation, therefore, highlighted the performance of the clown roles, or Chou, in which Didi and Gogo exchange ideas – with entertaining exaggeration and using various chanting tunes from Beijing opera – about their impatience in waiting. The emphasis on the clown roles implies that the life of "Chinese little men," represented by Didi and Gogo, was full of ironies to which they are subject but not aware of. What is interesting is that Wu eliminated many other elements of the traditional Chinese opera and focused solely on the acting of the two protagonists. In terms of setting, Wu and Ke-hua Lin, his stage designer, simplified the colorful Chinese stage to its possible extent – in black and white only. As to the performance, the clown roles, which are usually fringe characters in most Chinese operas, were allowed to express themselves freely and seriously in their own voices. According to Wu, the forbidden use of music, given as an instruction by Beckett's performing rights agency, was initially "unsettling," as he admitted in an interview, while he later realized that the performers could "sing from the very bottom of life" without the need for additional stage devices.[32] The most difficult part, as Wu admitted, was the adaptation of Christian concepts in the Chinese context, since the core of Chinese religions is very different from that of western monotheism. His solution was to replace the idea of "God might be dead" with the question of "the making of Buddha beyond transmigration," or "li-di-cheng-fo" in Chinese Mandarin.[33] The orientalizaton of *Waiting for Godot* was further stressed by the sound of a Chinese violin played before and after the actual performance, which did not contradict the no-music instruction.

It is fair to say that Wu has creatively employed an anti-play, namely *Waiting for Godot*, to break through the set dramaturgy of the Beijing opera, as well as to seek new possibilities of giving a western theatrical classic a Chinese mask. Not exactly abandoning the Chinese performing approach, Wu refreshed it by blending the features of both theatres and creating a novel aesthetics that has attracted favorable attention from many critics. According to Walter Asmus, previously assistant to Beckett and Dean of the College of Music and Theatre of Hanover, Wu's production presented a "perfect blending of poetics and drama... and rightly decoded the message of Beckett's play, which outshone [any] other adaptations I have seen. I must bring it to Germany" ("Shanghai" A9).

To look at Wu's adaptation from a postcolonial viewpoint, although the efforts that Wu made in blending different theatrical modes are indeed worthy of applause, the promotion of the arts of the Beijing opera to a western audience was eventually achieved by reproducing a foreign repertoire. Put another way, an Asian director of traditional arts had to courageously, under the pressure of cultural conservatives, open the door of those arts to the artistic Other of the West, so as to strategically entertain a western audience unfamiliar with the Chinese stage. One

---

[32]   Quoted in a review of *Waiting for Godot*, performed at the Shanghai Dramatic Arts Centre, China, on 21 April 2006.

[33]   The Chinese proverb, "li-di-cheng-fo," refers to the Buddhist story in which a butcher becomes a Buddha the moment he drops his cleaver.

may defend Wu and his fellow artists in that they have contributed to the diversification of the Chinese theatre, and popularized it through using modern marketing approaches as a backlash against the cultural imperialism that conventionally caters to the interests of the first-world countries of the West. It could not be refuted that there are still only a few western theatre troupes that have made the theatrical experiment of adapting a traditional Asian drama for performance in the style of western dramaturgy. Regardless of whether it is due to the superiority of the western theatre or lack of confidence, the achievement that the Contemporary Legend Theatre has made in the past twenty years, in adapting Greek, Shakespearean, and Beckett's dramas, shows that the cultural gap is not unbridgeable but is rather a matter of creativity.

Photograph by Yi-chuen Tsai. Endgame, *by Tainaner Theatre, 2006, Taiwan.*

The Contemporary Legend Theatre is not the only troupe in Taiwan that has the ambition of reproducing Beckett's drama with distinct Asian cultural elements and "exporting" it to the west. In 1987, three years later than the Contemporary Legend Theatre, the Tainaner Theatre was established in the south of Taiwan, where the Minnan vernacular, rather than Mandarin, was/is the major language of communication. According to its establisher and director, Po-shen Lu, the founding principle of his experimental theatre was, on the one hand, to show that "the repertoire which the Minnan vernacular can perform is beyond regional realistic drama, including poetic drama"; on the other hand, "the non-Minnan-speaking audience could thus simply enjoy the varieties and beauty of a dramatic voice in Minnan .... Native speakers could realize that their colloquial language [has] potential for performance" (qtd in Shen 52).[34] One of their approaches, apart from performing new plays featuring Taiwanese history, culture, and social phenomena, was to adapt western classics, not in Beijing Mandarin as the Contemporary Legend Theatre has done, but in Minnan, a popular, non-official language of Taiwan.[35] Beckett's *Endgame* was one of the plays that won local praise and was taken to Paris in 2004.[36]

Some particulars of this production can be expounded as follows. First, the preferred choice of language of the Tainaner Theatre, in terms of cultural politics, was a reaction to the popularity of the dominant Beijing Mandarin in Taiwan, which was once enthusiastically promoted through a number of national mechanisms before martial law was lifted. Partially to revive the language, partially to arouse the awareness of native identity, and partially to demonstrate that a vernacular can be spoken elegantly on stage, this theatre group translated *Endgame* into Minnan verse as an experiment. What is worthy of notice is that their choice of a non-official language might be, to some extent, similar to Beckett's choice of French for writing most of his works. Beckett's preference for French was not because he was not capable of writing in English as his mother tongue, but because he thought that "English was too easy. I wanted the discipline" (32). It was also not because he was not confident in Irish cultural matters and preferred to focus on universal subjects. It was probably because it was "easy" to be subject to the hidden cultural ideology of a more familiar language. Joyce, as Beckett's mentor, had commented on the potential imprisonment of a language: "I cannot express myself in English without enclosing in a tradition" (qtd in Ellmann 410). The undesirability of English, for an Irish writer in particular, might also result from the fact that: "the language and literary tradition of the conqueror carry the

---

[34]   Lu received an MA in Drama from Royal Holloway College, University of London.

[35]   *Endgame* was not the first western classic that the Tainaner Theatre adapted in Minnan. They have adapted *The Gap*, by Eugene Ionesco, and *The Marriage Proposal*, by Anton Chekov, in 1998. In 2001, the Greek tragedy *Antigone*, by Sophocles, was performed and received wide recognition for its success. *Macbeth*, *Hamlet*, and *Romeo and Juliet*, by William Shakespeare, were performed in 2003, 2004, and 2005 respectively. In 2006, the adaptation of Aeschylus's *The Suppliant Women*, by Charles L. Mee, a contemporary American playwright, was produced at the National Theatre, Taipei. Their repertoire attests to the recent ambition of this theatre group in reproducing western classics in the Taiwanese context and seeking new possibilities of performance in the Minnan vernacular.

[36]   It was performed at the auditorium of the Bureau de Representation de Taipei en France on 25-27 Nov. 2004.

hegemony or ideology of the conqueror and would necessarily be inimical to the conquered if used as a medium for self-expression" (Golden 411). The avoidance of using Beijing Mandarin for the Tainaner Theatre was, presumably, a counteraction against the symbolic status of this language and its associated cultural mechanisms, so the aim was to re-create the unique, artistic style of the Minnan vernacular and to secure a political identity different from that of those mainlanders whose culture and language could not be more dominant on this island.

In terms of genre, it could be argued that Lu's production outshone most of his predecessors and contemporaries, as he and Ding-bang Zhou, a Minnan poet, managed to translate *Endgame*, created by Beckett with musicality in its lines as poetic drama, into the verse of the Taiwanese vernacular. More specifically, differently from those previous productions in Mandarin, his production tends to more accurately represent the rhythms and tones of the original script by employing the traditional eight-tone chanting. The purpose of this reproduction of poetic lyrics was, according to Lu,

> ... to revive the poetics of drama that has been slighted after the rise of theatrical realism. Beckett's language, though appealing to the everyday, has a rigorous rhythm in style and musicality. In other words, the musicality of the language determines not only the performance of his rhythmic plays but also the actors' logics and emotions. Hopefully, our production in the Minnan vernacular can well represent the features of Beckett's dramatic language and be closer to the cadence of the original play as a poetic piece.[37]

It can safely be said that those productions prior to Lu's, though original in different ways, were not as well-considered as this one in terms of the poetic language. The production by the Contemporary Legend Theatre was adapted to incorporate chanting in verse, although this was not a major emphasis but an introduction of the performing skills of the Beijing Opera. Lu's production, as a result, should be seen as a more thoughtful one in regard to the inherent quality of the Beckettian language and dramaturgy.

Observing the localization of Beckett's drama from a postcolonial viewpoint, we might contend that Lu's refusal to adopt Mandarin as a would-be "foreign" language for Minnan speakers is more than a reclaiming of the elegance of a vernacular. Moreover, it was probably a gesture that called for the awakening of nativism amidst the enthusiastic democratic movement after martial law ended in Taiwan. People whose first language was Minnan were very interested in reasserting their cultural status through the restoration of this previously oppressed language. Their

---

[37]   Quoted from the website of the Tainaner Theatre on the performance of *Endgame*.

ambition was/is, to some extent, similar to that of Irish revivalists in the early twentieth century as a movement against the over-dominant English language and its culture. Nonetheless, it is undeniable that any set of accepted social conventions, or ideology, must bring forth more polemic, despite the fact that it could facilitate the process of social and political development, and *vice versa*. The theatre groups which this chapter has analyzed, not necessarily coincidentally, were however important participants in the campaigns of social reform in the different time and space of Taiwan. Beckett's absurdist theatre, interestingly, provides a platform on which these aspiring directors could attest to their creativity, challenge the existing cultural conventions, and produce a fresh theatrical style by bridging the theatres of the Far East and the West.

It is well known that the Irish colonial experience eventually caused many Irish writers, though writing mostly in English, to be alienated "from the language they use of a people who were forced to abandon their own," while their cynicism about the English language became "the primary rhetoric structuring the Irish use of [it]" (Golden 441). Beckett's drama in French, evidently, resulted from his alienation from both English – a mother tongue but a foreign one – and Gaelic – not a competent language of his – that would confine his creativity to cultural ideologies. French, as his language of proficiency, therefore serves as a medium through which he created a "third space of enunciation," as Bhabha described and this chapter demonstrated earlier. That his theatrical legacy could benefit Taiwanese directors across the continents and decades since the 1960s is probably because of this "third space," an ambivalent site on which cultural practices, norms, identities and values are revisable, negotiable and renewable. It was even more predictable that the transcultural representations of Beckett's drama, rather than simply translating and duplicating the original production, will never cease to bring about more promising theatrical styles on the global stage.

X. The Irish at Home and Abroad: Transnational Practices

Perhaps there is no country quite like Ireland, whose many epithets can testify to how drastically the nation has been transformed during the past few centuries. One notable byname has been "the Emerald Isle," conveying a soothing and poetic image of a garden of greenery blessed by rain and mist all the year round.

However, Ireland has also been described in much less flattering terms. In the nineteenth century, Dublin was referred to as "a backward deposed ex-capital of empire" (Kiberd 293). During World War I, the country was deemed "the back door to England" through which Germany could seek to attack England (Taylor 13). A decade ago southern Ireland was caricatured by a Northern Irish politician as a poverty-stricken, priest-ridden "potato Republic".[1] The large number of young and jobless Irish emigrants also contributed to another derogatory term, namely "emigrant nursery."[2] Surely no pejorative can be worse than being described as the "Poorest of the Rich" on the cover of *The Economist* in 1988.[3] Nevertheless, it is somehow elevating that a decade later the tide started to turn for Ireland. The rise of the "Celtic tiger" economy earned Ireland a new title as "Europe's shining light" – also printed in a large font on the cover of *The Economist* in 1997, followed by a series of special reports on its experience of success, although this shining light looked to have dimmed somewhat by 2008.[4]

These appellations show how Ireland has been changed rapidly by several social and economic factors that were present before the turn of the century – a largely agricultural state became a multiethnic and multicultural nation heavily dependent on multilateral trade. Metaphorically, the color that represents Ireland is no longer just emerald green but now resembles a tapestry of different colors and patterns – including economic migrants and professionals as well as refugees from the third world.

---

[1]   David Trimble, the First Minister of Northern Ireland, once unjustly described southern Ireland as a "priest-ridden potato Republic" (*The Irish Times*, 16 March 2002, 4).

[2]   See Jim MacLaughlin's *Ireland: The Emigrant Nursery and the World Economy* (1994).

[3]   For details, see "'Poorest of the Rich', A Survey of the Republic of Ireland," *The Economist*, issue 7533, 16 Jan. 1988.

[4]   For details, see "Ireland Shines" and "Ireland: Europe's Tiger Economy," *The Economist*, issue 8017, 17 May 1997.

Nonetheless, the flows of Irish emigrants and newcomers, and the boom and collapse of the Celtic Tiger, cannot erase the fact that the number of Irish people and their descendants who form a diaspora in foreign countries outnumbers the entire population of Ireland. This has led Ireland in recent decades to become "a first-world country, but with a third-world memory" (Gibbon 27). This haunting memory has inevitably triggered "schizophrenic behavior in certain situations" (Gibbon 27), for instance when the nation has become a top destination choice for asylum seekers and has had to accommodate them for humanitarian reasons.

It can be seen that a series of economic expansions and reforms has effectively revitalized the Irish economy, with the result that migrants have returned and new immigrants have settled in the country. New and existing residents have then experienced a culture shock as they go through "a process of estrangement [whereby] home has become as unfamiliar as abroad [...] Everything begins to exist in a state of internal exile" (O'Toole 173). This might be true for those who remain at home but suddenly find themselves surrounded everywhere by foreign faces and accents. For newcomers, however, this first-world country with a third-world memory threatens clashes of values and racial conflicts that can, despite their best efforts to resist it, give them a sense of insecurity that is with them everywhere. For both old and new dwellers in Ireland, their conflicting sentiments may explain why globalization always fails to homogenize different cultures and instead makes "the seams [...] ever more apparent culturally and politically as well as economically" (Gardels 5). Inevitably, the gaps between the "seams" only become more visible when a multi-racial, multi-national and multi-cultural Ireland is laid bare for examination.

Having compared and analyzed contemporary Irish plays that feature migrant workers, or disadvantaged people in international political and economic situations, this book illustrates what has been on the edges of the gaps or has already fallen through them. It examines a series of themed plays in an attempt to show Irish playwrights' engagements with local and international crises in the present or the past, and the profound cross-cultural influences of these plays across boundaries. It also uses examples of drama to show how Asian countries, for instance Taiwan, can serve as mirrors to each other in terms of theatrical and social developments in the twentieth-first century.

Homely and Un-homely: Staging Migrants' Dilemmas

Home has become an unsettling concept for the Irish ever since the drive for independence at the turn of the twentieth century, when Irish nationalists started to differentiate Ireland from their British ruler.

However, widely different perceptions of home, as George Bernard Shaw illustrated in *John Bull's Other Island* (1904), were apparent on either side of the Irish Sea, despite the fact that his play criticizes both English colonialism and Irish parochialism. The conflicting understandings of home, as Shaw comments through his character Peter Keegan, arise from the fact that the English and Irish rarely see their own home for what it is: "I did not know what my own house was like, because I had never been outside it" (95). Ignorance or a false image of what one's home is like prompt the Irish and the English to keep reproducing stereotypes, even though they live next to each other and share reciprocal benefits. In *John Bull's Other Island*, the Irish protagonist is further astonished on learning how his people have been regarded as objects of wonderment by their English neighbors.

The highly critical nature of a play about how the Irish create/ imagine themselves and are wrongly perceived by the English, would be an understandable reason for it not to be favored by the Abbey Theatre, Dublin, alongside the excessive length of the play. W.B. Yeats's declining of Shaw's play was therefore presumably a prudent decision, for it was a sensitive issue as to how Ireland should be understood by native and foreign audiences; a play which is "fundamentally ugly and shapeless, but certainly keeps everybody amused," as Yeats described it to Lady Gregory in a letter, could only be discarded (*Letters*, 1954, 442). In this era of globalization, the analogy between Shaw's observation of a nationalistic Ireland and the concept of a transnational Ireland lies in their false presentation of the country, despite the fact that all such presentations – whether aimed at Irish natives, migrants or the international community – have always been in the English language.

The analogy extends further into the ways in which the Other is perceived and accommodated. Judging by the increasing number of racial conflicts, the Irish Citizenship Referendum of 2004, and the refugee policies of the government, it may not be correct to claim that Ireland has been comfortable about itself in recent years, when the consequences of globalization have been changing the country "minute by minute" into becoming a multi-ethnic state.[5] Historically, the collective fear of being

---

[5]   On 11 June 2004, a citizenship referendum was held on tightening the citizenship laws that aimed to prevent "citizenship tourism" under which foreign women could travel to Ireland (without an Irish spouse or partner) to give birth, so as to get automatic Irish citizenship and an EU passport for their baby. The turnout rate was 59.95%, and 79.1% of voters wanted to end such practices. Opposition parties, including the Labour Party, Sinn Féin and the Greens, maintained that "the government is playing politics with the delicate issue of race and immigration [...] The number of women coming to Ireland to give birth is so small that it does not warrant a poll" ("Ireland votes to end birth right," par. 11, 13). A referendum of this nature on racial issues explains why

intimidated by whatever is foreign or unorthodox has arisen in part from the idea of decolonization – steered by the Catholic nationalist government ever since the establishment of the Irish Free State. An official "Irish-Irish identity" had led not only to cultural protectionism, under the auspices of censorship, but also to "a narrow, insular and triumphalist category" in the Irish psyche (Smyth 146). It is interesting to note that this conservative, hierarchical social climate has not completely suffocated Irish playwrights of the mid-twentieth century but has inspired them to turn a sharper eye on what has become an atrophied society.

Plays by Brian Friel and Tom Murphy, among others, have often gone beyond the constraints of local culture and shown concern for the wider world outside, in order to illustrate how the Irish have behaved in a xenophobic way through lack of confidence. John B. Keane's *Many Young Men of Twenty* (1961), Tom Murphy's *A Whistle in the Dark* (1961), *A Crucial Week in the Life of a Grocer's Assistant* (1969), and *Conversations on a Homecoming* (1985), Brian Friel's *The Enemy Within* (1962), *Philadelphia, Here I Come!* (1964), *The Loves of Cass McGuire* (1966), and *Faith Healer* (1979), have all, directly or indirectly, exhibited how church-affiliated Irishness has yet to be counteracted by foreign cultural inputs, despite the protagonists having to bear the burden of a series of crises in personal faith and self-recognition.

Friel's 2005 play, *The Home Place*, a Chekhovian play that explores the collapse of a landed Anglo-Irish family at the outbreak of the Land War in 1878, may be seen as a theatrical response to the 2004 citizenship referendum on the birthright of newborns of newly-arrived immigrants. This play depicts how a Victorian anthropologist applies craniological methods to measure the "negroness" of Aran Islands dwellers by checking the shapes and sizes of their skulls. This racist yet pseudoscientific hypothesis ignites the rancor of the townsfolk, against the background of the murder of an English landlord. Departing from Friel's early work *Translations* (1980), *The Home Place* further accentuates the ambiguity of being Anglo-Irish by serving the English establishment and its role in India, South America and Africa, colonial references to which are constantly made in *The Home Place*.

Specifically, the Irish, though residing in their "home place," are subject to the use of anthropometric science aimed at them, and are treated as a sub-race within British imperial demography. It could thus be suggested that that the production of this play in 2005 was an apparent

---

George Seremba, a Ugandan playwright who arrived in Ireland as a refugee, said he had "enough evidence of very overt and also covert racism. I can smell it. I can smell it a mile away" (qtd in King 119).

critique of the Irish Citizenship Referendum as mentioned earlier, in that those people in the play who are forced to have their heads measured, or real people who voted against in the Referendum, are powerless and voiceless within colonial politics or global economics. That said, the truth about Irish history being "fragmentary and hybrid, marked by the struggle between imperial rule and national resistance, and by economic, social and political inequalities" should be given greater stress rather than being ignored by the media and the government (McMullan 65), if Ireland is to come to terms with its unfortunate history of having being an emigrant nursery and now being a globalized state with relevant responsibilities.

A notable breakthrough at an early stage of the Celtic Tiger period was that playwrights often shifted their attention from stories with Irish characters *only* to include newly-arrived immigrants and other disadvantaged social groups. The interest in migrants has led a number of playwrights to document, unveil or research Irish experiences with foreigners in both historical and present-day contexts.

Sebastian Barry's *White Woman Street* (1992), set in 1916 in the wilds of Ohio, dramatizes a gang of robbers – Irish, Russian, Chinese, African and American-Indian – who attack trains during the Gold Rush, and the rape of an Indian child virgin. Donal O'Kelly's *Asylum! Asylum!* (1994) journalistically presents how Ugandan refugees are mistreated by Irish bureaucracy and repatriated, in spite of the fact that they will be killed by the government back home if this happens; Martin McDonagh's *The Cripple of Inismaan* (1996) is about how an Irish youngster is lulled by the American Dream, and criticizes how the Irish are stereotyped by Hollywood's film industry. John Barrett's *Borrowed Robes* (1998) reexamines anti-Semitism in Cork in 1904, pointing to the racist attitudes and hypocrisy of the Catholic Church. Theatre practitioners' concerns for cultural and racial conflicts also led *The Dilemma of a Ghost* (1965), written by Ama Ata Aidoo, a Ghanaian woman playwright, to be staged in Dublin in 2007.

The Celtic Tiger economy triggered not only an economic boom but also productions of new Irish plays. According to Patrick Lonergan's survey, 263 new Irish plays were produced between 2001 and 2007, and twenty-two plays were premiered abroad; almost every major playwright in Ireland contributed to this theatrical accomplishment, alongside many younger dramatists.[6] It should be emphasized that many plays were

---

[6]   Lonergan surveyed the Irish Playography website and came up with this figure. The major playwrights include Tom Murphy, Sebastian Barry, Marina Carr, Martin McDonagh, Mark O'Rowe, Enda Walsh, Marie Jones and Frank McGuinness. For details, see Lonergan's "Irish Theatre and Globalisation: A Faustian Pact?," p. 182.

"explicitly about globalization" (Lonergan 182).[7] On the other hand, the fact that younger playwrights tend to look for overseas venues in which to premier their works may be due to their desire to open a door to other English-speaking countries – offering fresh topics to wider audiences. Significantly, many young dramatists, breaking with nationalistic sub-themes, present various Irish experiences as regards the transformation of the country, unveiling the darker aspects behind the façade of this newly globalized state, ranging from illegal migration, international economic crimes and drug smuggling to capital flight, job cuts and other phenomena. These transnational phenomena are a significant motivating force in the Irish theatre in a manner that mirrors what is happening elsewhere in the world, as contributed by Irish playwrights.

Globalization, Racial Stereotypes and Imaginations of Home

Modern technology has redefined the traditional concept of national boundaries; information can be exchanged instantly and cultures are reenergized without the constraints of borders. For the Irish who have striven hard and made many sacrifices for nationalist causes, globalization has gradually reshaped the concept of being Irish, rerouting this island country from being a distant corner of Europe to a pivotal gateway – helped by having English as a common language – for transnational enterprises in North America.

However, the worry for people in Ireland is how to maintain the ties with the cultural past that have defined their Irish identity. These perplexing questions about who I am and where the country is going unavoidably build a sense of public disquiet when the nation is being economically and culturally re-formulated under the pressures of rapid globalization. What Ireland is now going through, from a meta-historical perspective, is a kind of continuation of imperialism in another form – with more centers of attraction across the world and more relocation of displaced people. The illegal immigrants that try to move to these centers may resemble what Edward Said says about a modern age which, "with its modern warfare,

---

[7] Lonergan gives a full list of these plays with globalization as a theme, including Sebastian Barry's *The Pride of Parnell Street* and *Hinterland*, Marina Carr's *Woman and Scarecrow*, Stella Feehily's *Duck* and *O Go My Man*, Marie Jones's *Rock Doves*, Owen McCaffery's *Scenes from the Big Picture*, Martin McDonagh's *The Lieutenant of Inishmore* and *The Pillowman*, Frank McGuinness' *Speaking like Magpies* and *There Came A Gypsy Riding*, Conor McPherson's *Shining City*, *Port Authority* and *The Seafarer*, Gary Mitchell's *Loyal Women*, Tom Murphy's *Alice Trilogy*, Edna O'Brien's *Triptych*, Christian O'Reilly's *Is This About Sex?*, Mark O'Rowe's *Made in China*, Colin Teevan's *How Many Miles to Basra?*, and Enda Walsh's *The New Electric Ballroom* and *The Small Things*. For details, see Lonergan's "Irish Theatre and Globalisation: A Faustian Pact?," p. 182.

imperialism and the quasi-theological ambitions of totalitarian rulers – is indeed the age of the refugee, the displaced person, mass immigration" (174). For Irish natives, their home is accommodating new yet unfamiliar/ strange faces; new immigrants are surrounded by unspoken animosity and isolation in their new home.[8] If this modern warfare does exist, it has broken out quietly but not with any less antagonism; globalization shifts not only people but the cores of different cultures and traditions.

Globalization has speeded up cultural exchanges within Ireland, but it has not erased ethnic divides, especially given that a large number of non-white migrants, tourists and students have arrived in this formerly purely Caucasian country. Elisa Joy White, a professor from the University of Hawaii, recalled how she was insulted at Dublin airport by a group of boys shouting: "'hands up, nigger bitch'" – with fingers pointing at her like guns (102). In her estimation, the "guns" embodied the "racialised immigration rhetoric conflated with skewed understandings of Black experience," and what prompted the boys to pretend to shoot a black woman may rest on the frightening impression given by the media that "the last shreds of Irish culture [are about to be polluted by] the murky waters of difference and diversity" (White 103). Needless to say, the criminalization of immigrants (about how they waste public resources) has been repeatedly drummed into the public consciousness.

It can be argued that the antipathy of the Irish against the Other can be attributed partly to the historical sectarianism that has divided society. That said, the religious and political sectarianism that created social divides in the era of globalization has been transformed into focusing on ethnic differences which are more obviously seen than political loyalties. As Seamus Deane foresaw in 1991, "when a culture is politically homogeneous, like that of Britain, the sectarianism is directed externally rather than internally and is usually xenophobic in character" (682). It is interesting that Deane discovered this to be an Irish phenomenon after years of decolonization, particularly when globalization had diluted internal antagonisms and contributed to a better political climate (e.g. the Peace Process), economic success (e.g. Ireland was at one time the second richest European country after Luxembourg), and new demographic structures (e.g. the arrival of economic migrants and refugees).

The sectarianism that formed an individual's religious and political values has turned into a new criterion for judgment that concerns the

---

[8] The Celtic Tiger economy relied heavily on economic migrants, as is evident from government reports. As Martine Pelletier summarizes, between 1996 and 2002 more than 153,000 people, including returning migrants, moved to the Republic. In 2003 alone, 47,000 employment visas were issued to foreign nationals; between 1999 and 2004, "there was a 600 per cent rise in the number of work visas granted" (Pelletier 99).

divides between Caucasian Irish and non-white ethnicities, and between the financially advantaged and those who abuse social welfare. Although the Northern Ireland Troubles have seemingly been settled in recent years, a sense of insecurity is still inherent within different social strata in various ethnic communities. This sentiment has notably inspired playwrights to depict the new troubles in Irish society, and incidentally prepare for a new page of theatre history.

A renewed understanding of frontiers in the era of globalization should prompt an old question to be reviewed in relation to nation formation. Given that globalization has acted as a catalyst in the transformation of Ireland – from a largely homogenous entity into a culturally multifarious and demographically hybrid state – we should bear in mind that Ireland has never been a country with a single culture and ethnicity, but it is a destination where "there is [...] always the distracting presence of another temporality that disturbs the contemporaneity of the national present" (Bhabha, *Location* 143). Globalization therefore unveils "the [looming] presence of another temporality" in Ireland, which allows audiences to reflect on the experience of Ireland, in terms of migration, and the making of a nation: "nations are in fact a response to the hybrid nature of living conditions, yet for all their claim to essential unity, they create even further hybridities" (Kiberd 313). However, not all threads of hybridity have been given equal value, and many protectionist social welfare policies have resulted, as have different forms of violence against non-white people.

Compared with Great Britain, and other former imperial powers, Ireland is still a relatively new country searching for its own global role and negotiating with emerging forces. Its rapid transformation in the past few decades has, unfortunately, not allowed ordinary Irish people much time to review their own history of migration but has given rise to enmity towards the ethnic Other, be they non-white migrants, refugees, or less advantaged individuals or communities.

Therefore, what the Irish theatre produced during the later decades of the twentieth century was not only evidence of the painful process of social transformation but a platform on which cultural nationalism was deconstructed. One notable example was Martin McDonagh's *The Cripple of Inishmaan* (1996), a dark comedy set on Inis Meáin, one of the Aran Islands, and satirizing the kind of Irishness stereotyped by the Hollywood film industry, illustrating how neo-colonialism takes advantage of economically unprivileged countries by non-militant means.[9]

---

[9]   Specifically, this play is a critique of how *Man of Aran*, a 1934 British fictional documentary, was filmed under the directorship of Robert J. Flaherty. For instance, the film presented fishing skills that had not been employed for fifty years at the time, and the actors were not family members as the documentary suggested.

Although primitive Irishness does contribute to an enticing prototype for tourism, the promotion of Irish life by untrue means simply reveals disrespect of and intellectual violence on dwellers of the Aran Islands, Irish cinema viewers and foreign audiences. On the other hand, as *The Cripple of Inishmaan* is a critique of the British fictional documentary *Man of Aran* (1934), this play challenges the notion of cultural nativism and the romantic stereotypes that have been molded by Irish Revivalists. The protagonist's failure to star in the documentary suggests how the Irish have been manipulated by the stereotypes in which they have acquiesced and by Hollywood as a neo-colonial superpower. In this regard, the play serves as a double-sided mirror through which the Irish audience can see how Ireland is inappropriately regarded by foreign enterprises for marketing purposes, and how the Irish themselves participate in that parochial image without offering much challenge to it.

The changes that globalization has brought to Ireland include interactions of greater intensity between playwrights and the audience, and realizations of the significance of older plays in the classic Irish canon. This was particularly true of the 2011 production of Sean O'Casey's *The Plough and the Stars* (1926) at the Abbey Theatre. This classic play was critical of nationalistic ferment during the early twentieth century and its impact on slum dwellers. This new production, interestingly, was timely in that people related it to the then current Irish financial situation, and audiences could easily find many lines that corresponded to what they were experiencing and witnessing, for instance the high youth unemployment rate that was deeply troubling the country. Although this play mainly featured the consequences of Irish nationalism, rather than cross-border activities or the like, the merits of the play were further illuminated when considered alongside globalization, even though it played down the "shining light" of Ireland.[10] It can thus be argued that the excessive credit expansion before 2008 resembled the political ideals of radical nationalism, in that they both promised the Irish unrealistic dreams about the future, which were followed by not only personal bankruptcy, broken families and a market bubble, but resentment at the government of the day.

The imagined prospect of a new home in a foreign country is also an important theme in contemporary Irish drama. This imagination has prompted many playwrights since the mid-twentieth century to reflect on the repressive and insular nature of Irish culture by casting doubts on nationalist rule and the Church's domination in Ireland. Brian Friel's early work, *Philadelphia, Here I Come!* (1964), presents an emigrant-to-be who is haunted by his sense of guilt that is conditioned by the Catholic

---

[10]   See note 4.

doctrines that pervaded his upbringing. Hugh Leonard's *Da* (1978) illustrates how Irish parochialism follows the protagonist like a phantom, such that he only wants to escape from home.

These presentations of Ireland in relation to other countries and cultures have the potential to subvert the traditional nationalist historiography, in that the making of Ireland, in the eyes of these playwrights, is an unstable and problematic national myth, and they expect audiences to see beyond the myth. For instance, Friel's *Translations* (1980) and *Making History* (1988), among others, testify to the kind of "nets" that keep the Irish bound by political ideologies and religious doctrines. These plays can all be seen to deepen the public's perception of Irish history by unearthing embarrassing truths in Anglo-Irish relations. More importantly, Irish experiences in counteracting and negotiating with foreign powers and influences can be an object lesson for other countries that are still enmeshed in the processes of decolonization and globalization.

Interestingly, the playwrights' shared attempts to dramatize stories about or beyond borders is most effective when they try to reach new audiences overseas. Frank McGuinness, Thomas Kilroy, Tom Murphy, Colin Teevan and Brian Friel have all written works that were either set overseas or were adapted from classic plays by Henrik Ibsen, Bertolt Brecht, Anton Chekhov or Ivan Turgenev.

Furthermore, some playwrights have re-characterized figures from classical mythology, giving them multidimensional masks for modern audiences, and some of their versions have been translated into foreign languages. To name only a few: Friel's *Living Quarters* (1977), Tom Paulin's *The Riot Act* (1985), Marina Carr's *The Mai* (1995) and *On Raftery's Hill* (2000), and Seamus Heaney's *The Burial at Thebes: Sophocles' Antigone* (2004).[11] These plays all demonstrate how the playwrights' considerations of themes have not been limited to Irish locations or references but have crossed beyond the barriers of time and language – using characters that travel across the centuries to meet new audiences at home and overseas, as the next section will demonstrate.

Transposing the Exotic

It could be said that the initial aim of W.B. Yeats's cultural nationalism was to remove the impasse in Irish politics at the turn of the twentieth century and to enable republicans of different hues to gain a tacit understanding of political realities. In his view, fundamental nationalism –

---

[11]   For details, see Arkin Brian's *Irish appropriation of Greek tragedy* (2010) and *Amid our troubles: Irish versions of Greek tragedy* (2002), edited by Marianne McDonald and J. Michael Walton.

which demanded political and economic autonomy and independence from the United Kingdom – would be unlikely to benefit the nation because of its lack of "universalism." For Yeats, "universalism" could be attained "through what is near you, your nation, or […] your village and the cobwebs on your walls […] One can only reach out to the universe with a gloved hand – that glove is one's nation, the only thing one knows even a little of" (*Letters*, 1934, 36). It is apparent that Yeats's cultural nationalism in relation to "universalism" was so narrow that his romantic proposal eventually confirmed the sentiments of Irish nativists by placing Irish culture in the foreground rather than considering foreign cultures.

Cultural nationalism has been a tremendous benefit to Ireland, although there has also been a price to pay. The Irish Free State, or later the Republic, soon served as the guardian of the cultural revival and, as "(Eamonn) de Valera's Gaelic Eden," Ireland very much isolated itself from concurrent literary developments on the European Continent and in the rest of the world (Brown 159). This partially paved the way for the Censorship of Publications Act of 1929, which sought to confirm "the mores and attitudes of a nation of farmers and shopkeepers, [and to] denounce all developments in society that might have threatened a rigid conformism in a strictly enforced sexual code" (Brown 39).[12]

It is very interesting to note that the cultural vacuum that resulted from the censorship did not entirely prevent Irish playwrights from finding models to follow that were written in foreign languages. Despite not being able to read Russian, Greek, German and Norwegian, some of them managed to obtain translations from which they acquired the experimentalism that had become a virtual norm in twentieth-century European theatre. They then adapted and repackaged European works with an Irish ambiance.

More significantly, many of these playwrights became interested in works that were highly critical of existing social conventions, hierarchy, class distinction and corruption. For instance, Frank McGuinness adapted a series of Ibsen's plays, including *Rosmersholm*, *Peer Gynt*, *Hedda Gabler*, *A Doll's House* and *John Gabriel Borkman* as well as Chekhov's *Three Sisters* and *Uncle Vanya*, among others.[13] Thomas Kilroy rewrote

---

[12] Statistics show that between 1928 and 1944, 77 books by 44 Irish writers were banned in Ireland, alongside many works by non-Irish writers. Many canonical Irish figures, such as James Joyce, Samuel Beckett and George Bernard Shaw, were on the censored list. Not until the late 1970s was the censorship gradually relaxed. For details, see Michael Adams's *Censorship: The Irish Experience* (1968), p. 215.

[13] Nonetheless, Chekhov's works did not have a smooth journey to Ireland. It was not until 1925 that the Abbey Theatre first produced his play *The Proposal* (1890), a one-act farce. Notably, the concerns were for the political correctness of Chekhov's and experimental European plays. In order to introduce more European dramas, Edward

Ibsen's *Ghosts*, subtitling it "After Ibsen," and Chekhov's *The Seagull*. Colin Teevan had Ibsen's *Peer Gynt* retranslated and staged. Tom Murphy's *The House* (2000) is thematically based on Chekhov's *The Cherry Orchard*, which he adapted for another version in 2004, whereas the former play is set in the countryside of Ireland in the 1950s. Brian Friel had Turgenev's *A Month in the Country* and Chekhov's *Uncle Vanya* retranslated. His own play *Aristocrats* (1979) and *The Yalta Game* (2001) are notably Chekhovian; the latter was inspired by Chekhov's short story, "The Lady with the Dog."[14]

The search by twentieth-century Irish playwrights for models and inspiration from authors not writing in English can be dated back to Sean O'Casey's *The Dublin Trilogy*, which applied Ibsenian realism when critiquing Irish nationalism and social phenomena. Perhaps it is surprising that, after nearly one hundred years, these European dramatists still hold a key role in the making of Irish theatre. This may suggest that Ireland and their European neighbors share, to some extent, corresponding cultural symptoms and political beliefs, in that industrialization and democratization have made dominant and irreversible impacts on every rung of the social ladder.

Irish playwrights do not simply reproduce canonical works but try to refine them through a new translation or adaption that is in homage to their models. Each new translation or adaptation presents, if not a misappropriation of original texts, Irish playwrights' cross-cultural engagement with their overseas role models. The reason why they would re-translate and adapt a work which already has an English equivalent probably rests on the definition of being faithful to the original text. For them, of greater importance would be how foreign ideas and cultural contexts are delivered to and re-appropriated for an audience with a different language background, rather than presenting a literal translation line by line. Tom Murphy, who adapted Chekhov's *The Cherry Orchard* in

---

Martyn and John McDonagh had to establish The Irish Theatre Company (1914-1920) as a rival enterprise to the Abbey Theatre. However, their production of *The Cherry Orchard* in 1919 was castigated in *The Leader* (5 July 1919) for having produced a Russian play in an Irish theatre. For more details, see Dixon's "Chekhov Bogged Down? Tom Kilroy's Version of *The Seagull*," and Mária Kurdi's "An Interview with Tom Murphy."

14 For details on Ibsen's and Chekhov's influences on Irish dramatists, see Ros Dixon's "Chekhov Bogged Down? Tom Kilroy's Version of *The Seagull*"; Heing Kosok's "Adaptation-Translocation-Acculturation-Appropriation: Contemporary Irish Play-wrights and Continental Drama; Robert Tracy's "The Russian Connection: Friel and Chekhov"; *Ibsen and Chekhov on the Irish Stage*, edited by Ros Dixon and Irina Malone, etc.

two different versions, explained his aesthetics in approaching a Russian play as follows:[15]

> A version, as I see it, is more subjective and more interpretively open; it is speculative in its considerations of the 'spirit' of the original and seeks to translate that 'spirit' into a language and movement that have their own dynamic; the ordering in the version attempts to re-create what was alive, musical and vibrant in the original. (2)

Consequently, a proper appropriation should, in his words, come closer to an adaptation and "avoid looking like the back of the tapestry" (Murphy 2). Thomas Kilroy, also a veteran in adapting Chekhov's and Ibsen's dramas, expressed a consonant attitude about transposing foreign plays to an Anglo-Irish setting in that "an Irish setting would more easily allow the rawness of passion of the original to emerge, the kind of semi-farcical hysteria which Chekhov uses in [his works]" (80).

For both Murphy and Kilroy, a *literal* translation into English would not adequately project the critical essence of and sentiments in a drama written in a foreign language. A proper appropriation should therefore, to some degree, relate the historical or relevant experiences of an Irish/new audience, even though the plot would inevitably be altered. This strategy is used in Murphy's *The House*, staged at the Abbey Theatre in 2000 and with a plot corresponding to but not exactly the same as that of *The Cherry Orchard*. However, *The House* does not convey the essential comic ambiance of *The Cherry Orchard* but instead features the downfall of a family from the Anglo-Irish landed class and the rise of *nouveau riches*. This illustrates not only how an Irish dramatist can conceive a motif from a foreign play but also how Irishness, of which the Anglo-Irish legacy presumably plays a part, informs a new Irish work on the English-speaking stage.

Brian Friel also has a relatively long list of works to his name that bear a noticeable relationship to works by European playwrights, including adaptations of Chekhov's *Three Sisters, Uncle Vanya, The Yalta Game* and *The Bear* in 1981, 1998, 2001 and 2002 respectively, alongside Turgenev's *Fathers and Sons* in 1987, *A Month in the Country* in 1992 and Ibsen's *Hedda Gabler* in 2008. Notably, the shadow of Russian playwrights also looms over much of Friel's earlier *oeuvre*, including *Living Quarters* and *Aristocrats*. Thematically, these plays both present a father or mother of a landed family who is as domineering, but helpless, as Mme Ranevsky in *The Cherry Orchard*. There is an even greater degree of conformity among

---

[15]   Murphy published a new version of his translation of *The Cherry Orchard* in 2004 to mark the centenary of the original's premiere at the Moscow Art Theatre in 1904, the year in which Chekhov died. He had previously adapted and published this play as *The House* in 2000. Both plays were staged at the Abbey Theatre.

these plays in that the family troubles in each are all closely or distantly subject to the protagonists' former experiences abroad which have led to the making of a perspective or decision. For instance, Frank Butler in *Living Quarters*, as a retelling of the Theseus/Hippolytus/Phaedra myth in a contemporary Irish setting, was formerly a commandant serving the United Nations as part of Middle East peacekeeping. *Aristocrats*, featuring an American scholar who is conducting field research on Irish Roman Catholic nobility, depicts the financial collapse of this once-privileged family – but adds an over-romantic perspective as an outsider.

The Chekhovian element of these plays is the mental struggle of the protagonists in the face of powerful social changes in relation to transnational activities and democratization. These characters are either returning home from or leaving for a foreign post, and taking part in a quiet revolution that significantly reroutes their lives. In this context, the intertextuality of these plays rests on thematic similarities that transcend time, space and culture, along with the playwrights' critical observations on globalization/industrialization versus personal values and traditions.

Staging Ethnicities in Contemporary Irish Theatre

Globalization, as a catalyst for the Irish economy, made a massive contribution to the rise of the Celtic Tiger from the late 1980s, transforming the Emerald Isle "from an emigrant sending to an immigrant receiving society" (King 23). Nonetheless, the rising number of ethnic newcomers, including economic migrants, refugees, tourists, international students and scholars, has not had the effect of removing the xenophobia that has been culturally planted in Irish life and has led to new forms of racism. As Robbie McVeigh observes, the "re-emergence of racialised imperialisms" has given rise to a "new world order" within which "capital, labour, goods and services are distributed and moved in ways that remain inherently racialised" (406).

Major resources are still administered by economic superpowers, and public sector organizations not only prefer to endorse an old, advantaged social order but continue to code race, ethnicity and nationality into newly passed immigration laws and policies, so as to more easily distinguish between national/non-national, citizen/non-citizen, labor/non-labor, and legal/illegal. On the other hand, the rapid social changes that prompted Ireland to become an immigrant receiving destination have not allowed much time for the Irish to reflect properly on the racial discriminations that troubled their forefathers.[16] This may therefore be the reason why the

---

[16] Some disturbing stereotypes about the Irish include the image of "human chimpanzees," as Charles Kingsley, a renowned Victorian novelist and university professor, described them in his travelogue of Ireland (107). In his eyes, "to see white chimpanzees is

ethnic Other's way into Ireland is far from smooth and pleasant at the turn of the twenty-first century, they being no more welcome than Bloom, the son of a Jewish Hungarian immigrant, in Joyce's *Ulysses*. They remain the unacquainted Other that is yet to come under the spotlight of justice.

Many contemporary Irish playwrights are sensitive about the visible and invisible prejudices against ethnic minorities in newly globalized Ireland. Their new works often focus on the "immigration phenomenon and its implications for Ireland's identity and self-image and these have, in turn, become the object of critical inquiry" (Pelletier 100). Some theatre companies were established to dramatize racial issues in particular, in an attempt to draw the public's attention to the human rights of people who are politically and economically disadvantaged.

Calypso Productions, for instance, established in 1993 by Donal O'Kelly but which has now ceased operation, aimed to promote the notion of "world citizen" and "world family" as its "simple, practical and humble" mission, with which "[we should] nurture their inheritance – social, political, artistic, environmental and sacred [...] [With being] world citizens [...] comes a responsibility to defend them for ourselves and for others." (qtd in Merriman 280).[17] Differently from other Irish theatre groups, such as Field Day, that feature issues that are more Irish-related than international, Calypso was known for its focus on refugees, Third World countries, the international arms trade, and socially marginalized communities, and some of its plays were set overseas, for example *Hughie on the Wires* (1993) in El Salvador and *Trickledown Town* (1994) in Jamaica. Its theatrical experiments included a parade, called *Féile Fáilte* (1997), from Temple Bar to the Civic Offices at Wood Quay in Dublin, to demonstrate how the Celtic Tiger economy was built at the expense of the interests of refugees and those less well off. It ended with ethnic music and firework displays as a gesture to celebrate racial diversity in Ireland. Calypso's production of *Rosie and Starwars* (1997), written by Charlie O'Neill and based on true events, presented the social

---

dreadful; if they were black, one would not feel it so much, but their skins, except where tanned by exposure, are as white as ours" (107). The phrase, "No Irish Need Apply," in job advertisements in newspapers on both sides of the Atlantic ever since the mid-eighteenth century, perpetuated employers' beliefs that the Irish were not reliable as workers. Roddy Doyle, in his 1991 novel *The Commitments*, points out that "the Irish are the niggers of Europe ... An' Dubliners are the niggers of Ireland ... An' the northside Dubliners are the niggers o' Dublin" (13). It can be assumed that these traditional racialized categories were still being perpetuated by former colonizers; even worse, the Irish shifted the meaning to refer to economically deprived people in their homeland.

17 For more details, see the website of Calypso Productions: <http://homepage.tinet. ie/~calypso/about.html>.

exclusion of and prejudice against Irish Travellers in County Clare, while Ireland was booming in economic exuberance.

Established in 2003, Arambe Productions has adapted a number of Irish plays using Black actors, mostly immigrants from Africa, in an attempt to encourage a different image of Irish identity given that more and more newcomers are arriving in Ireland from distant locations.[18] In 2007, the founder, Bisi Adigun, co-adapted *The Playboy of the Western World* with Roddy Doyle for a new version in which Christy Mahon is replaced by a Nigerian, Christopher Malomo, who has to tell a story convincing enough to be granted the status of refugee. The production received mixed reactions from the audiences as it touched on a sensitive issue as regards the official asylum-seeking policy, thus revealing the extent to which public attitudes have changed towards the ethnic Other.

The play also exhibits a modern-day Ireland that includes both racial conflicts and lingerie shops. Significantly, this play challenges the notion of being Irish by giving Black actors Irish names and relevant (Irish) experiences. That said, Irish identity in the era of globalization can scarcely maintain its narrow definition as a racialized concept but must instead take account of a medley of cultural and ethnic constituents. This version of *The Playboy of the Western World* also points to the existing phenomenon of some Irish children now having an African or Indian surname. They will grow up needing to have a cross-cultural understanding of themselves and their existence points to a more complicated social future for Ireland.

The development of Arambe is also testament to the growing number of non-white actors and directors involved in contemporary Irish theatre. Arambe's 2013 production, *The Paddies of Parnell Street*, was adapted from Jimmy Murphy's *The Kings of the Kilburn High Road* (2000), featuring the pain, loneliness and nostalgia of Irish migrants in London, while the cast was entirely composed of Black immigrant actors living in Ireland. According to the director, Bisi Adigun, some members of the Irish audience expressed their irritation at finding Black actors playing Irish roles, pointing out that "those people are not Irish."[19] Reactions of this kind show that native Irish people have had to grapple with the fact that "the African population [has gone] from almost zero to over 50,000" in a relatively short time (Murphy, "Our Stage"), and they still find it hard

---

[18]   The name Arambe, meaning "there are wonders that I want to perform," is taken from a Yoruba proverb: "Ara m be ti mo fe da, k'aiye ma pa kadara mi da," which means "all things being equal, there are wonders that I will perform." Yoruba is an ethnic group of southwestern Nigeria and southern Benin in West Africa. For more details, see the website of Arambe Productions: < http://www.arambeproductions.com>.

[19]   Adigun described how he was confronted and how he reacted in his talk available on Youtube: <http://www.youtube.com/watch?v=PxSYLtB4YzU>.

to accept Irish plays being performed with foreign or culturally/politically incorrect accents.

However, this situation has not prevented contemporary Irish playwrights from producing new works that feature the neglected experiences of migrants in Ireland. Some playwrights have introduced cross-cultural perspectives, some have unearthed almost forgotten historical events that involve ethnic minorities, and some have dramatized concurrent incidents in a journalistic manner.

For example, Donal O'Kelly's *Asylum! Asylum!* (1994) reveals the bureaucracy of the Irish immigration system in processing the appeal of an asylum seeker from Uganda, despite the risk of him receiving the death penalty if he is repatriated. John Barrett's *Borrowed Robes* (1998) and Elizabeth Kuti's *Treehouses* (2000) illustrate the Jews' painful past in the 1904 Limerick Pogrom and the Holocaust during World War II, respectively. Roddy Doyle's *Guess Who's Coming for Dinner* (2001) presents a dyed-in-the-Green father who finds it hard to accept his future Black son-in-law from Nigeria. Dermot Bolger and Kazem Shahryari, the latter being a Paris-based Iranian writer in exile, co-authored *Départ et Arrivée* (2004) to document the devastating experiences of Kurds.[20] In 2006 the Pan Pan Theatre adapted J.M. Synge's classic, *The Playboy of the Western World* (1907), setting it in the Beijing suburbs with a cast of Chinese actors, to illustrate a different cultural image and the universality of the story.[21] The IRA assassin's story in Sean's O'Casey's *The Shadow of a Gunman* (1923) serves as a motif in Declan Corghan's *Paddy Irishman, Paddy English, Paddy ...?* (1999), through which the playwright portrays the neglected experiences of Irish migrant laborers in London and their doubts about their cultural allegiance to Ireland, among other questions in relation to nationality, heroism, ethnic prejudice, republicanism and personal freedom.

As a whole, these new plays and adaptations bear witness to contemporary Irish dramatists' critical interest in examining different forms of racism in Ireland and historical and contemporary experiences

---

[20]   The play is set in a hotel room in Dublin, featuring an Irish and a Kurdish young woman living in 1963 and 2003 respectively. They are both pregnant and attempting to escape from their homelands so as to find a better life for their babies. The script was published in French. For details, see <http://www.numilog.com/106257/Depart-et-Arrivee.ebook>.

[21]   Pan Pan Theatre, established by co-directors Gavin Quinn and Aedín Cosgrove, produced a Chinese language version of *The Playboy of the Western World* in 2006, and had it set in a foot massage parlor on the outskirts of Beijing. The production toured in Beijing and Dublin. In 2007, Adigun, a Nigerian migrant living in Dublin as mentioned earlier, adapted this play in which Giles Terrera, a Black actor, played the role of Christy Mohan. This production was staged at the Abbey Theatre.

involving migrants, as well as the ethnic and cultural integrations needed for a globalized Ireland. Moreover, the staging of these new Irish plays demonstrates a painful yet largely ignored facet of contemporary Ireland during its transformation, and the playwrights' urgency in seeking to redress its possible wrongs in relation to economic deprivation, social exclusion and racism in Ireland.

A less discussed but important facet of Irish drama concerns presentations of Jews, despite the fact that everyone knows Bloom from *Ulysses* to differing degrees. The long underrepresentation of Jews in Irish society may be due to religious and cultural causes, although the final decades of the twentieth century witnessed the emergence of several Jewish characters on the Irish stage.

"Fishamble: The New Play Company", established in 1988 with the aim of promoting new writing, produced Gavin Kostick's *The Ash Fire* in 1992.[22] The play dramatizes interactions between native Irish people and Polish Jews who moved to the working-class areas of the northside of Dublin in the 1930s, and how the latter managed to maintain their Jewish tradition but were also assimilated into the urban life of Dublin.[23] It is important to note that, according to the playwright's directions, "the director should not be too quick to search for actors that look 'Jewish' to play the [roles]" (Kostick 94). Presumably this could be because the playwright, an Irish Jew, intended to redress Jewish stereotypes, in that his people, after centuries of migration and mixed marriages, vary significantly in their appearance. On the other hand, it can also be said that the Jewish experience of being uprooted and relocated is parallel to the Irish one, for there is not really a stereotype of how the Irish should look. It is therefore justifiable to state that the actors chosen for the play should have just the average faces that could be seen in the streets of any European city.

A more interesting aspect is that the newborn child in this play is given an Irish first name, and the language used in the Jewish migrant family includes Russian, German and Polish expressions, despite the play being performed in English. It is also significant that the characterizations of

---

22   When first established in 1988, Fishamble was originally named "Pigsback." It was renamed 'Fishamble' in 1997 in honor of Fishamble Street in Dublin.

23   A limited number of productions about Jews include Harvey Fierstein's *Torch Song Trilogy* (1982), performed by the Kabosh Theatre Company in 1996. It is an American comedy about a gay Jewish man – doubly marginalized due to his sexual orientation and ethnic identity – in New York searching for love and respect. John Barrett's *The Borrowed Robes* (1988) is based on the religious bigotry against Jews in Cork during the Limerick Pogrom in 1904; John Banville's *Conversation in the Mountains* (2008) concerns the antagonism between Paul Celan, a Jewish poet, and the philosopher Martin Heidegger.

Jews in *The Ash Fire* vary from one to another – there is one who denies his Jewish links; one who is religiously and sexually deviant; one who is supportive of socialism. Significantly, the play seems to suggest that the Jews, through centuries of migration, might be the first people who have quietly put globalization into practice by internalizing every local culture they have encountered. On the other hand, *The Ash Fire* may prompt an Irish audience to relate the Jewish question to the Irish one, in that the Jews' quandaries in maintaining their religious practices and cultural identity are no different from what the Irish are experiencing because of migration, urbanization and globalization. How the Jews have accommodated multiculturalism, historically, might inspire a new perspective for understanding Ireland within a global context.

The latter decades of the twentieth century witnessed the evolution of the Irish theatre from being inward-looking to a more multicultural approach. The change, on the one hand, allows fresh perspectives on how migrants perceive themselves among the native Irish, and *vice versa*. On the other hand, it should broaden the ways in which Irish history is projected on the international/British stage, especially by offering an ethnic viewpoint that is not familiar to the audience.

In particular, transnational migration has been a catalyst for transforming contemporary Irish theatre into a multi-faceted forum in which Irish and ethnic audiences can acquire an onlooker's point of view in order to observe sectarian divides, whether religious, political or cultural. Plays about migration should therefore give rise to a critical comparison between the current movement towards globalization and the history of British imperialism, both of which have made significant impacts on human civilization. The irreversible changes that have occurred have inspired many contemporary Irish dramatists, whether newcomers or more established, to demonstrate their creativity and to keep Irish theatre always at the forefront of social conscience.

Conclusion: Visualizing the Invisible

To a large extent, the plays discussed in this book help theatergoers visualize the experiences of socially marginalized characters by temporarily liberating them from their political and hierarchical oppression. These plays not only question the notion of the home to which the characters belong or are trying to return, but demonstrate how their existence is hampered by violent intimidation and mental abuse. Some characters become internal exiles, despite being "at home." Their mental processes become more acute as a result of oppression, as is shown in many of these plays through monologues or conversations with an imaginary listener. That said, social divides can confine these disadvantaged characters, as portrayed by contemporary Irish playwrights, to invisible places where all social restraints are removed.

In general, the selection of dramatic texts for discussion in this book had the ultimate aim of demonstrating the possibilities of understanding a play, or a collection of them, in an intertextual and intercultural framework. The momentum that validates this notion is the increasingly powerful force of globalization. The latter can either suggest different interpretations or incorporate one text with another in a creative way.

This points to Julia Kristeva's argument about the intertextuality of artistic works: "any text is constructed as a mosaic of quotations; any text is the absorption and transformation of another. The notion of intertextuality replaces that of intersubjectivity, and poetic language is read as at least double" (37). In other words, the corpus of this book acquires significance beyond subject matter or themes: it project new perspectives and unheard voices into a kaleidoscope of enlightening or disturbing effects. Moreover, by adapting different source materials to another context, through either repetition or alteration or both, these plays ensure that the competing voices of the oppressed can be observed more critically.

The study of Irish drama within and beyond geopolitical borders, or across different historical eras, illuminates how "we live not only in a world of influence, but also in a world of dependency" (Jordan xiv). When one shows the contradictions inherent in this struggle of cultural and political exchange, human history becomes an open text rather than a closed system of codes.

As a whole, this book can serve as a challenge to the system of cultural signifiers that have conditioned received ideas of national drama and related dramaturgies. In other words, within a global framework, Irish drama has been hybridized, decentralized, fragmented, or/and syncretized with American, English, South African, Taiwanese, Lebanese and Iraqi cultural subtleties, thereby constructing a new cultural collage that has yet to be fully described. The encounter with different cultures is not always a pleasant experience; it proves painful as social hierarchy, power struggle and economic exploitation can migrate and be used by the new subjugator over the subjugated as a set of interiorized values.

Research on plays pertaining to intercultural and inter-ethnic signifiers is thus a "direct response to this steadily shrinking world" (Bharucha 1). As this book has hopefully shown, this type of research enables one to observe with critical distance the alarming gaps between the privileged and the unprivileged. Thus, once can gain a transcendent view of power mechanisms conditioned by history, race, gender and language.

Roy Foster once commented that "in Ireland everyone is a historian, using the past for the purposes of the present and the future" (186). Nevertheless, globalization may offer a different perspective on Ireland, from being inward-looking to accepting unfamiliar ethnic cultures. It may fulfil what Bernard Shaw proposed in his *John Bull's Other Island*, namely that only when one leaves one's lodging can one appreciate what one's home looks like. In this connection, a catalyst for change in how the general public views itself, as well as the darker corners of Irish society, is being provided by contemporary playwrights who are extending their moral sphere to encompass silenced, socially marginalized groups. Irish theatre may therefore benefit from multiculturalism and individual differences, greeting them enthusiastically as chances to enter the kaleidoscope of the world without leaving home.

Bibliography

"About Arambe." Arambe Productions. 13 Oct. 2013. 28 Nov. 2014. <http://www.arambeproductions.com>.

"About Calypso." *Calypso Productions*. 13 Oct. 2013. 28 Nov. 2014. <http://homepage.tinet.ie/~calypso/about.html>.

Adams, Michael. *Censorship: The Irish Experience*. Dublin: Scepter Books, 1968.

Adigun, Olabisi. "An Irish Joke, a Nigerian Laughter." *The Power of Laughter: Comedy and Contemporary Irish Theatre*. Ed. Eric Weitz. Dublin: Carysfort, 2004. 76-86. Print.

—. "Arambe Productions: An African's Response to the Recent Portrayal of the Fear Gorm in Irish Drama." *Performing Global Networks*. Eds. Karen Fricker and Ronit Lentin. Newcastle: Cambridge Scholars, 2007. 52-65. Print.

—. "Re-Writing Synge's Playboy – Christy's Metamorphosis, A Hundred Years On." *Synge and His Influences: Centenary Essays from the Synge Summer School*. Dublin: Carysfort, 2011. 259-268. Print.

Aidoo, Ama Ata. *The Dilemma of a Ghost*. Accra: Longman, 1965. Print.

Akenson, Donald H. *Occasional Papers on the Irish in South Africa*. Grahamstown: Rhodes UP, 1991. Print.

Apollodorus. *The Library*. Trans. James George Frazer. 1921. Cambridge, Mass.: Harvard UP, 1990. Print.

Ashcroft, Bill, Gareth Griffiths, and Helen Tiffin. *Key Concepts in Post-Colonial Studies*. London: Routledge, 1998. Print.

Barge, Laura. "Out of Ireland: Revisionist Strategies in Beckett's Drama." *Comparative Drama* 34.2 (2000): 175-209. Print.

Barry, Sebastian. *Plays 1*. London: Methuen, 1997. Print.

Beckett, Samuel. Interview. *Conversations with and about Beckett*. By Mel Gussow. New York: Grove, 1996. Print.

"Beckett in an Old House: Six Short Plays Exploring Life." *United Daily News* 17 May 1988: 5. Print.

Behan, Brendan. "The Big House." *The Complete Plays*. New York: Grove Weidenfeld, 1978. 359-384. Print.

—. "Meet the Quare Fella." *Brendan Behan: Interviews and Recollections*. Ed. E.H. Mikhail. Vol. 1. London: Gill and Macmillan, 1982. 142-148. Print.

Ben-Zvi, Linda. *Women in Beckett: Performance and Critical Perspectives*. Urbana: U of Illinois P, 1992. Print.

Bermel, Albert. "Art and Life in Apposition." *New Leader* 82.15 (1999): 31-32. Print.

Bhabha, Homi K. *The Location of Culture*. London and New York: Routledge, 1994. Print.

—. "Dissemination: Time, Narrative and the Margins of the Modern Nation." *Nation and Narration*. Ed. Bhabha. London: Routledge, 1990. 291-322. Print.

—. "Locations of Culture." *The Transnational Studies Readers: Intersections and Innovations*. Eds. Sanjeev Khagram and Peggy Levitt. New York, Routledge, 2008. 333-338. Print.

Billington, Michael. "Which Side Are You On, Boys?" *The Guardian* 13 Oct. 2001. 28 June 2014. <http://www.guardian.co.uk/culture/2001/oct/13/artsfeatures1>.

Bogard, Travis. *Contour in Time: The Plays of Eugene O'Neill*. New York: Oxford UP, 1972. Print.

Bolger, Dermot, ed. *Druids, Dudes and Beauty Queens: The Changing Face of Irish Theatre*. Dublin: New Island, 2001. Print.

Boucicault, Dion. "The Shaughraun." *Plays by Dion Boucicault*. Ed. Peter Thomson. Cambridge: Cambridge UP, 1984. 171-219. Print.

Bowles, Patrick. "Another Biblical Parallel in Desire Under the Elms." *Eugene O'Neill Newsletter* 2.3 (1979): 10-12. Print.

Bristol, Michael D. "In Search of the Bear: Spatiotemporal Form and the Heteroegeneity of Economics in *The Winter's Tale*." *Shakespeare Quarterly* 41.2 (1991): 145-168. Print.

Brown, Terence. *Ireland: A Social and Cultural History 1922-1985*. London: Fontana, 1985. Print.

Budgen, Frank. *Myselves When Young*. New York: Oxford UP, 1970. Print.

Burch, Steven Dedalus. "Historical Invisibility: the Vexatious A. P. Wilson and the Abbey Theatre." *Theatre History Studies* 23 (2003): 65-76. Print.

Butler, Guy. *Demea*. Cape Town: David Philip, 1990. Print.

Butler, Judith. *Bodies That Matter: on the Discursive Limits of "Sex."* New York: Routledge, 1993. Print.

Byrne, Patricia. "Traveling with J. M. Synge. *Hungarian Journal of English and American Studies* 15.2 (2009): 448-451. Print.

Cai, Pei-huo. *A History of the Taiwanese Nationalist Movement*. Taipei: Independence Times Publishing, 1971. Print.

Carlson, Julia, ed. *Banned in Ireland: Censorship & The Irish Writer*. London: Routledge, 1990. Print.

Cave, Richard Allen. "Staging the Irishman." *Acts of Supremacy: The British Empire and the Stage, 1790-1930*. Ed. J.M. MacKenzie. Manchester: Manchester UP, 1991. 150-178. Print.

Chen, Yao-Qi. "Words for the First Performance of Hwang Chen's 'Prophet'." *Theatre Quarterly* 4 (1966): 277-278. Print.

Chen, Ying-Zhen. "Recollection of the Theatre Quarterly." *Youth Literary* 71.5 (1990): 28-31. Print.

Chen, Yun-wen. *Radio Drama in Taiwan: 1930s-1990s*. M.A. National Taiwan University, 1999. Print.

Chi, Hui-Ling. "Lai's Reproduction of Doctoral Presentation." *Min-Sheng Daily* 1 Aug. 2001: A6. Print.

Chiu, Kuen-liang. *Old and New Dramas: A Study of Taiwan's Dramas under Japanese Rule (1895-1945)*. Taipei: Independence Times Publishing, 1991. Print.

—. *Taiwan Theatre and Cultural Development: Memories and Civil Perspectives.* Taipei: Tai-Yuan, 1997. Print.

—. "Floating Stage: The Development of Taiwanese Professional Theatre." *Correspondence of Taiwan History and Relics* 36 (2000): 226-241. Print.

—. "The Story of the Nei-wan Train Line." *Anthology of Civil Literature: Drama*. Ed. Qu-mei Wang. Vol. 2. Taipei: Yu-Shan. 68-99. Print.

Chung, Chiao. *The Homesickness of Body*. Taipei: Morning Star, 1999. Print.

—. *Magic Tent Theatre: Four Plays*. Taipei: Yan-zhi, 2003. Print.

"Classical Si-hey-yuan versus Western Modern Drama." *Min-Sheng Daily* 23 May: 9. *Contemporary Legend Theatre*. Taipei: Contemporary Legend Theatre, 2006.

Coleman, Michael. "Representations of American Indians and the Irish in Educational Reports, 1850s-1920s." *Irish Historical Studies* 33.129 (2002): 33-51. Print.

Colum, Pádraic. *Arthur Griffith*. Dublin: Browne & Nolan, 1959. Print.

"The Contemporary Legend Theatre in Shanghie." *Min-Sheng Daily* 24 April 2006: A9. Print.

Csikai, Zsuzsa. "Recreating the Front of the Tapestry: Murphy's Version of *The Cherry Orchard*." *"Alive in Time": The Enduring Drama of Tom Murphy: New Essays*. Ed. Christopher Murray. Dublin: Carysfort, 2010. 203-217. Print.

Cullingford, Elizabeth Butler. *Ireland's Others: Ethnicity and Gender in Irish Literature and Popular Culture*. Cork: Cork UP, 2001. Print.

Curtis, L. Perry. *Apes and Angels: The Irishman in Victorian Caricature*. Washington: Smithsonian Institution Press, 1997. Print.

Davitt, Michael. *The Boer Fight for Freedom*. London: Funk & Wagnails, 1902. Print.

Deane, Seamus, ed. *Nationalism, Colonialism, and Literature*. Derry: Field Day, 1990. Print.

Deane, Seamus. "Political Writings and Speeches 1900-1988." *The Field Day Anthology of Irish Writing*. Eds. Deane *et al*. Vol. 3. Derry: Field Day, 1991. 3 vols. 681-685. Print.

Delaney, Edna. *Demography, State and Society: Irish Migration to Britain, 1921-1971*. Montreal: McGill-Queen's UP, 2000. Print.

—. "Emigration and Immigration Since 1950." *Encyclopedia of Irish History and Culture.* Ed. James S. Donnelly, Jr. 2 vols. Detroit: Macmillan, 2004. 439-442. Print.

Deleuze, Gilles, and Félix Guattari. *Anti-Oedipus: Capitalism and Schizophrenia.* 1983. Minneapolis: U of Minnesota P, 1990. Print.

Dewhurst, Madeline, "'Theatre and the Impossible'. An Interview with Colin Teevan." *Contemporary Theatre Review* 15(2) 2005: 246-251. Print.

Dixon, Ros. "Chekhov Bogged Down or Not? Tom Kilroy's Version of *The Seagull." Renegotiating and Resisting Nationalism in 20th-Century Irish Drama.* Ed. Scott Boltwood, Gerrards Cross: Colin Smythe, 2009. 97-109. Print.

Dixon, Ros and Malone, Irina (eds). *Ibsen and Chekhov on the Irish Stage.* Dublin: Carysfort, 2012. Print.

Doyle, Roddy. *The Commitments.* Dublin: King Farouk, 1987. Print.

"Dramatic Insights for Pentagon." *The Times Higher Education Supplement* 27 Jan. 2011. Print.

Dubost, Thierry, ed. *Drama Reinvented. Theatre Adaptation in Ireland and Irish Drama.* New York: Peter Lang, 2007. Print.

Eamon, Maher. *Cultural Perspectives on Globalisation and Ireland.* New York: Peter Lang, 2009. Print.

"Endgame." *Tainan Jen Theatre.* 28 June 2014. 28 Nov. 2014. <http://www. tainanjen.org.tw/2004_Endgame.htm.>

Ellis, Sylvia A. "The Historical Significance of President Kennedy's Visit to Ireland in June 1963." *Irish Studies Review* 16.2 (2008): 113-130. Print.

Ellmann, Richard. *James Joyce.* New York: Oxford UP, 1959. Print.

Esslin, Martin. *The Theatre of the Absurd.* Garden City, N.Y.: Anchor, 1961. Print.

Fabulous Beast Dance Theatre [online]. 28 June 2013. 28 Nov. 2014. <http:// danceworks.net/fabulous-beast-dance-theatre>.

Ferriter, Diarmuid. "Paddies' Pain: The Film That Captures Lonely Lives of Men Who Built Britain." *Irish Examiner* 27 Sept. 2007. 28 June 2013. <http://www. irishexaminer.com/archives/2007/0927/ireland/paddies-pain-the-film-that-captures-lonely-lives-of-men-who-built-britain-43673.html>.

Finson, John W. *Edward Harrigan and David Braham: Collected Songs 1873-1882.* Madison: A-R Editions, 1997. Print.

Fisher, Jean. "Editor's Note." *Global Visions: Towards a New Internationalism in the Visual Arts.* Ed. Fisher. London: Institute for the International Visual Arts, 1994. x-xiv. Print.

Foley, Frederic J.. Rev. of *Waiting for Godot.* Trans. Zhuang Ling. Theatre Quarterly Group. Tien Educational Center, Taipei. *Theatre Quarterly* 4 (1966): 271-272. Print.

"Footfalls – Beckett in an Old Courtyard." *Min-Sheng Daily* 2 May 1988: 9. Print.

Foster, R.F. *Modern Ireland 1600-1972.* London: Penguin, 1989. Print.

Foster, Roy. "Re-inventing the Past." *Re-imagining Ireland*. Ed. Andrew Higgins Wyndham. Charlottesville: U of Virginia P, 2006. 186-190. Print.

Foucault, Michel. *Introduction. Anti-Oedipus: Capitalism and Schizophrenia*. By Gilles Deleuze and Félix Guattari. 1983. Minneapolis: U of Minnesota P, 1990. xi-xiv. Print.

Fox, Robert Elliot. "Ulysses in Africa." *Okike: An African Journal of New Writing* 24 (1983): 24. Print.

Frenz, Horst, ed. *Nobel Lectures: Literature*. 4 Vols. Amsterdam: Elsvier, 1997. Print.

Freud, Sigmund. *On Sexuality*. London: Penguin, 1956. Print.

—. *Introductory Lectures on Psychoanalysis*. Trans. James Strachey. Vol. 1. 1975. London: Imago, 1986. Print.

Freud, Sigmund. *Writings on Art and Literature*. Stanford, CA: Stanford UP, 1997.

Fugard, Athol. *The Blood Knot*. London: French, 1984. Print.

Gallagher, Kent G. *The Foreigner in Early American Drama: A Study in Attitudes*. The Hague: Mouton, 1966. Print.

Gardels, Nathan. "Post-Globalization." *New Perspective Quarterly* 25.2 (2008). 2-5. Print.

Gibbons, Luke. "Ireland and the Colonization of Theory." *Interventions* 1.1 (1998). 27. Print.

Gibson, Florence E. *The Attitudes of the New York Irish toward State and National Affairs, 1848-1892*. New York: Columbia UP, 1951. Print.

Gidden, Anthony. *The Consequences of Modernity*, Cambridge: Polity, 1990. Print.

Golden, Sean. "Familiars in a Ruinstrewn Land: Endgame as Political Allegory." *Contemporary Literature* 22 (1981): 425-455. Print.

Gregory, Augusta. "Our Irish Theatre." *Modern and Contemporary Irish Drama*. Ed. John P. Harrington. 1991. New York: Norton, 2009. 401-409. Print.

Grene, Nicholas. "Out of History: from *The Steward of Christendom* to *Annie Dunne*." *Out of History: Essay on the writing of Sebastian Barry*. Ed. Christina Hunt Mahony. Dublin: Carysfort, 2006. 167-182. Print.

—. "Synge in Performance." *The Cambridge Companion to J. M. Synge*. Cambridge: Cambridge University Press, 2009. 149-162. Print.

Grene, Nicholas, and Chris Morash. *Irish Theatre on Tour*. Dublin: Carysfort, 2005. Print.

Grene, Nicholas, and Patrick Lonergan, eds. *Irish Drama: Local and Global Perspectives*. Dublin: Carysfort, 2012. Print.

Hall, Stuart. "The Formation of a Diasporic Intellectual. An Interview with Stuart Hall by Kuan-Hsing Chen." *Stuart Hall: Critical Dialogues in Cultural Studies*. Eds. D. Morlet and K.H. Chen. London: Routledge, 1996. 474-503. Print.

—. "Thinking the Diaspora: Home-Thoughts from Abroad." Ed. Gauraw Desai and Supriya Nair. *Postcolonialisms: An Anthology of Cultural Theory and Criticism.* Oxford: Berg, 2005. 543-560. Print.

Harrigan, Edward. "The Mulligan Guard Ball." *Drama from the American Theatre: 1762-1909.* Ed. Richard Moody. Boston: Houghton Mifflin, 1969. 549-565. Print.

Harrington, John P. *The Irish Beckett.* New York: Syracuse UP, 1991. Print.

Hennessy, Mark. "Irish-born population in England and Wales falls sharply in last decade." *Irish Times* 12 Dec. 2012. 2 Jan. 2013. <http://www.irishtimes.com/ newspaper/ireland/2012/1212/1224327773596.html>.

Hewison, Robert. "Spirits rise above less than zero; Drama." *Sunday Times,* 19 July 1992, 8. Print.

Hezser, Catherine. "'Are You Protestant Jews or Roman Catholic Jews?' *Literary Representations of Being Jewish in Ireland.*" Modern Judaism 25.2 (2005): 159-188. Print.

Higgins, Michael D., and Declan Kiberd. "Culture and Exile: The Global Irish." *New Hibernia Review* 1.3 (1997): 9-22. Print.

Hoare, John Edward. "Ireland's National Drama." *The North American Review* 194.671 (1911): 566-575. Print.

Hoogvelt, Ankie. *Globalization and the Postcolonial World: The New Political Economy of Development.* Baltimore: John Hopkins UP, 1997. Print.

Howells, William Dean. "Editor's Study." *Harper's New Monthly Magazine* 73 (1886): 315-317. Print.

Huang, Shuan-fan. *Language, Society, and Ethnic Awareness.* Taipei: Crane, 1991. Print.

Hurtley, Jacqueline. "Frank McGuinness." *Ireland in Writing: Interviews with Writers and Academics.* Eds. Jacqueline Hurtley, Rosa Gonzelez, Ines Praga, Esther Aiaga. Amsterdam-Atlanta: Rodopi, 1998. 51-70. Print.

Ignatiev, Noel. *How the Irish Became White.* New York: Routledge, 1995. Print.

"Ireland votes to end birth right." *BBC.* 13 June 2004. 2 Oct. 2013. <http://news. bbc.co.uk/2/hi/europe/3801839.stm>.

James, David. "Testing Transnationalism." *Contemporary Literature* 52.1 (2011): 190-209. Print.

James, Henry. *The Portrait of a Lady.* New York: Norton, 1975. Print.

Jay, Paul. *Global Matters: The Transnational Turn in Literary Studies.* Ithaca and London: Cornell UP, 2010. Print.

Ji, Hui-ling. "Await Godot for Fifty Years – Incessant Echo in Taiwan." *Min-Sheng Daily* 9 Jan. 2003: A12. Print.

Jian Guo-xian. "The Wall." *Jian Guo-xian. 1946.* Ed. Chung chaio. Taipei: Council for Cultural Affairs, 2006, 159-176. Print.

Jiang Mo-chun. *New Theater Research "Castrated Rooster": The Comparison of Presentational Activities Between 1940's and 1990's*. M.A. National Taipei University of Education, 1997. Print.

Jordan, Eamonn. *The Feast of Famine: The Plays of Frank McGuinness*. Berlin: Peter Lang, 1997. Print.

—. "The Theatrical Representation of Incest in Marina Carr's On Raftery's Hill." *Journal of Applied Social Care* 3.1 (2001): 138-150. Print.

—. "Frank McGuinness." *The Methuen Drama Guide to Contemporary Irish Playwrights*. Eds. Martin Middeke and Peter Paul Schnierer. London: Methuen, 2010. 234-250. Print.

Kearney, Richard. *Transitions: Narratives in Modern Irish Culture*. Manchester: Manchester UP, 1988. Print.

Keenan, Brian. *An Evil Cradling*. London: Vintage, 1993. Print.

Kennedy, Sighle. "Sourals of Need: Irish Prototypes in Samuel Beckett's Fiction." *Yeats, Joyce, and Beckett: New Light on Three Modern Irish Writers*. Eds. Kathleen McGrory and John Unterecker. London: Associated UP, 1976. 153-166. Print.

Kiberd, Declan. "Story-Telling: The Gaelic Tradition." *The Irish Short Story*. Eds. Patrick Rafroidi and Terence Brown. Gerrards Cross: Colin Smythe, 1979. 13-27. Print.

—. "Strangers in their Own Country: Multi-Culturalism in Ireland." *Multi-Culturalism: the View from the Two Irelands*. By Kiberd and Edna Longley. Cork: Cork UP, 2001. 45-74. Print.

—. *Inventing Ireland: The Literature of the Modern Nation*. 1988. London: Vintage, 1996. Print.

—. "The City in Irish Culture." *City* 6.2 (2002): 219-228. Print.

—. *The Irish Writer and the World*. Cambridge: Cambridge UP, 2005. Print.

Kilroy, Thomas. "The Seagull: an Adaptation." *The Cambridge Companion to Chekhov*. Eds. Vera Gottlieb and Paul Allain. Cambridge: Cambridge UP, 2000. 80-90. Print.

Kimmel, Michael S. "Masculinity as Homophobia: Fear, Shame, and Silence in the Construction of Gender Identity." *Theorizing Masculinities*. Eds. Harry Brod and Michael Kaufman. Thousand Oaks, California: Sage, 1994. 119-141. Print.

King, Jason. "Canadian, Irish and Ugandan Theatre Links: An Interview with George Seremba." *Canadian Journal of Irish Studies* 31.1 (2005). 117-121. Print.

—. "Interculturalism and Irish Theatre: The Portrayal of Immigrants on the Irish Stage." *The Irish Review* 33 (2005). 23-39. Print.

Kingsley, Charles. *Charles Kingsley: His Letters and Memories of His Life*. Vol. 2. London: Henry S. King, 1877. 2 vols. 2012. 28 Nov. 2014. <http://ebooks.cambridge.org/ebook.jsf?bid=CBO9781139084499>.

Kosok, Heinz. "Adaptation-Translocation-Acculturation-Appropriation: Contemporary Irish Playwrights and Continental Drama." *Hungarian Journal of English and American Studies* 10.1/2 (2004). 41-50. Print.

—. *The Theatre of War: The First World War in British and Irish Drama.* Basingstoke: Palgrave Macmillan, 2007. Print.

Kostick, Gavin. "The Ash Fire." *Fishamble/Pigsback: First Plays.* Dublin: New Island, 2002. 91-165. Print.

Kristeva, Julia. *The Kristeva Reader.* Ed. Toril Moi. Oxford: Blackwell, 1986. Print.

Krutch, Joseph Wood. Introduction. *Nine Plays by Eugene O'Neill.* New York: 1954. xi-xxii. Print.

Kurdi, Mária. "An Interview with Tom Murphy." *Irish Studies Review* 12.2 (2004). 233-240. Print.

—. "'Really All Danger': An Interview with Sebastian Barry." *New Hibernia Review* 8:1 (2004): 41-53. Print.

—. *Literary and Cultural Relations: Ireland, Hungary, and Central and Eastern Europe.* Dublin: Carysfort, 2009. Print.

—. *Codes and Masks: Aspects of Identity in Contemporary Irish Plays in an Intercultural Context.* New York: Peter Lang, 2000. Print.

Lan, Bo-Zhou."Looking for the Flagman: Song Fei-wo." *Unitas* 9.6 (1993): 23-27. Print.

—. *The Writers Who Disappear in the Mist of History.* Taipei: Unitas, 2001. Print.

—. *Song Fei-wo.* Taipei: Council for Cultural Affairs, 2006. Print.

Lauren Onkey. "'A Melee and a Curtain': Black-Irish Relations in Ned Harrigan's *The Mulligan Guard Ball.*" *Jouvert* 4.1 (1999). 28 June 2013. 28 Nov. 2014. <http://english.chass.ncsu.edu/jouvert/v4i1/onkey.htm>.

Lee, J.J. "Emigration: A Contemporary Perspective." *Migrations: The Irish at Home & Abroad.* Ed. Richard Kearney. Dublin: Wolfhound, 1990. 33-44. Print.

Lee, Ou-fan. "Modernism in Chinese Modernist Literature – A Comparative Research on Literary History." Ed. Yao-Te Lin. *Contemporary Literary Criticism in Taiwan: Trends & topographies of Recent Taiwanese Writing.* Taipei: Zheng Zhong, 1993. 121-158. Print.

Leeney, Cathy. "Feminist Meanings of Presence and Performance in Theatre: Marina Carr's *Portia Coughlan.*" *Opening the Field: Irish Women, Texts and Contexts.* Eds. Patricia Boyle Haberstroh and Christine St. Peter. Cork: Cork UP, 2007. 92-101. Print.

Lentin, Ronit, and Robbie McVeigh. "Situated Racism: A Theoretical Introduction." *Racism and Anti-Racism in Ireland.* Eds. Ronit and McVeigh. Belfast: Beyond the Pale, 2002. 11-48.

Leverich, Jean Maire. "Engendering the Nation: Nationalism, Feminism and the Writing of Modern Irish Literary History." Diss. U of Michigan, 1996. Print.

Lewis, Aidan "America's New Irish Immigrants." *BBC News Magazine*. 18 Dec. 2013. 28 Nov. 2014. < http://www.bbc.com/news/magazine-25360424 >.

Lion of Kabul Roars His Last." *BBC* 26 Jan. 2002. 1 July 2013. <http://news.bbc. co.uk/2/hi/south_asia/1783910.stm>.

Liu, Da-ren. "A Note before Performance." *Theatre Quarterly* 4 (1966): 266. Print.

Lonergan, Patrick. "Irish Theatre and Globalisation: A Faustian Pact?" *Cultural Perspectives on Globalisation and Ireland*. Ed. Eamon Maher. Berlin: Peter Lang, 2009. 177-190. Print.

—. *Theatre and Globalization: Irish Drama in the Celtic Tiger Era*. New York: Palgrave Macmillan, 2009. Print.

Lu, Ai-ling. "Where is Godot? When will he come? – A few French Productions of *Waiting for Godot*." *Performing Arts Reviews*. Nov. 1995: 37-38. Print.

Lu, Su-shang. *A History of Cinema and Drama in Taiwan*. Taipei: Yin-Hua, 1961. Print.

Lyons, F.S.L. *Ireland Since the Famine*. London: Fontana, 1985. Print.

MacArdle, Dorothy. "The Dual Nature of Man." The Irish Press 18 April 1934: 5. Rpt. in *Eugene O'Neill's Critics: Voices from Abroad*. Eds. Horst Frenz and Susan Tuck. Carbondale: Southern Illinois UP, 1984. 54-56. Print.

Mau, Steffen. *Social Transnationalism: Lifeworlds Beyond The Nation-State*. New York: Routledge, 2010. Print.

Mark, Peter. "'Great Game: Afghanistan' takes an exhaustive look at a much fought-over land." *The Washington Post* 20 Sept. 2010. 6 July 2013. <http://www. washingtonpost.com/wp-dyn/content/article/2010/09/19/AR2010091904274. html>.

Martinovich, M.K. "The Mythical and the Macabre: The Study of Greeks and Ghosts in the Shaping of the American premiere of *By the Bog of Cats....*" *The Theatre of Marina Carr: "before rules was made."* Eds. Cathy Leeney and Anna McMullan. Dublin: Carysfort, 2003. 114-127. Print.

McCaffrey, Lawrence J. *Textures of Irish America*. New York: Syracuse, 1992. Print.

McCracken, Donal P. *The Irish Pro-Boers, 1877-1902*. Johannesburg: Perskor. 1989. Print.

—. "Irish Settlement and Identity in South Africa before 1910." *Irish Historical Studies* 28.110 (1992): 139-149. Print.

—. "The Irish Literary Movement, Irish Doggerel and the Boer War." *Etudes Irlandaises* 20 (1995): 97-115. Print.

—. "Irish Identity in Twentieth-Century South Africa." *Ireland and South African in Modern Times*. Ed. McCracken. Durban: University of Durban-Westville. 1996. 7-45. Print.

—. *Forgotten Protest: Ireland and the Anglo-Boer War*. Belfast: Ulster Historical Foundation. 2003. Print.

McCracken, Patricia A. McCracken. "Arthur Griffith's South African Sabbatical." *South African Irish Studies* 3 (1996): 227-262. Print.

McDonald, Marianne. "Classics as Celtic Firebrand: Greek Tragedy, Irish Playwrights, and Colonialism." *Theatre Stuff: Critical Essays on Contemporary Irish Theatre*. Ed. Eamonn Jordan. Dublin: Carysfort, 2000. 16-27. Print.

Meagher, Timothy. *The Columbia Guide to Irish American History*. New York: Columbia UP, 2005. Print.

Mercier, Vivian. "An Irish School of Criticism?" *Studies: An Irish Quarterly Review* 45.1 (1956): 84-87. Print.

—. "Ireland / The World: Beckett's Irishness." *Yeats, Joyce, and Beckett: New Light on Three Modern Irish Writers*. Eds. Kathleen McGrory and John Unterecker. London: Associated UP, 1976. 147-152. Print.

Merrill, Charles A. "Eugene O'Neill, World-Famous Dramatist, and Family Live in Abandoned Coast Guard Station on Cape God." *Boston Sunday Globe* 8 July 1923: 1. Rpt. in *Conversations with Eugene O'Neill*. Ed. Mark W. Estrin. Jackson: UP of Mississippi, 1990. 38-43. Print.

Merriman, Victor. "Songs of Possible Worlds: Nation, Representation and Citizenship in the Work of Calypso Productions." *Theatre Stuff: Critical Essays on Contemporary Irish Theatre*. Ed. Eamonn Jordan. Dublin: Carysfort, 2000. 280-291. Print.

—. "Poetry Shite: A Postcolonial Reading of Portia Coughlan and Hester Swayne." *The Theatre of Marina Carr: "Before Rules Was Made"*. Eds. C. Leeney and A. McMullan. Dublin: Carysfort, 2003. 145-159. Print.

—. "Songs of Possible Worlds: Nation, Representation and Citizenship in the Work of Calypso Productions." *Theatre Stuff: Critical Essays on Contemporary Irish Theatre*. Ed. Eamonn Jordan. Dublin: Carysfort, 2000. 280-291. Print.

—. *'Because We Are Poor': Irish Theatre in the 1990s*. Dublin: Carysfort, 2011. Print.

McFeely, Deirdre. "Between Two Worlds: Boucicault's *The Shaughraun* and Its New York Audience." *Irish Theatre in American: Essays on Irish Theatrical Diaspora*. Ed. John P. Harrington. Syracuse: Syracuse UP, 2009. 54-65. Print.

McGrew, Anthony. "A Global Society." *Modernity and Its Futures*. Eds. Stuart Hall, David Held and Tony McGrew. Cambridge: Open UP, 1992. 61-117. Print.

McGuinness, Frank. *Plays 2*. London: Faber & Faber, 2002. Print.

McGuire, Stryker. "Ireland's New Face: A Surge In Non-Eu Immigration Has Transformed A Once Homogenous Nation." *Newsweek* 15 Dec. 2003: 26-27. Print.

MacLaughlin, Jim. *Ireland: The Emigrant Nursery and the World Economy*. Cork: Cork University Press, 1994. Print.

McLuhan, Marshall. "Introduction." *Explorations in Communication*. Eds. M Marshall and E. Carpenter. Boston: Beacon, 1960. ix-xii. Print.

—. McLuhan, Marshall. *The Gutenberg Galaxy: The Making of Typographic Man*. Toronto: Toronto University Press, 1962. Print.

McMahon, Deirdre. "Ireland, the Empire, and the Commonwealth." *Ireland and the British Empire.* Ed. Kevin Kenny. Oxford: Oxford UP, 2004. 182-219. Print.

McMullan, Anna. "Brian Friel's The Home Place: Unhomely Inheritances." *Irish Theatre International* 2.1 (2009). 62-68. Print.

McVeigh, Robert. "Racism and Sectarianism in Northern Ireland." *Contemporary Ireland: A Sociological Map.* Ed. Sara O'Sullivan. Dublin: UCD Press, 2007. 402-416. Print.

Mikami, Hiroko. *Frank McGuinness and His Theatre of Paradox.* Gerrards Cross: Colin Smythe, 2002. Print.

Mikos, Michael, and David Mulroy. "Reymont's The Peasants: A Probable Influence on Desire Under the Elms." *Eugene O'Neill Newsletter* 10.1 (1985): 4-15. Print.

Miller, Rory. "Why the Irish Support Palestine." *Foreign Policy* 23 June 2010. 3 July 2013. <http://www.foreignpolicy.com/articles/2010/06/23/why_the_irish_support_palestine>.

Moody, Richard. "Introduction to *The Mulligan Guard Ball,* Harrigan Edward." *Dramas from the American Theatre: 1762-1909.* Ed. Moody. Boston: Houghton Mifflin Company 1969. 535-544. Print.

Mooney, Sinead. Rev. of *Tragedy and Irish Literature: Synge, O'Casey, Beckett,* by Ronan McDonald. *MLA* 99.2 (2004): 477-478. Print.

Murray, Christopher. "Drama 1690-1800." *Field Day Anthology of Irish Writing.* Vol. 1. Gen. ed. Seamus Deane. Derry: Field Day, 1991. 500-7. 3 vols. Print.

—. *Twentieth-century Irish Drama: Mirror up to nation.* Manchester: Manchester UP, 1997. Print.

Murphy, Colin. "Our stage will be a poorer place after losing one of its few African voices." *The Irish Independent.* 24 August 2013. 13 Oct. 2013. <http://www.independent.ie/entertainment/books-arts/our-stage-will-be-a-poorer-place-after-losing-one-of-its-few-african-voices-29524300.html>.

Murphy, Jimmy. *The Kings of the Kilburn High Road.* London: Oberon, 2001. Print.

—. "The Kings of the Kilburn High Road." *Two Plays.* London: Oberon, 2001. 7-66. Print.

Murphy, Maureen. "From Scapegrace to Grasta: Popular Attitudes and Stereotypes in Irish American Drama." *Irish Theatre in American: Essays on Irish Theatrical Diaspora.* Ed. John P. Harrington. Syracuse: Syracuse UP, 2009. 19-37. Print.

Murphy, Mike, and Cliodhna Ni Anluain. *Reading the Future: Irish Writers in Conversation with Mike Murphy.* Dublin: Lilliput, 2000. Print.

Murphy, Tom. Foreword. *The Cherry Orchard.* By Anton Chekhov. London: Methuen, 2004. Print.

—. "Conversations on a Homecoming." *Plays 1.* London: Methuen. 1-87. Print.

—. "Interview with Tom Murphy." *Reading the Future: Irish Writers in Conversation with Mike Murphy.* Ed. Cliodhna Ni Anluain. Dublin: Lilliput, 2000. 173-188. Print.

Naficy, Hamid. "Introduction: Framing Exile from Homeland to Homepage Home." *Exile, Homeland: Film, Media, and the Politics of Place.* Ed. Naficy. New York and London: Routledge, 1999. 1-13. Print.

Nixon, Mark. "'A Brief glow in the dark': Samuel Beckett's Presence in Modern Irish Poetry." *The Yearbook of English Studies* 35.1 (2005): 43-57. Print.

Nolan, Hugh J. *The Most Reverend Francis Patrick Kenrick: Third Bishop of Philadelphia, 1830-1851.* Washington D.C: Catholic U of America P, 1948. Print.

O'Brien, Eoin. "Beckett Centenary." *The Irish Times* 16 June 2006: 8. Print.

O'Casey, Sean. *Plays.* London: Faber and Faber, 1998. Print.

—. *Pictures in the Hallway.* London: Pan, 1942. Print.

Odell, George C.D. *Annals of the New York Stage.* Vol. 9. New York: Columbia UP, 1937. 15 vols. Print.

O'Neill, Eugene. *Three Plays.* New York: Vintage, 1959. Print.

—. and Whitney J. Oates, ed. *Seven Famous Greek Plays.* 1938. New York: Modern Library, 1950. Print.

O'Toole, Fintan. *Tom Murphy: The Politics of Magic.* Dublin: New Island, 1994. Print.

—. "Cultural Capital in Intercultural Theatre: A Study of Pan Pan Theatre Company's *The Playboy of the Western World*." *Target: International Journal on Translation Studies* 25.3 (2013): 407-426. Print.

"Paddies of Parnell Street." *AfricaWorld* TV. 28 Aug 1013. 13 Oct. 2013. <http://www.youtube.com/watch?v=PxSYLtB4YzU>.

Paulin, Tom. "Cultural Struggle and Memory: Palestine-Israel, South Africa and Northern Ireland in Historical Perspective." *Holy Land Studies* 4.1, 2005: 5-16. Print.

Pelletier, Martine. "'New Articulations of Irishness and otherness' on the contemporary Irish Stage." *Irish Literature Since 1990: Diverse Voices.* Eds. Scott Brewster and Michael Parker. Manchester: Manchester UP, 2009. 98-117. Print.

Peng, Ya-ling. "We are Here." *Anthology of Civil Literature: Drama.* Ed. Wang Qu-mei. Vol. 2. Taipei: Yu-Shan, 2002. 236-291. Print.

Perng, Ching-hsi. Rev. of *Waiting for Godot.* Performing Workshop. National Theatre, Taipei. 14 Sept 2006. 28 Nov. 2014. <http://www.pwshop.com/portfolio-cht/zht-theater/%E7%AD%89%E5%BE%85%E7%8B%97%E9%A0%AD%EF%BC%882001%EF%BC%89/>.

Pfefferkorn, Kristin. "Searching for Home in O'Neill's America." *Eugene O'Neill's Century: Centennial Views on America's Foremost Tragic Dramatist.* Ed. Richard F. Moorton, Jr. Westport, CT: Greenwood, 1991. 119-143. Print.

Pine, Richard. "Frank McGuinness: A Profile." *Irish Literary Supplement* 10.1 (1991): 29-30. Print.

"'Poorest of the Rich', A Survey of the Republic of Ireland." *The Economist.* 16 Jan. 1988. Print.

Pratt, Mary-Louise. *Imperial Eyes: Travel Writing and Transculturation.* London & New York: Routledge, 1992. Print.

Purcell, Deirdre. Interview. *The Sunday Tribune* 15 May 1988. 17. Print.

Raleigh, John Henry. "O'Neill's *Long Day's Journey into Night* and New England Irish-Catholicism." *O'Neill: A Collection of Critical Essays.* Ed. John Gassner. Englewood Cliffs, N.J.: Prentice-Hall, 1964. 124-141. Print.

Rev. of *Waiting for Godot*, the Contemporary Legend Theatre. Shanghie Drama Arts Centre, Shanghie. Chinese Theatre Association 21 April 2006. 17 Sept., 2007. <http://www.chinatheatre.org/zwxj.asp?id=12>.

Richards, Jeffery H.. *Drama, Theatre, and Identity in the American New Republic.* Cambridge: Cambridge UP, 2005. Print.

Robertson, Roland. "Glocalization: Time-Space and Homogenity-Heterogeneity." *Global Modernities.* Eds. Mike Featherstone, Scott Lash, and Robertson. London: Sage, 1995. 25-44. Print.

Roof, Judith. "Playing Outside with Samuel Beckett." *A Century of Irish Drama: Widening the Stage.* Eds. Stephen Watt, Eileen Morgan, and Shakir Mustafa. Bloomington: Indiana UP, 2000. 146-159. Print.

Rosenau, James N. *Turbulence in World Politics: A Theory of Change and Continuity.* Brighton: Harvester Wheatsheaf, 1990. Print.

Ruda, R. "The Irish Transvaal Brigades." *Irish Sword* 11.45 (1974): 201-211. Print.

Ryan, Fred. "The Laying of the Foundations." *Lost Plays of the Irish Renaissance.* Eds. R. Hogan and J. Kilroy. Newark: Proscenium, 1902. 23-38. Print.

Ryan, Jean and Michael Hayes. *Postcolonial Identities: Constructing the "New Irish."* Newcastle: Cambridge Scholars, 2006. Print.

Said, Edward. W. "The Mind of Winter: Reflections on life in exile." *Harpers* 269.161 (1984): 49-55. Print.

—. *Reflections on Exile and Other Essays.* Cambridge: Harvard UP, 2000. Print.

—. "Yeats and Decolonization." *Nationalism, Colonialism, and Literature.* Minneapolis: U of Minnesota P, 1990. 69-95. Print.

—. *Power, Politics, and Culture: Interviews with Edward W. Said.* Ed. Gauri Viswanathan. New York: Vintage, 2001. Print.

—. "Afterword: Reflections on Ireland and Postcolonialism." *Ireland and Postcolonial Theory.* Eds. Clare Carroll and Patricia King. Notre Dame: University of Notre Dame Press, 2003. 177-185. Print.

—. *Reflections on Exile and Other Essays.* Cambridge, Mass.: Harvard UP, 2000. 174-186. Print.

Schwarze, Tracey Teets. "Silencing Stephen: Colonial Pathologies in Victorian Dublin." *Twentieth Century Literature* 43.3 (1997): 243-263. Print.

Seigneuret, Jean-Charles, *et al.*, eds. "Incest." *Dictionary of Literary Themes and Motifs A-J*. 2vols. New York: Greenwood, 1988. 651-665. Print.

Sexton, David. "Interest in Conflict Radio." *Sunday Telegraph* 18 July 2004. 1.

Shakespeare, William. *King Henry V*. Ed. Andrew Curr. Cambridge: Cambridge UP, 1992. Print.

Shaw, George Bernard. *John Bull's Other Island*. 1907. London: Penguin, 1984. Print.

Sheaffer, Louis. *O'Neill: Son and Playwright*. Boston: Little Brown, 1969. Print.

Shen, Ling-Ling. *The Research on the Administration and Development of Tainan Jen Theatre and the Criticism of Its Works: 1987-2004*. MA thesis. Cheng-Keng U, 2005. Print.

Sihra, Melissa. Introduction. *Women in Irish Drama: A Century of Authorship and Representation*. New York: Palgrave Macmillian, 2007. 1-22. Print.

Smyth, Damian. *Soldiers of the Queen*. Belfast: Lagan, 2002. Print.

Smyth, Gerry. *Decolonisation and Criticism: The Construction of Irish Literature*. London: Pluto Press, 1998. Print.

Stephens, Simon. "Canopy of Stars." *The Great Game: Afghanistan*. London: Oberon, 2011. Print.

Spivak, Gatatri Chakravorty. "Can the Subaltern Speak." *Marxism and the Interpretation of Culture*. Eds. Cary Nelson and Lawrence Grossberg. Urbana: U of Illinois P, 1998. 271, 281. Print.

Synge, J.M. *The Playboy of the Western World*. New York: W.W. Norton, 1997. Print.

Tanaka, Mariko Hori. "The Legacy of Beckett in the Contemporary Japanese Theatre." *Drawing on Beckett: Portraits, Performances, and Cultural Contexts*. Ed. Linda Ben-Zvi. Tel Aviv: Assaph, 2003. 47-59. Print.

Taylor, Peter. *Brits: The War Against the IRA*. London: Bloomsbury, 2002. Print.

Teevan, Colin. *How Many Miles to Basra?* London: Oberon, 2006. Print.

—. "The Boards and The Border: Myths and Mythtakes in the Criticism of Northern Irish Drama." *The Irish Review* 25 (1999): 60. Print.

—. *Iph...: a new version from the Greek of Iphigeneia in Aulis*. London: Oberon, 2005. Print.

—. *How Many Miles to Basra?*. London: Oberon, 2008. Print.

—. "The Lion of Kabul." *The Great Game: Afghanistan*. London: Oberon, 2011. 151-169. Print.

—. "There Was A Man, There Was No Man." *The Bomb: A Partial History*. London: Oberon, 2011. 133-156. Print.

Temple-Thurston, Barbara. "The Reader as Absentminded Beggar: Recovering South Africa in Ulysses." *James Joyce Quarterly* 28.1 (1990): 247-256. Print.

Townsend, Sarah L. "Cosmopolitanism at Home: Ireland's Playboys from Celtic Revival to Celtic Tiger." *Journal of Modern Literature* 34.2 (2011): 45-64. Print.

Tracy, Robert. "The Russian Connection: Friel and Chekhov." *Irish University Review* 29.1 (1999): 64-77. Print.

Truniger, Annelise. *Paddy and the Paycock: A Study of the Stage Irishman from Shakespeare to O'Casey.* Bern: Francke, 1976. Print.

Umberto, Eco. *Interpretation and Overinterpretation.* Cambridge: Cambridge UP, 1992. Print.

van Onselen, Charles. *Masked Raiders: Irish Banditry in Southern Africa 1880-1899.* Cape Town: Zebra, 2010. Print.

Waiting for Godot. Videocassette. Writ. Samuel Beckett. Dir. Jing-Mei Zhu. National Taiwan U. 1997. 90 min.

"Waiting for Godot." *Performing Workshop.* 14 Sept 2006. 28 Nov. 2014. <http://www.pwshop.com/portfolio-cht/zht-theater/%E7%AD%89%E5%BE%85%E7%8B%97%E9%A0%AD%EF%BC%882001%EF%BC%89/>.

Walshe, Dolores. "In the Talking Dark." *Seen and Heard: Six New Plays by Irish Women.* Ed. Cathy Leeney. Dublin: Carysfort, 2001. 225-324. Print.

Wang, Mo-lin. Rev. of *Waiting for Godot.* Performing Workshop. Taipei. *Min-Sheng Daily.* 25 Oct. 2001: A12. Print.

Weitz, Eric. "Who's Laughing Now? Comic Currents for a New Irish Audience." *Crossroads: Performance Studies and Irish Culture.* Eds. Sara Brady and Fintan Walsh. London: Palgrave MacMillan, 2009. 225-236. Print.

White, Elisa Joy. "The new Irish storytelling: Media, representations and racialised identities." *Racism and Anti-Racism in Ireland.* Eds. R. Lentin and R. McVeigh. Belfast: Beyond the Pale Publications, 2002. 102-115. Print.

White, Hayden. "Historical Emplotment and the Problem of Truth." *The Postmodern History Reader.* Ed. Keith Jenkins. London: Routledge, 1997. 392-396. Print.

Williams, Raymond. *Drama from Ibsen to Brecht.* London: Penguin, 1978. Print.

Winther, Sophus Keith. "Desire Under the Elms, A Modern Tragedy." *Modern Drama* 3 (1960): 326-32. Belfast: Beyond the Pale Publications, 2002. 102-115. Print.

Wittke, Carl. *The Irish in America.* New York: Russell & Russell, 1956. Print.

Woof, Virginia. "Professions for Women." *The Virginia Woolf Reader.* 1931. Ed. M.A. Leaska. New York: Harcourt, 1984. 280. Print.

Yang, Du. *Taiwan's New Theatre Movement under Japanese Rule.* Taipei: China Times Publishing. 1994. Print.

Yao Yi-Wei. Rev. of *Waiting for Godot.* Theatre Quarterly Group. Tien Educational Center, Taipei. *Theatre Quarterly* 4 (1966): 271-272. Print.

Yeats, W.B., and Lady Gregory. "Cathleen Ni Houlihan." *Modern and Contemporary Irish Drama*. Ed. John P. Harrington. 1991. New York: W.W. Norton, 2009. 3-11. Print.

Yeats, W. B. *Letters to the New Island*. Ed. Horace Reynolds. Cambridge, Mass.: Harvard UP, 1934. Print.

—. *Selected Plays*. London: Macmillan, 1974. Print.

—. *Letters of W. B. Yeats*. Ed. Allan Wade. London: Rupert Hart-Davis. 1954. Print.

—. *Collected Plays*. London: Macmillan, 1966. Print.

Younger, Kelly. "Irish Antigones: Burying the Colonial Symptom." *Colloquy: Text Theory Critique* 11 (2006): 148-162. Print.

Zhang, Wen-huan, and Lin Tuan-qiu. "Castrated Rooster." *Zhang Wen-huan: Complete Works*. Ed. Chen Wan-yi. Vol. 2. 1943. Taichung: Taichung County Cultural Center, 2002. 239-287. Print.

Index

UNIVERSITY OF WINCHESTER
LIBRARY

UNIVERSITY OF WINCHESTER
LIBRARY

DRAMATURGIES

TEXTS, CULTURES AND PERFORMANCES

This series presents innovative research work in the dramaturgies of the twentieth and twenty-first centuries. Its main purpose is to re-assess the complex relationship between textual studies, cultural and/or performance aspects at the dawn of this new multicultural millennium. The series offers discussions of the link between drama and multiculturalism (studies of "minority" playwrights — ethnic, Aboriginal, gay, and lesbian), reconsiderations of established playwrights in the light of contemporary critical theories, studies of the interface between theatre practice and textual analysis, studies of marginalized theatrical practices (circus, vaudeville, etc.), explorations of emerging postcolonial drama, research into new modes of dramatic expressions and comparative or theoretical drama studies.

The Series Editor, **Marc MAUFORT***, is Professor of English literature and drama at the Université Libre de Bruxelles.*

Series Titles

No.27 – Sébastien RUFFO, *Jeux d'acteurs comparés. Les voix de Belmondo, Depardieu, Lebeau et Nadon en Cyrano de Bergerac*, 2011, ISBN 978-90-5201-657-3

No.26 – Catherine BOUKO, *Théâtre et réception. Le spectateur postdramatique*, 2010, ISBN 978-90-5201-653-5

No.25 – Marc MAUFORT, *Labyrinth of Hybridities. Avatars of O'Neillian Realism in Multi-ethnic American Drama (1972-2003)*, 2010, ISBN 978-90-5201-033-5

No.24 – Marc MAUFORT & Caroline DE WAGTER (eds.), *Signatures of the Past. Cultural Memory in Contemporary Anglophone North American Drama*, 2008, ISBN 978-90-5201-454-8

No.23 – Maya E. ROTH & Sara FREEMAN (eds.), *International Dramaturgy. Translation & Transformations in the Theatre of Timberlake Wertenbaker*, 2008, ISBN 978-90-5201-396-1

No.22 – Marc MAUFORT & David O'DONNELL (eds.), *Performing Aotearoa. New Zealand Theatre and Drama in an Age of Transition*, 2007, ISBN 978-90-5201-359-6

No.21 – Johan CALLENS, *Dis/Figuring Sam Shepard*, 2007, ISBN 978-90-5201-352-7

No.20 – Gay MCAULEY (ed.), *Unstable Ground. Performance and the Politics of Place*, 2006 (2e tirage 2008), ISBN 978-90-5201-036-6

No.19 – Geoffrey V. DAVIS & Anne FUCHS (eds.), *Staging New Britain. Aspects of Black and South Asian British Theatre Practice*, 2006, ISBN 978-90-5201-042-7

No.18 – André HELBO, *Signes du spectacle. Des arts vivants aux médias*, 2006, ISBN 978-90-5201-322-0

No.17 – Barbara OZIEBLO & María Dolores NARBONA-CARRIÓN (eds.), *Codifying the National Self. Spectators, Actors and the American Dramatic Text*, 2006, ISBN 978-90-5201-028-1

No.16 – Rachel FENSHAM, *To Watch Theatre. Essays on Genre and Corporeality*, 2009, ISBN 978-90-5201-027-4

No.15 – Véronique LEMAIRE, with the help of/avec la collaboration de René HAINAUX, *Theatre and Architecture – Stage Design – Costume. A Bibliographic Guide in Five languages (1970-2000) / Théâtre et Architecture – Scénographie – Costume. Guide bibliographique en cinq langues (1970-2000)*, 2006, ISBN 978-90-5201-281-0

No.14 – Valérie BADA, *Mnemopoetics. Memory and Slavery in African-American Drama*, 2008, ISBN 978-90-5201-276-6

No.13 – Johan CALLENS (ed.), *The Wooster Group and Its Traditions*, 2004, ISBN 978-90-5201-270-4

No.12 – Malgorzata BARTULA & Stefan SCHROER, *On Improvisation. Nine Conversations with Roberto Ciulli*, 2003, ISBN 978-90-5201-185-1

www.peterlang.com